BETWEEN MODES AND KEYS

German Theory 1592-1802

To the memory of my mother

BETWEEN MODES AND KEYS

German Theory 1592-1802

by

Joel Lester

HARMONOLOGIA SERIES No. 3

PENDRAGON PRESS
STUYVESANT, NY

OTHER TITLES IN THE HARMONOLOGIA SERIES

No. 1 *Heinrich Schenker: Index to Analyses* by Larry Laskowski (1978) ISBN 978-0-918728-06-7

No. 2 *Marpurg's* Thoroughbass and Composition Handbook: *a narrative translation and critical study* by David A. Sheldon (1989) ISBN 0-918728-55-5

No. 4 *Music Theory from Zarlino to Schenker: A Bibliography and Guide* by David Damschroder and David Russell Williams (1991) ISBN 978-0-918728-99-9

No. 5 *Musical Time: The Sense of Order* by Barbara Barry (1990) ISBN 978-0-945193-01-2

Library of Congress Cataloging-in-Publication Data

Lester, Joel.
Between Modes and Keys.
(Harmonologia Series ; no. 3
1. Composition (Music)--Germany--17th century--History and Criticism. 2. Composition (Music)--Germany--18th century--History and Criticism. 3. Music--Germany--Theory--17th century--History and Criticism. 4.
Music--Germany--Theory--18th century--History and Criticism. I. Title II. Series.
ML430.L47 1989 781. 6'1'0943 87-14864
Isbn 978-0-918728-77-7 (lib. bldg.)

Contents

Introduction   vii
History and the Historian, vii
The Modes and Modal Terminology, xii
Modes versus Keys, xv
Solmization and its Terminology, xvii
Harmonic and Arithmetic Division, xix
Tuning Systems, xx
Acknowledgements, xxiv

Chapter 1, The Legacy of the Sixteenth Century   1
Modal Theory in Glarean and Zarlino, 1

Chapter 2, German Theorists Before Lippius   21
Sethus Calvisius, 21
German Modal Theory Around 1600, 24
Growing Recognition of the Triad, 28

Chapter 3, Johannes Lippius   37
Modes, 41

Chapter 4, The Mid-Seventeenth Century   47
Johann Crüger as Transmitter of Lippius's
Theories, 52
The Maintenance of Traditional Modal Theory, 59

Chapter 5, Toward Twenty-Four Keys   77
The Church Keys, 77
Expanded Listings of Keys, 83
Andreas Werckmeister, 86
Evolution from the Modes, 94

Chapter 6, Twenty-Four Keys   97
    French and English Presentations of the Keys, 97
    German Works, 104

Chapter 7, Mattheson's Aftermath   119
    Buttstett's Response, 119
    The *Orchestre* Defended, 121
    Die Orchestre-Kanzeley, 125

Chapter 8, The Persistence of Modal Theory   133
    Walther's *Lexicon* and Its Influence, 135
    The Mid and Late Eighteenth Century, 140

Chapter 9, Epilogue   149

Appendix 1, Translation of articles from *Clavis ad thesaurum magnae artis musicae* by Thomas Balthasar Janowka   163

Appendix 2, Mattheson's Tuning System   179

Appendix 3, Translations from *Gradus ad parnassum* by Johann Joseph Fux   183

Appendix 4, Translation of the article *Modus musicus* from the *Lexicon* of Johann Gottfried Walther   211

Index   235

Introduction

History and the Historian

Though we may often think of history as an objective chronicle of the factual record of the past, there is a direct correlation between the biases of historians and the history they write. Scholars exploring the past seek those aspects that are of interest to their contemporary perspectives, thereby determining both the limits and the focus of inquiry. A given history thus illuminates not only the era under examination, but also the era and personal interests of the historian.

Such biases are perhaps most obvious in revisionist histories, whether written by totalitarian regimes to hide their past or by liberationists to uncover their roots. But the history of music too is not immune. Nineteenth-century and early twentieth-century musicologists established the history of music theory as we know it. For these historians, tonality was a natural language toward which music had evolved for over a millennium. The history of pretonal theory was a chronicle detailing the evolution of ideas toward the tonal future. In the view of these historians, their task was to locate crucial tenets of tonal theory in the works of supposedly representative theorists, thereby highlighting the main stages in the evolutionary process.

Nowhere are these ethnocentric and progressive biases more pervasive than in Hugo Riemann's *Geschichte der Musiktheorie im IX.—XIX. Jahrhundert*, a work that remains the sole attempt at a comprehensive history of theory: "I have endeavored at the least to omit nothing essential to the course of evolution, and to give a continuous presentation of the genesis of the individual concepts of today's teachings."[1] Many commentators, ranging from Matthew

---

[1] (Leipzig, 1898), p. vi: "...habe ich mich aber bestrebt, wenigstens nichts wesentlich den Gang der Entwicklung Bestimmendes auszulassen und eine zusammenhängende Darstellung der Genesis der einzelnen Begriffe der heutigen Lehre zu geben."

Shirlaw in 1917[2] to Carl Dahlhaus in 1957,[3] have criticized flaws in Riemann's discussion of Zarlino, for instance. Yet, despite the recognition of numerous flaws in Riemann's work, his central thesis of a progressive history of music theory remains relatively unchallenged. Witness the recent English translations of the *Geschichte...*,offered not as an historical document, but as an authoritative research tool.[4]

The progressive bias in the history of music theory arises not only from early historical studies, but from other sources as well. Numerous modern articles, especially those that derive from graduate seminar reports and dissertations, fall prey to this bias. Scholars dutifully read works by their chosen theorist, and often works by a few contemporaries and predecessors. But without a comprehensive knowledge of the historical era, the theorist's predecessors, what the theorist included because it was routine to do so, what he significantly omitted, whether he wrote to oppose an old-fashioned or a new idea, and so forth—without a grasp of these aspects, the resulting study is at best an accurate chronicle of the contents of the treatises. At worst, and all too often, scholars, eager to prove that their charge was not out of step with the march of history, emphasize supposedly progressive features of the works under study.

Tracing the progressive development of a concept from one generation of theorists to another may well be one proper goal of historians of music theory. But we should not expect that perspective to inform us of the conceptual universe within which any given generation of musicians resided. To take a single instance, it is one thing to cite Zarlino's conception of a major-minor differentiation of harmony and modes as it influenced later theorists. It is quite another to take the handful of lines that Zarlino devoted to this subject in two widely separated passages in his *Istitutioni harmoniche*, both amid other discussions, and make these tenets the core of his theories, or the primary noteworthy features, as some standard music histories do.

---

[2] *The Theory of Harmony* (London, 1917); most recent edition under the title *The Theory and Nature of Harmony* (Sarasota: Birchard Coar, 1970), chapter 2.

[3] "War Zarlino Dualist?" in *Die Musikforschung* 10 (1957): 286–90.

[4] Translation of Books I and II by Raymond H. Haggh (Lincoln: University of Nebraska Press, 1962). Translation of Book III by William Mickelson (Lincoln: University of Nebraska Press, 1977).

Such a progressive approach to the history of music theory will not serve us well if we wish to understand the gradual evolution of one set of concepts into another over several generations. For such a study, it is not sufficient merely to cite the origins of the later beliefs. The locus of these tenets within a theory, the transmission of that tenet from one theorist to another, the degree to which that tenet is disseminated among a number of contemporary theorists, the degree to which it is included in practical as opposed to speculative works, whether a tenet appearing in print for the first time is announced with fanfare or appears in an obscure location, whether a tenet appearing in print for the first time can be traced to an earlier oral tradition—these issues become primary. After all, the earlier formulations of later beliefs must have arisen in the context of those earlier eras because they made sense to the musicians of that earlier era in terms of their own conceptions of music. In addition to the meaning or importance of the tenet for later eras, we must also understand its place in the era in which it arose. From this perspective, which is the basis of the present study, the aim of a history of music theory is to recreate the conceptual universe within which musicians of the past lived and created.

To return with this perspective to Zarlino and his major- minor differentiation of the affects of the modes, there may not seem to be much difference between stating that Zarlino differentiated modes into major and minor according to the quality of their tonic triads or that Zarlino differentiated the affects of the modes based on the quality of thirds and sixths above crucial notes in the mode. But the differences between these statements concern more than mere semantics. The modern musician conceives of the "triad" as a harmonic unit with three possible positions. For Zarlino to have conceived of such a unit as a basis for the differentiation of modal affect would have violated several foundations of his conceptual universe. His is primarily a contrapuntal theory based on intervals, not a harmonic theory based on chords. Thus for him the harmony that we call the first inversion of a major triad is a *minor* chord because it has two *minor* imperfect consonances over the bass. Likewise, what we call the first inversion of a minor triad has two *major* imperfect consonances over the bass. Zarlino relates these "first inversion chords" to the "root position triad" of the *same* bass, which chords share the same quality of imperfect consonances over the bass. It is only later harmonic theory that supersedes the immediate sound of these first inversion chords and insists on finding the "root" of the sonority before determining its quality. (Indeed, the difference between total interval content of a harmonic structure and the interval structure over the lowest sounding note continues to be a problematic and often unexplored area in tonal theory as well as in contemporary atonal theory.) Zarlino is more concerned with the sound of a sonority than he is with relating it to a hypothetically parent root sonority. His interest in modal affect concerns the actual intervals that appear over a few crucial bass pitches in each mode, not how entirely different bass pitches might share chords that differ in intervallic quality. And yet, the tenor is still the center of the composition for Zarlino. He cannot incorporate into his formal theories a concept founded on the primacy of the bass voice.

Thus, Zarlino does not incorporate the major-minor differentiation of modal affect into his formal discussion of mode, but retains it as a rule of thumb useful in composition, especially text-setting. Zarlino's or any other theorist's stature as a theorist derives in no small part from the realization that a proper theory of music is not merely a presentation of true statements about music. That a statement is true is often far less significant than how it is integrated into the entire theory and related to other significant statements. Zarlino creates in his treatises a mighty edifice of theoretical knowledge. But the signal evidence of Zarlino's commanding greatness is his realization that many of his intuitions about music could not be integrated fully into his formal theories. His inclusion of these nonsystematic suggestions into the study of composition informs us not only of the cogency of his overall conception of musical structure, but also of the valuable role played by tenets that would not otherwise be subsumed by that conception, thereby elevating his treatises above all others of their generation; indeed, above those of so many other generations as well.

My curiosity about the status of modal theory during the seventeenth and eighteenth centuries dates to my awareness of the letter exchange of the 1710's between Johann Joseph Fux and Johann Mattheson.[5] I was amazed to find that in the early eighteenth century a composer and theorist of the stature of Fux was not only rejecting a presentation of the twenty-four major and minor keys, but was

---

[5] See p. 127 re this letter exchange, and *Current Musicology* 24 (1977): 37–62 for an annotated English translation by this author.

actually defending the system of twelve church modes *as the founda-tion of contemporary music* and, even more remarkably, was advocat-ing the medieval system of six-syllable solmization with mutation of hexachords *as an invaluable pedagogical tool for teaching children to sing*. In the light of this letter exchange, I began to wonder whether the use of modes in Fux's *Gradus ad parnassum* (1725) was part of his attempt to create (or maintain) an archaic style for strict counter-point, as is commonly believed, or whether Fux believed that he was presenting the foundations of the music of his time. My subsequent research into another classic of the early eighteenth century, Johann Gottfried Walther's monumental *Lexicon* (1732), made it clear to me that skepticism about the adequacy of the major and minor keys to explain the basis of contemporary music was quite prevalent in central Europe during the high Baroque, and was not confined to any single school of musical thought. Many aspects of modal theory were still a part of contemporary musical thought. How could this be accommodated with standard reference works that ascribed recognition of major and minor to the works of Glarean and Zarlino over a century and a half earlier?[6]

The present study attempts to answer this question by defining the changing status of modal as opposed to major-minor thinking in German theory from the late sixteenth through the end of the eighteenth century. For much of this period, theories that we or-dinarily think of as centuries apart coexisted. The 1710's, for instance, saw the first appearance in print of the circle of keys and other presentations of twenty-four keys, vigorous defenses of modal theory and six-syllable solmization, and the last editions of a *Lateinschul* manual whose earliest editions appeared in 1548.[7] A chronicle of the change from modal to major-minor thinking must come to grips with these historical realities.

---

[6] Manfred Bukofzer, *Music in the Baroque Era* (New York: Norton, 1947), p. 387: "The contrast of major and minor [was] discussed as early as Glareanus and Zarlino..." Gustave Reese, *Music in the Renaissance* (New York: Norton, 1959), p. 377: "Like Glareanus, Zarlino lists twelve [modes] but, unlike him, places the Ionian and Hypoionian first and the Aeolian and Hypoaeolian last... He thus not only recognizes major and minor, like the Swiss theorist, but places them in positions of special prominence."

[7] Johann Quirsfeld's *Breviarum musicum...* (Dresden, several editions from 1675-1717) is quite close in content to Heinrich Faber's *Compendiolum musicae pro incipientibus* (first edition, Braunschweig, 1548). See pp. 68-75 for a discussion of these works.

To be sure, my approach to the history of theory is decidedly late twentieth-century in perspective. We no longer live in a tonal universe, or, for that matter, in a universe limited to music of only a few generations. Contemporary compositional styles range from tonal to just about anything. A concert-goer in any major cultural center (indeed, in any culturally active university) can hear music from every era in Western history as well as a wide cross-section of the musics of other cultures. A musician may, in a single day, teach simple diatonic tonal music, rehearse a recent creation, and attend a performance of medieval music. What a different attitude from that articulated by Tinctoris in 1477, when he dismissed from consideration all music except that composed in the last forty years![8]

Living in this musical universe, I am quite comfortable in describing a seventeenth-century and eighteenth-century climate in which a variety of musics coexisted. But I do not believe that I have imposed on the seventeenth and eighteenth centuries a musical diversity that better reflects our own times than that era. The Baroque in Central Europe, like many eras elsewhere, encompassed great contrasts. Older musical styles and attitudes existed alongside new creations that challenged the very basis of musical traditions. As in virtually all historical eras, each generation of musicians and theorists included some who upheld the past and ridiculed the new and others who launched the new and ridiculed the past. What was new and what was traditional changed from generation to generation, but the vibrant diversity remained. This study explores this diversity as it affected the retention of traditional notions of modes and the exploration of new ideas of major and minor.

Before we begin the history itself, this introduction surveys a few preliminaries, including terminology and concepts that arise later.

The Modes and Modal Terminology

Modern disagreements about the origins, the essence, and the meaning of mode, as well as of the relevance of mode to the structure or the classification of Western music of the Middle Ages and Renaissance need not concern us here. What matters for the present study

---

[8] Johannes Tinctoris, *Liber de arte contrapuncti* (Naples, 1477), English translation by Albert Seay as *The Art of Counterpoint* (N.p.: American Institute of Musicology, 1961). The remarks on the superiority of recent music close the dedication.

Example I-1. The Eight Traditional Modes

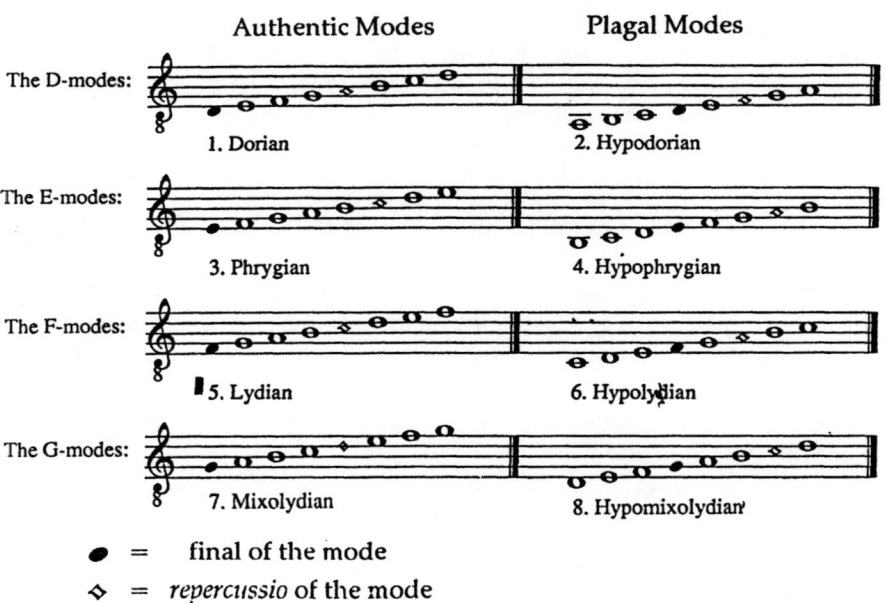

Authentic Modes   Plagal Modes

The D-modes:
1. Dorian   2. Hypodorian

The E-modes:
3. Phrygian   4. Hypophrygian

The F-modes:
5. Lydian   6. Hypolydian

The G-modes:
7. Mixolydian   8. Hypomixolydian

● = final of the mode

◇ = *repercussio* of the mode

is the status of modal theory during the sixteenth century. Prior to the writings of Glarean and Zarlino in 1547 and 1558, theorists commonly recognized four primary modes, each one existing in two forms: *authentic* and *plagal*. See example I-1., above.

The difference between authentic and plagal modes is a difference of *ambitus* or range. The ambitus of each authentic mode is the white-note scale filling an ascending octave from the *final* of the mode (indicated by black noteheads in example I-1). The ambitus of each plagal mode lies a fourth lower than that of the corresponding authentic mode.

The term ambitus refers both to the range of the mode and also to the notes that make up the scale of the mode. In Dorian mode, for example, an F above the high D would be said to exceed the ambitus of the mode just as would a G-sharp in the scale.

The ambitus of each mode comprises a *species* or type of fifth plus a *species* of fourth. Fifth-species and fourth-species differ in the placement of their semitone. Thus Dorian and Mixolydian have the same fourth species (A to D and D to G, each with a semitone after the second degree), but have different fifth species. Authentic and plagal modes with the same final share identical fifth- and fourth-species, but reverse their disposition. Thus Dorian and Hypodorian share the same fifth-species (D to A) and fourth-species (A to D); in Dorian the fourth-species lies above the fifth-species, in Hypodorian it lies below.

In each mode the concluding note is the *final* of the mode. The important note generally lying a fifth above the final in authentic modes and a third above the final in plagal modes is called the *reciting tone*, the *repercussio*, or, later, the *dominant*. The terms reciting tone and repercussio arose because this note of the mode was intoned in the psalm tones. The term dominant arose in French writings of the seventeenth century because the reciting tone dominated in melodies in that mode.

Beginning with Glarean in 1547, sixteenth-century and later theorists often added the four modes listed in example I- 2.[9]

Example I-2. The Four Modes Added by Glarean in 1547

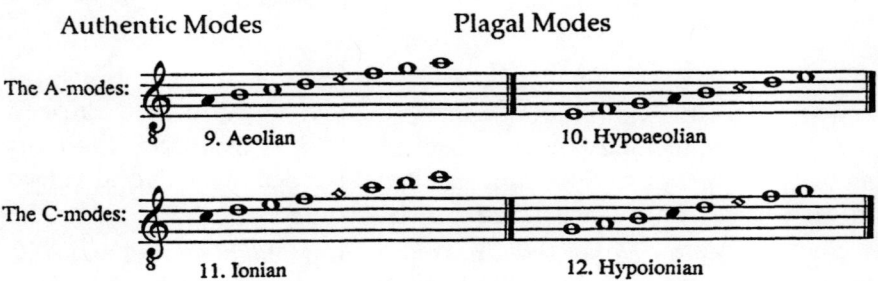

Authentic Modes   Plagal Modes

The A-modes: 9. Aeolian   10. Hypoaeolian

The C-modes: 11. Ionian   12. Hypoionian

● =   final of the mode

◇ =   *repercussio* of the mode

Each mode presents a different organization of tones and semi-tones in relation to the final. These different scales were known as *octave species*—literally meaning the types or species of scales filling in an octave.

---

[9] For Glarean's reasons for adding these modes, see pp. 1-7 of the present study.

Modes versus Keys

The transition from recognition of modes to recognition of major and minor keys is the change from a melodic to a harmonic conception of the differentiation of modes. During the Middle Ages and Renaissance, theorists differentiated modes from one another according to melodic patterns or the placement of semitones within the scale. These are melodic distinctions—all modes have the same number of tones and semitones, major and minor thirds, perfect fourths, the single tritone between F and B, and the inversions of all these intervals. But in each mode, these intervals are arranged differently in relation to the final (and also, of course, in relation to all other degrees of the modal scale). As shown in example I-3, the D-mode differs in construction from the G-mode as well as from the A-mode by the placement of a single semitone.

Example I-3.

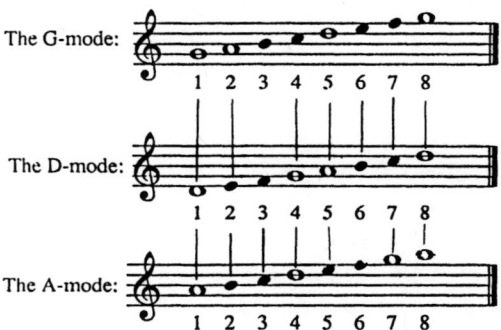

Black noteheads indicate semitones

The differing positions of intervals in relation to a given scale degree in each mode give rise to the different melodic and structural possibilities in the various modes. In the D-mode, for instance, skipping or outlining scale degrees 1-5-2 presents no problems with the tritone F to B. But in the E-mode, such a scale-degree succession is not possible without encountering the problematic tritone. Similarly, the E-modes, because they have a semitone above the final, cannot use the cadence patterns common in all the other modes. And so forth. Such distinctions entail differences in the structure of compositions in the various modes.

This aspect of mode is reflected by the term itself, which carries a meaning not dissimilar to its nonmusical meaning of "a manner of doing or being; method, form; fashion."[10] Early in the seventeenth century Michael Praetorius speaks of pieces in the Dorian, Phrygian, and Lydian modes "as one might say nowadays, 'This is a Polish dance, an Italian, French, or German dance or melody.'"[11] Although Praetorius offers here his interpretation of the ancient Greek usage of the term, this attitude underlies the usage of "modes" by his contemporaries as well. When theorists refer to the Phrygian or the E-mode, they are not merely referring to the final on E, with the octave species of the white-note scale E-e. In addition, they are referring to the entire range of compositional possibilities uniquely available in this mode: the melodic lines, skips, ambitus, cadences, points of imitation, and so forth. Contrapuntal theory covered the interaction of notes and lines with one another. But only modal theory covered the unique structural possibilities of each mode. A differentiation of modes based on a single interval over the final is alien to modal theory, whether the distinction be made on the basis of a major or minor third, a major or minor second, or any other interval.

As a result, the study of mode was central to many treatises on music. Under the rubric of modal theory, practical aspects of music as diverse as melodic structure, cadence patterns, and the ranges of voices in polyphonic compositions were studied. This is in part the reason for the extensive discussions of mode in many Renaissance treatises. Almost all of Glarean's *Dodecachordon* (1547) is devoted to the modes. In Zarlino's encyclopedic *Istitutioni harmoniche* (1558),[12] the treatment of mode is one third as long as the discussion of counterpoint and composition. What tonal theorist would spend one fourth of his composition treatise merely listing the major and minor keys and giving examples in them? With the rise of tonality and the reduction of the number of modes to two, the differences between the types of modes no longer required such extensive treatment. Many subjects previously treated under the heading of mode received separate discussions.

[10] *Webster's New International Dictionary*, second edition.

[11] Michael Praetorius, *Syntagma musicum*, I (Wittenberg, 1614-1615), p. 183: "Dorius, Phrygius & Lydius (als wie man itzo sagen möchte/ diss ist ein Polnischer Tanz/ ein Welscher/ Frantzösischer/ Deutscher Tanz/ oder Melodey.)"

[12] See pp. 7-20 of the present study for a discussion of Zarluno's modal theories.

Key distinctions in tonal music are made in two parts. The pitch name ("in the key of C") merely gives the level of transposition of the tonic. Hence the term *key* (a translation of the Latin *clavis*), indicating the note on the keyboard. In addition, a modal distinction is made between the major and minor keys. But in contrast to the melodic differentiation of the traditional modes, the distinction between major and minor is harmonic. The major scale and natural minor scale contain the same number of tones and semitones, major and minor thirds, perfect fourths, and the tritone. In addition, they contain the same number of major and minor triads, and the same number of each type of seventh chord. It is the quality of the third above the tonic that determines the quality of the mode—major or minor. The major scale and the ascending melodic minor are identical in structure save for the third scale degree. Yet the one is clearly major and the other clearly minor. Review example I-3. The D-mode may differ from both the A-mode and the G-mode by the placement of only a single semitone. But from a major-minor perspective, the G-mode is major and the D-mode and A-mode are minor solely because of the quality of the third over the final.

The third scale degree is so important to the distinction between major and minor modes because of the importance of the triad as a harmonic unit in tonal music. Thus the transition from modes to keys is also the transition from an intervallic to a chordal conception of harmony. Several recent studies explore harmonic theories of the late sixteenth and early seventeenth centuries. These studies have uncovered well-developed harmonic theories over a century before Rameau's *Traité...* of 1722, allowing us to understand better shifts in modal theories of the period. Chapter 2 surveys these recent discoveries.

Solmization and its Terminology

A colleague of mine recently related a discussion she had had with her young son's sight-singing teacher concerning fixed and movable "do" systems. Our discussion of the pros and cons of various systems of solmization must have recreated innumerable such exchanges over the past millennium. Ever since Guido formulated the hexachordal sequence *ut re mi fa sol la* with its single semitone,[13]

[13] See Oliver Strunk, *Source Readings in Music History* (New York: Norton, 1950), pp. 121–125, for the relevant portions of Guido's letter to Brother Michael.

emendations or alternative systems have been proposed, attacked, defended, and occasionally adopted widely. Principal changes in the original formulation include a system of three hexachords (one on C, one on F with B-flat, and one on G with B-natural) with mutation (change from one hexachord to another) to account for melodies that exceeded the range of a single hexachord,[14] the proposal of a new system of seven syllables by Ramos de Pareja in his *Musica practica* (1482)[15] to avoid mutation, the similar system of bocedisation introduced by the Belgian Hubert Waelrant in the next century,[16] the addition of a seventh syllable (*bi*) to the original Guidonian hexachord around the turn of the seventeenth century,[17] as well as recommendations for using pitch names instead of solmization syllables.[18]

The structures of solmization systems answer the needs of the tonal or modal system of an era. In Medieval and Renaissance music, where eight modes were recognized, there were four possible scale arrangements above the final of a mode. The Guidonian hexachord provided a norm in the form of a scale segment whose semitone placement was invariable. The hexachord was chosen as the largest diatonic scale segment without a tritone or diminished fifth. Mutation from one hexachord to another when a melody exceeded the range of a single hexachord may have been clumsy. But a hexachordal system avoided having to teach four different types of scales. With the reduction of modal possibilities to two in the major and minor keys, the need for hexachordal solmization disappeared: only two scalar patterns needed to be learned. Proponents of the traditional modes into the eighteenth century often continued to defend the use of hexachordal solmization including the system of mutation.

The terminology of the hexachords was later used for several different purposes. The terms *durus* and *mollis* for the hexachords on G and F arose at first because of the shape of the notes B-natural and B-flat. B was written with square shape, B-flat with a round figure—hence the terms *hard* (*dur*) and *soft* (*moll*).

---

[14] See the article on solmization by Andrew Hughes in *The New Grove*.

[15] Facsimile edition (Bologna: G. Vecchi, 1969).

[16] See Gustave Reese, *Music in the Renaissance* (New York: Norton, 1959), p. 396.

[17] See Erycius Puteanus (1574–1646), *Modulata Pallas* (Milan, 1599).

[18] See, for example, Johann Mattheson's letter to Johann Joseph Fux, translated by this author, in "The Fux-Mattheson Correspondence: An Annotated Translation," in *Current Musicology* 24 (1977): 40–41, 54.

The term *mollis* was soon transferred to refer to modes or melodies transposed to a one-flat signature. A song transposed into a one-flat signature was considered to be transposed from *cantus durus* or *cantus naturalis* into *cantus mollis*. The term *mollis* thereby came to mean *flat* for some theorists. Thus in the seventeenth century the note A-flat might be referred to as *A moll*. Some theorists in the late seventeenth and early eighteenth centuries extended this usage so that *mollis* referred to compositions written with flats and *durus* to compositions with sharps or only naturals. Thus for some theorists E-flat major was a *mollis* key, while F-sharp minor was a *durus* key.[19]

Zarlino used the Italian word *molle* in its meaning of soft, delicate, and tender to describe the quality of songs in those modes with minor imperfect consonances over the final and fifth.[20] Lippius in 1612 extended this usage to describe the quality of the minor third and minor sixth, the minor triad, and the modes with a minor triad on the final.[21] Later in the seventeenth century the term *dur* was associated by contrast with major intervals, major triads, and the major mode.[22] This is the meaning of the terms *dur* and *moll* that has survived until today.

Harmonic and Arithmetic Division

From antiquity through the period under study here, interval sizes were investigated according to divisions of strings on the monochord. Two types of string divisions were used. In the Arithmetic Division the string was divided successively into equal parts: into halves, quarters, and so forth. In the Harmonic Division (or Geometric Division) the string was divided according to the number series: one half, one third, one quarter, and so forth.

As shown in example I-4, next page, arithmetic division of an octave outlines the final and repercussio of a plagal mode, while

---

[19] See the discussions of Georg Falck and Daniel Speer on pp. 83-4 of this study.

[20] Zarlino, *Istitutioni harmoniche*, second edition (Venice, 1573), p. 182 (Book III, chapter 10): "it [the quality of the minor imperfect consonances] renders the entire song tender." "...che rende tutta la cantilena molle." See also the discussion on pp. 13-20 of the present study.

[21] Johannes Lippius, *Synopsis musicae novae* (Strasbourg, 1612), fols. E7r, F5v, I1r, *passim*. See also chapter 3.

[22] See Andreas Werckmeister, *Musicae mathematicae* (Frankfurt and Leipzig, 1687), p. 125. See also chapter 5.

Example I-4. Division of the Octave

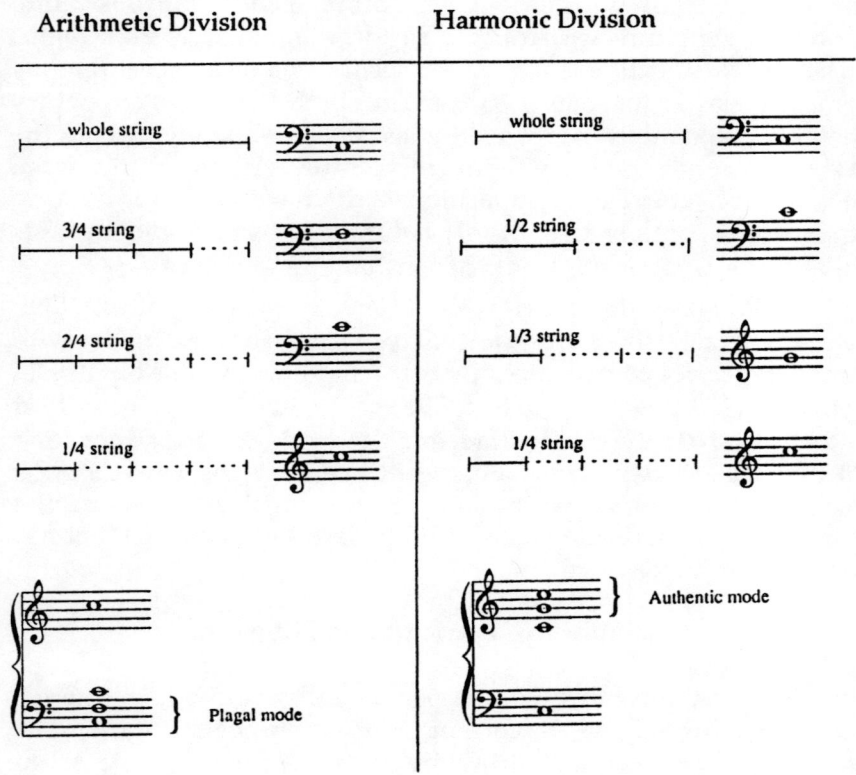

harmonic division outlines the final and repercussio of an authentic mode. The harmonic division of a perfect fifth gives rise to the major triad; the arithmetic division of a perfect fifth gives rise to the minor triad. See example I-5, opposite.

Tuning Systems

During the periods under study here, numerous systems of tuning and temperament were proposed, and numerous such systems were in use. In all tuning systems other than equal temperament, instances of the same interval (except for the octave) may not be of the same size.

Example I-5. Division of the Perfect Fifth

Arithmetic Division | Harmonic Division

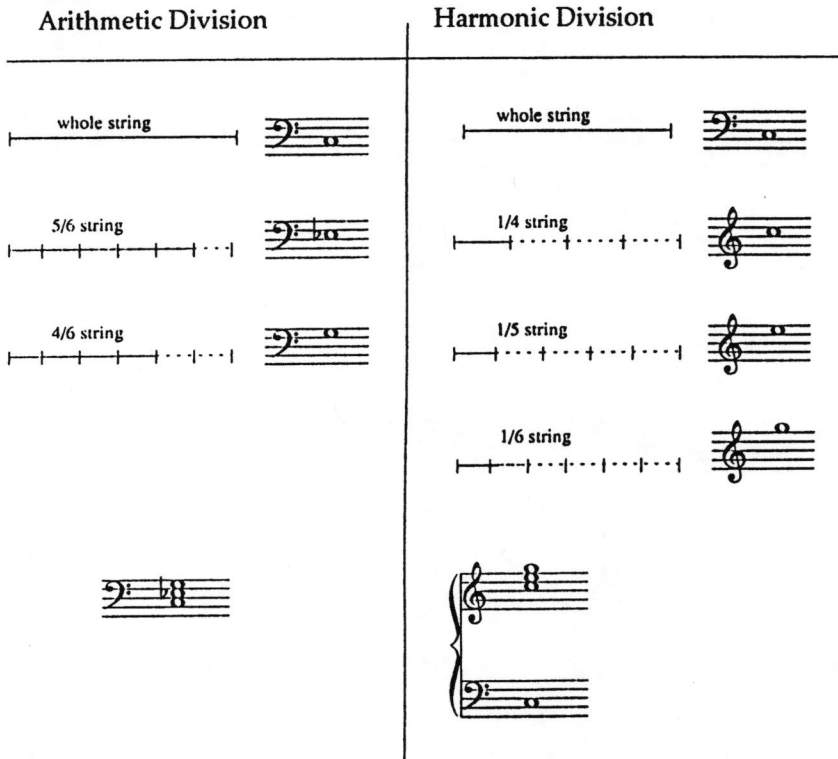

In the Pythagorean system of tuning, all the notes are tuned in a series of pure perfect fifths up and down from the starting pitch (presumably C). As a result, all thirds are quite out-of-tune in relation to their acoustical models. This system, which had proponents during the Middle Ages, was rejected once musical styles demanded consonant thirds. See Example I-6 , next page.

Example I-6. Pythagorean Tuning
Tuned as all perfect fifths ($\frac{3}{2}$)

$$\frac{2}{3} \qquad 1 \qquad \frac{3}{2} \qquad \frac{9}{4} \qquad \frac{27}{8} \qquad \frac{81}{16} \qquad \frac{243}{32}$$

Scale Tuning:

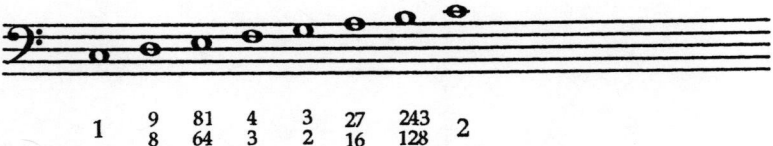

$$1 \quad \frac{9}{8} \quad \frac{81}{64} \quad \frac{4}{3} \quad \frac{3}{2} \quad \frac{27}{16} \quad \frac{243}{128} \quad 2$$

All semitones are $\frac{256}{243}$, also called the *limma* or the *diesis*.

All whole tones are $\frac{9}{8}$, the major tone.

All minor thirds are $\frac{32}{27}$, which is $\frac{81}{80}$ (the syntonic comma) smaller than the pure minor third ($\frac{6}{5}$).

All major thirds are $\frac{81}{64}$, which is $\frac{81}{80}$ (the syntonic comma) larger than a pure major third ($\frac{5}{4}$).

All perfect fourths are, of course, pure ($\frac{4}{3}$).

All perfect fifths are, of course, pure ($\frac{3}{2}$).

The tuning system supported by Zarlino, and one commonly used in theoretical discussions, is the syntonic system, also known as pure tuning. In this system, the notes of the diatonic scale are tuned by pure fifths (3:2) and pure major thirds (5:4)—see example I-7. This results in two different sizes of whole steps: 9:8 (the major

Example I-7. Syntonic Tuning

Tuned as a pure fifth down from C and two pure fifths up (3/2). The
 remaining notes (A, E, B) are tuned as pure major thirds (5/4) up from
 F, C, and G

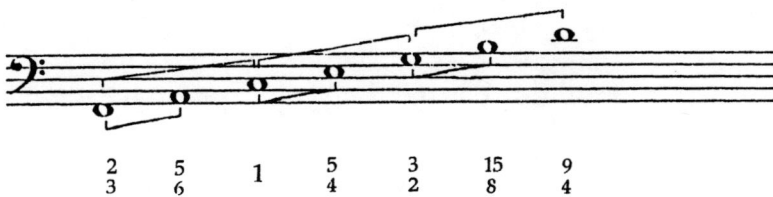

$$\frac{2}{3} \quad \frac{5}{6} \quad 1 \quad \frac{5}{4} \quad \frac{3}{2} \quad \frac{15}{8} \quad \frac{9}{4}$$

Scale Tuning:

$$1 \quad \frac{9}{8} \quad \frac{5}{4} \quad \frac{4}{3} \quad \frac{3}{2} \quad \frac{5}{3} \quad \frac{15}{8} \quad 2$$

All semitones are $\frac{15}{16}$.

There are two sizes of whole tones: $\frac{9}{8}$ —major tone (the sum of two perfect fifths); and $\frac{10}{9}$ —the minor tone (the difference between a pure
 major third [$\frac{5}{4}$] and a major tone).

The minor thirds occur in two sizes: $\frac{6}{5}$ —the pure minor third; and $\frac{32}{27}$ between D and F, which is smaller than a pure minor third by $\frac{81}{80}$ (the
 syntonic comma).

The major thirds are all pure ($\frac{5}{4}$).

The perfect fourths are all pure ($\frac{4}{3}$ except for A to D, which is larger than
 a pure perfect fourth by $\frac{81}{80}$ (the syntonic comma).

The perfect fifths are all pure ($\frac{3}{2}$) except for D to A, which is smaller than
 a pure perfect fifth by $\frac{81}{80}$ (the syntonic comma).

tone) and 10:9 (the minor tone). In addition, one of the perfect fifths
in the diatonic scale (from D to A if the system is tuned from the note
C) is rather flat.

Of the numerous other tuning systems proposed and in use,
only two ever arose as factors in discussions of modes or keys. One

was an approximation of equal temperament described by Andreas Werckmeister in his *Musicalische Temperatur* (Frankfurt and Leipzig, 1691). The development of approximations of equal temperament both allowed the use of more keys on keyboard instruments and recognized the increasing use of distant keys on keyboard instruments. The other tuning system that merits our attention was an extension of pure tuning proposed by Mattheson. The tuning system is described in Appendix 2; its significance for Mattheson's tonal theories is discussed in chapters 6 and 7.

Acknowledgements

A substantial portion of the material in this book appeared in two articles: "Major-Minor Concepts and Modal Theory in Germany, 1592-1680" *Journal of the American Musicological Society* 30 [1977]: 208-53) and "The Recognition of Major and Minor Keys in German Theory: 1680-1730" (*Journal of Music Theory* 22 [1978]: 65-103). In the present book I place the findings of these articles in a large perspective that is possible only in a single study. There is in addition a great deal of hitherto unpublished research, primarily on the mid and late eighteenth century, and a number of hitherto unpublished translations. I am most grateful to the editors of both journals for allowing me unrestricted use of my earlier articles.

I am also indebted to the staffs of numerous libraries, among them The New York Public Library Music Research Division, The Library of Congress, the Herzog August Bibliothek in Wolfenbüttel, the Stadtarchiv Heilbronn, the Österreichische Nationalbibliothek in Vienna, the Stadtarchiv and Rats- und Konsistorial Bibliothek in Rothenburg ob Tauber, the Ratsschulbibliothek in Zwickau, the Stadtarchiv in Braunschweig, the Staatsbibliothek der Stiftung Preussischer Kulturbesitz in Berlin, and the Universitäts-Bibliothek of Humboldt-Universität in Berlin.

For their help with translations from Latin, I am indebted to Professors Stephen Daitz (Classics Department, The City College) and Raymond Erickson (Copland School of Music, Queens College).

Special thanks are due to Ms. Susan Somers of the New York Public Library Music Research Division, who for many years was always available to answer innumerable queries on bibliographical and other matters pertaining to this study.

And last but not least, I owe special thanks to Robert Kessler of Pendragon Press for his interest in publishing this study and all the special care that he put into its preparation.

CHAPTER 1

The Legacy of the Sixteenth Century

Modal Theory in Glarean and Zarlino

Understanding the achievements of early seventeenth-century German theorists requires knowledge of the status of modal theory and major-minor concepts in the sixteenth century—especially in the works of Glarean and Zarlino. The works of the latter, as transmitted to a German audience by Sethus Calvisius in writings dating from 1592, were a seminal influence on the developments of the first decade after 1600.

Heinrich Glarean (1488-1563). Glarean's *Dodecachordon* (Basel, 1547)[1] is an encyclopedic presentation of sixteenth-century modal theory. The treatise contains a full account of the traditional eight modes (in Book I) and Glarean's arguments for a system of twelve modes (Books II and III). See Figure 1-1, next page.

There is not a trace of major-minor thinking in the *Dodecachordon*, not in the generation of the modes, the differentiation of modes, the naming, the ordering, or the discussion of the characteristics of the modes. Glarean did indeed add modes with finals on A and C to the traditional modes with finals on D, E, F, and G—new modes whose octave species we recognize as the natural minor and the major scales. But far from trying to isolate the new Aeolian and Ionian modes as being based on a new perspective, Glarean argues that by introducing modes on A and C he is only trying to complete an imperfect system of eight modes—he is merely correcting a misunderstanding of the nature of mode as octave species. Although

---

[1]Facsm. ed. (New York: Broude, 1967). Passages quoted below in English are taken from the translation by Clement A. Miller (N.p.: American Institute of Musicology, 1965), unless otherwise noted. The treatise was completed in manuscript by 1539 (see Miller, p. 9).

1

Figure 1-1. The Twelve Modes as Presented by Glarean

No.	Authentic Modes	Plagal Modes	Final	Octave Species	
1	Dorian		D	D-D	
2		Hypodorian	D	A-A	
3	Phrygian		E	E-E	The eight
4		Hypophrygian	E	B-B	traditional
5	Lydian		F	F-F	modes
6		Hypolydian	F	C-C	
7	Mixolydian		G	G-G	
8		Hypomixolydian	G	D-D	
9	Aeolian		A	A-A	
10		Hypoaeolian	A	E-E	Glarean's
11	Ionian		C	C-C	four new
12		Hypoionian	C	G-G	modes
13	Hyperaeolian		B	B-B	Two modes
14		Hyperphrygian	B	F-F .	rejected be-cause of a tritone against the final

some of this attitude may be the disingenuous stance of a scholar trying to convince traditionalist skeptics, Glarean was certainly no musical radical. The first two books of the *Dodecachordon* discuss mode in terms of chant, and the introduction of the new modes is only applied to contemporary music in Book III after it has first been defended in terms of chant in Book II. In short, Glarean recognized the Ionian and Aeolian modes, not C major and A minor.

Melodic (scalar) considerations govern the generation of the traditional modes as well as the new modes. Traditional modal theory accepted the first eight modes in Figure 1-1. Any octave species not found among these eight modes had been explained as an inconsequential alteration of another species, not affecting the essential structure of the mode. That is, what Glarean called Aeolian had been considered Dorian with a lowered sixth step, and Ionian had been considered Lydian with a lowered fourth step. From a practical viewpoint, this certainly made sense, since pieces with a final on F as

2

a rule had a signature of one flat (or used B-flat throughout), and pieces with a final on D frequently had a signature of one flat or used B-flat. For Glarean, this approach suffered from inconsistency. Why should some octave species be modes and other octave species be alterations of modes? He tackles the problem head on in Book II, Chapter 6, complaining about those "superficial scholars" who contend

that the entire system is in nowise changed because of altering one or another of the semitones. For they say that this song is *synemmenon* and foreign, as it were, changing nothing in the substance of the mode... And so our eleventh and twelfth modes [the C modes] are not to be separated in any way from the old fifth and sixth modes [the F modes] because of changing a single semitone in the fifth [that is, changing the semitone in the lower fifth of the octave from between scale steps 4 and 5 to between scale steps 3 and 4]... Indeed, we have no quarrel with them concerning what they say in the beginning about the difference of a semitone, if they take it to mean the change of a single note. For we acknowledge that such a tone is used frequently, but as a foreign tone. If, however, they believe this with respect to an entire song, this opinion must be turned down.

We shall easily show in what manner this is false. For if the seventh mode [the G mode] drops the semitone in its fifth from the third position to the second position [that is, from between scale steps 3 and 4 to between scale steps 2 and 3] it will fall completely into the first mode [the D mode]... So in like manner if the third mode raises the semitone in its fifth by one position...it will fall into the system of the second mode. But it is also absurd in the writings of these men, that either the seventh mode is the same as the first, or the third mode is the same as the second. Therefore, the new fifth and sixth modes, or our eleventh and twelfth modes, are not the same as the old fifth and sixth modes...

This passage goes to the heart of the matter. For, if the placement of the semitones within the octave species is the factor differentiating one mode from another, who is to say which semitone alterations are essential and which are merely superficial?[2] Glarean himself is not willing to follow the argument to its conclusion and admit all semitone arrangements or even all diatonic semitone arran-

[2]All theorists who would differentiate modes by semitone placement are vulnerable to this argument. It is used nearly two centuries later by Mattheson in his controversy with Fux on whether there are twelve modes or twenty-four keys. See chapter 7.

gements, for he does not want to establish true modes with a final on B. Thus, he needs two criteria for the definition of mode: "Musical modes are nothing but the consonant species of the octave itself, and the very ones (species) which are joined together from the various species of [consonant] fifths and fourths as we have said above concerning intervals."[3] Since the diminished fifth (B-F) and the augmented fourth (F-B) are not included among the species of consonant fifths and fourths, the possibility of a final on B does not arise.

This definition is the foundation of the formal exposition of the twelve modes in chapter 3 of Book II: "How the twenty-four octave-species arise from the connection of the fourth and the fifth, from which species twelve are rejected and twelve are accepted." There are three species of perfect fourth (with the semitone between steps 1 and 2, 2 and 3, and 3 and 4) and four species of perfect fifth (with the semitone between steps 1 and 2, 2 and 3, 3 and 4, and 4 and 5). If the species of fourth can be placed above and below the species of fifth, there are twenty-four possible connections. Twelve of these are rejected because they give rise to successions of steps not found in a diatonic scale (that is, they are not "consonant species"): four or five whole tones in succession, two semitones in succession, or a single whole tone between two semitones. For instance, if the species of fourth with a semitone between steps 2 and 3 is placed above the species of fifth with the semitone between steps 1 and 2, four consecutive whole tones will arise, as shown in Example 1-1.

Example 1-1.

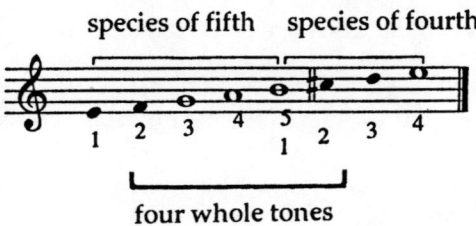

species of fifth   species of fourth

four whole tones

---

[3]Book I, chapter 11: "Modi musici nihil aliud sunt quam ipsius Diapason consonantiae species, quae et ipsae ex variis diapente ac diatessaron speciebus conflantur, ut supra de intervallis diximus." The translation of this sentence is taken from Edward Houghton's review of Clement Miller's translation, *Journal of the American Musicological Society* 20 (1967): 292–293.

And if the species of fourth with the semitone between steps 1 and 2 is placed above the species of fifth with the semitone between steps 4 and 5, two consecutive semitones will arise, as shown in Example 1- 2.

Example 1-2.

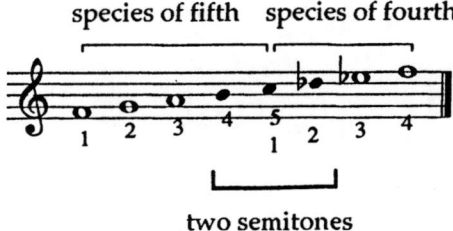

two semitones

The remaining twelve connections are the models for Glarean's six authentic and six plagal modes, modes 1-12 in Figure 1-1. The traditional Greek names of the original eight modes are retained. Glarean bestows names on the new modes in line with his argument that he is merely restoring the ancient teaching of the modes to its rightful place.

A second, less formal, generation of the modes appears in chapter 4 of Book II. The seven octave species are listed (A-a, B-b, and so forth). The fourth and fifth steps of each are examined to see if there is a tritone against the final. Two octave species are thus rejected: the authentic and plagal modes with a final on B. These two rejected modes are named Hyperaeolian (above Aeolian) for the authentic form and Hyperphrygian (above Phrygian) for the plagal form.[4]

As the foregoing demonstrates, melodic (scalar) considerations govern the generation of modes. Relationships among the modes, discussed in chapter 11 of Book II, also depend on melodic criteria:

Modes are also changed from one into another but not with equal success. For in some cases the change is scarcely clear even to a

[4]Glarean explains that there is no other name for the authentic mode on B (Book II, chapter 18). The plagal mode with a final on B could be named as other plagal modes, but as he wryly notes "no sensible person says Hypohyperaeolian" (Book II, chapter 25).

perceptive ear, indeed, often with pleasure to the listener, a fact which we have frequently declared is very common today in changing from the Lydian to the Ionian. Those who play instruments and who know how to sing readily the verses of poets according to a musical plan, understand this. Indeed, in this way they are frequently worthy of praise if they do it skillfully, especially if they change the Ionian into the Dorian. But in other cases the changing seems rough, and scarcely ever without a grave offense to the ears, as changing from the Dorian to the Phrygian... It is evident from the previous discussion that the entire difference between the modes arises from the changing of the fifth and the fourth within the octave in which all modes fit. But this variation arises from the different placing of the semitone, which alters the entire situation. It is also evident that the Lydian and Hypolydian modes have a common fifth, namely, the third species [of fifth]; the Phrygian and Hypophrygian have a common fifth, the second species, each of which includes the tritone, a hard interval, and somewhat unsuitable to the diatonic system... And thus if one changes the Ionian and Hypoionian into the Dorian and Hypodorian, the fifth is changed but is still without a tritone; for this reason the ears are not offended, but rather one will be pleased by the changing of the modes.

The major or minor third over the final is clearly not a factor in determining closely related modes. Ionian and Dorian are listed together because in both there is no tritone within the species of fifth. Lydian is shown to be changed to Ionian in order to remove the tritone from the fifth species, and Hypolydian is always changed to Hypoionian (Book III, chapters 20 and 21).

Nor do major and minor affect the ordering of the modes. In chapter 7 of Book II, Glarean notes that some theorists place Hypodorian first, since it is the first octave species (alphabetically, in that it is the octave A-a). But Hypodorian is not one of the modes supposedly dating back to the modes of the ancient Greeks. Of the three original Greek modes (Dorian, Phrygian, and Lydian), Dorian has the first octave species (alphabetically), and therefore was named the first mode by "our musicians." Glarean retains this ordering, with the addition of his four new modes. In chapter 15 of Book II and in the discussion of each mode separately in chapters 16-27, the modes are ordered alphabetically by octave species. But when each mode is referred to by number (the "first mode," etc.) the numbering is in the series beginning with Dorian.

In summary, mode for Glarean is a melodic concept. The major-minor duality of the Ionian and Aeolian modes, or of any other modes, plays no part in any of Glarean's thinking—not in the generation of the modes, their ordering, differentiation, relationships, or characteristics.

Gioseffo Zarlino (1517-1590). Zarlino is one of those rare theorists whose works not only organize the collected knowledge of an era, but also provide imaginative insights into hitherto unrecognized aspects of music. His *Istitutioni harmoniche* (Venice, 1558; second edition 1573)[5] is one of the landmarks of music theory, combining speculative theory, formal theoretical presentations, and a practical method of composition. The treatise divides into four parts: the divisions of music and necessary mathematical operations (Part I), intervals (Part II), instruction in composition and the art of counterpoint (Part III), and modes (Part IV). Within these formal presentations, Zarlino is the first theorist to recognize that harmonic criteria play a role in determining the affect of modes, the first theorist to recognize the fundamental nature of that harmony with a fifth and third over the bass, and the first theorist to recognize the polarity between the form of that harmony with a major third and that with a minor third. But for an accurate assessment of his accomplishments, it is essential to place each of these tenets in his theoretical framework.

Part IV of the *Istitutioni* contains Zarlino's formal presentation of the modes (chapters 1-31, pp. 359-419[6]). In its general approach to the modes, Zarlino's theory is similar, if not identical to Glarean's. Only eleven years after the publication of the *Dodecachordon*, Zarlino accepts the twelve modes with neither question nor acknowledgement. Following a discussion of the ancient Greek and medieval writers on mode (chapters 1-8, pp. 359-378), Zarlino discusses the division of the octave (chapter 9, p. 379), the generation of modes by the connection of the species of fifth with that of the fourth (chapter

[5]Facsimile of the first edition (New York: Broude, 1965). This edition of the treatise was reprinted in 1561, 1562, and 1572. A new edition appeared in 1573 (facsimile edition [Ridgewood, N.J.: Gregg, 1966]). References below are to the 1573 edition unless otherwise noted. Part III (1558 edition) is in English translation by Guy Marco and Claude Palisca under the title *The Art of Counterpoint* (New Haven: Yale University Press, 1968). Part IV is in English translation by Vered Cohen under the title *On the Modes* (New Haven: Yale University Press, 1983).
[6]Page 419 is incorrectly numbered 319 in the 1573 edition.

10, pp. 379-380)[7], and the second generation of the twelve modes by the division of the six octave species capable of harmonic and arithmetic division (chapter 11, pp. 380-383). He divides the modes into authentic and plagal categories (chapter 12, p. 384) and discusses range (chapters 13-14, pp. 384- 389). The modes are differentiated by the placement of the semitone within the octave species. If a semitone is changed by an accidental only a few times, then the mode is not considered to be changed. But if this alteration occurs throughout a composition, then the mode is changed (chapter 16, pp. 389-390). Transposition is treated in chapter 17 with greater freedom than in Glarean's *Dodecachordon*. Glarean had included only the transposition up a fourth to a signature with one flat—a transposition sanctioned by the inclusion of B-flat in the solmization hexachords. Zarlino notes in addition that transposition is particularly necessary when singing with organ or other instruments. The most common transposition is up or down by a fourth, but transpositions by a second "or another interval, not only by chromatic notes, but even enharmonic,"[8] are also possible. On the same page, a D mode melody appears in examples transposed down and up by a major second; first it appears with a signature of two flats and then with one of two sharps. In the individual discussions of each mode (chapters 18-29), however, only the transposition to a signature with one flat is listed. Other aspects treated for each mode include, in part, cadences, a list of compositions, and an example in two voices.

In the aspects of modal theory described above, Zarlino's presentation is either the same as Glarean's, or it differs only in minor ways. But there are two important issues on which there is an essential difference between the two theorists: one concerns the ordering of the modes, the other the differentiation of the modes on the basis of the imperfect consonances.

The question of the ordering of the modes arises in chapters 18-29 of Part IV, in which each mode is discussed in turn. In the prints from 1558 to 1572, Glarean's ordering is used: Dorian and

---

[7]"Se dalla unione, o compositione della Diapente con la Diatessaron nascono li Modi moderni..." (p. 379: "The modern modes arise from the union or composition of the fifth with the fourth").

[8]P. 391: "o per altro intervallo: ado perando non solamente le Chorde Chromatiche: ma anco le Enharmoniche."

Hypodorian are the first two modes. In the 1573 edition, however, the first mode discussed is the C mode. In chapter 20, Zarlino reaches the D mode, now third, "which was universally placed by musicians in the first place until now, though with little reason."[9] He refers the reader to the fifth *Ragionamento* of his *Dimostrationi harmoniche* (Venice, 1571)[10] for the reasoning behind the new ordering.

Definition 8 of the fifth *Ragionamento* is a listing of the seven octave species in the order C, D, E, F, G, A, B.[11] The discussion following this covers pages 270-273 and presents six reasons for the new ordering of the octave species, and, hence, the modes.

1. The model for pure tuning on the keyboard is the octave C-c.[12] Hence the C mode should be first.[13]

2. The second and third reasons concern the relationship between the modes and Guidonian solmization. "Our ancestors, having reduced the order of musical notes into hexachords, and having attributed to them that order of the syllables which you

[9]P. 396: "il quale fin hora dalla Università delli Musici è stato posto, con poca ragione, nel Primo luogo."

[10]Facsimile edition (Ridgewood, N.J.: Gregg, 1966).

[11]"La Prima specie della Diapason è quella, che tra la terza & la quarta chorda: & tra la settima & la ottava contiene il Semituono maggiore. La Seconda è quella..., procedendo sempre dalla parte grave alla acuta" (*Dimostrationi harmoniche*, p. 270: "The first species of octave is that which contains the major semitone between the third and fourth and seventh and eighth notes. The second is that..., always proceeding from the low part to the high").

[12]One of the innovations of the *Istitutioni* is Zarlino's strong advocacy of pure tuning (just intonation) as the model for intonation. Review the introduction of the present work for the details of this tuning system.

[13]"...dalla Divisione harmonicamente fatta della Diapason nelle sue parti...nasce uno ordine de intervalli: nel primo de i quali, che è il piu grave, si ritrova il Tuono maggiore: nel Secondo il minore: & nel Terzo il maggior Semituono. Simigliantemente di nuovo nel Quarto è collocato il Tuono maggiore: nel Quinto il minore: nel Sesto ancora il Tuono maggiore: & nel Settimo & ultimo posto nell' acuto si trova il Maggior semituono: chiaramente compresi, che tale Diapason: divisa secondo la natura del Numero harmonico: è collocata tra le nostre moderne chorde: C. D. E. F. G. a. ♮ & c" (*Dimostrationi harmoniche*, pp. 270–271, "From the harmonic division of the octave into its parts...an order of intervals arises: in the first or lowest position is found the major tone, in the second position the minor tone, and in the third the major semitone. Similarly, again in the fourth is placed the major tone, in the fifth the minor tone, in the sixth again the major tone, and in the seventh and last position at the top is found the major semitone. Clearly, it is understood that such an octave, divided according to the nature of the harmonic number, is placed between our modern notes C, D, E, F, G, a, b, c").

have named [*ut, re, mi, fa, sol, la*], they should sooner have given first place to those species of the first syllable *ut* than to those of *re*, which is the second, so that when the fourth species is reached in their manner, it would not be necessary to return and begin in the fourth place from the syllable *ut*—which for every reason should hold the first place, and not the last..."[14]

3. Zarlino then hypothesizes that A was originally selected as the first octave species since it was the first letter of the alphabet. *Re* was thus associated with the first mode. Since there can be no mode on B, however, D (also *re*) was selected as the final of the first mode. Zarlino, of course, does not accept this conclusion.

4. Zarlino notes that in the ordering beginning with C, there are no skips between the finals of successive authentic modes (C, D, E, F, G, A), whereas by beginning on D there is a skip between A and C (D, E, F, G, A, C).

5. By beginning on C, the finals of the modes follow the order of the hexachord: *ut, re, mi, fa, sol, la*.

6. Zarlino's final reason is that the ordering of the modes now follows the ordering as described by the ancient Greeks. According to his reading of Greek theorists, Dorian and Phrygian were distant from each other by a tone, as were Phrygian and Lydian. Zarlino gives these ancient modes the numbers 1, 2, and 3. His first three authentic modes are also distant from one another by whole steps, which is not true in the series begun on D.

As a consequence of these reasons, the authentic modes are given a new ordering: C, D, E, F, G, A. In Definition 14 of the *Dimostrationi* (pp. 275-277), the authentic modes receive the following names:

[14]"...nostri Maggiori ridutto l'ordine delle chorde musicali in Hexachordi: & havendoli attribuito quell' ordine de Voci, che nominato havete: piu tosto bisognava dar principio a queste Specie nella prima voce Ut: che nella Re, che è la Seconda: accioche quando si pervie, ne alla Quarta specie al modo loro: non si havesse à ritornare in dietro: & incominciare nel Quarto luogo di tale ordine dalla voce Ut: la quale, per ogni dovere, doverebbe tenere il primo, & non l'ultimo luogo" (*Dimostrationi harmoniche*, p. 271).

1. Dorian, the C mode
3. Phrygian, the D mode
5. Lydian, the E mode
7. Mixolydian or Locrian, the F mode
9. Ionian, the G mode
11. Aeolian, the A mode

All the names here differ from those of Glarean with the exception of Aeolian. Furthermore, the names of modes 3-10 do not agree with the names of the corresponding traditional eight church modes. Perhaps it was to prevent confusion that Zarlino avoided the use of Greek names elsewhere in his works and referred to the modes by number only, in the ordering C mode to A mode.[15] When later theorists discuss the modes, they generally use the traditional nomenclature, with Glarean's names for the modes on A and C. This is true even when theorists use different orderings.[16] In this study, the names always refer to Glarean's usage.

[15]Carl Dahlhaus, in *Untersuchungen über die Entstehung der harmonischen Tonalität* (Kassel: Bärenreiter, 1968), mentions only Zarlino's last reason for reordering the modes. He thereby ascribes the new ordering solely to a misunderstanding of Greek theory already present in the 1558 edition of the *Istitutioni*. It is because of this that Dahlhaus explains the use of numbers, not names for the modes even in that edition. Dahlhaus then wrongly attributes to Calvisius and Lippius the explanation of Ionian in first position because it is the "most natural." This is already presented in Zarlino's first reason, which is repeated by Calvisius. Furthermore, Lippius never argues for Ionian mode in the first position because it has the "natural triad" in the "natural position," as Dahlhaus asserts.

[16]Zarlino's nomenclature does occur in some later works, among which are: 1. Charles Guillet (?–1654), *Vingt quatre fantasies à quatre parties disposées selon l'ordre des douze modes* (1610). Guillet also wrote a manuscript treatise, *Institution harmonique* in 1642, concerning which see Herbert Schneider, *Die französische Kompositionslehre in der ersten Hälfte des 17. Jahrhunderts* (Tutzing: H. Schneider, 1972), pp. 189-192, *passim*. 2. Marin Mersenne (1588-1648) uses these names in several of his treatises. See Schneider, *op. cit.*, pp. 131ff. 3. The French lutenist Dénis Gaultier (ca. 1603-1672) ordered compositions in his *Rhétorique des dieux* (manuscript from 1652, facsimile edition with introduction by André Tessier and Jean Cordey, Publications de la Société française de musicologie, t. 6-7 [Paris, 1932]) according to twelve modes. The names agree with Zarlino except that Ionian and Aeolian are reversed, now with finals on G for the latter and A for the former. 4. Johann Fux, who otherwise referred to the modes by pitch in his *Gradus ad parnassum* (Vienna, 1725, facsimile editions [New York: Broude, 1966 and in *Fux Sämtliche Werke* 7/1, Kassel: Bärenreiter, 1967]), uses these names on p. 231.

I do not wish to examine here the logical flaws and historical errors in some of Zarlino's reasons. What matters for the present study are the reasons themselves as Zarlino understood them, not their validity. It should be clear that Zarlino's reasons for reordering the modes are in no way related to isolating Ionian and Aeolian or placing them in prominent positions, either because they represent "major and minor,"[17] or for any other reason. In fact, had Zarlino wished to emphasize "major and minor," he would have done better by using Glarean's ordering. Many a seventeenth-century and early eighteenth- century theorist would have chosen Glarean's ordering as a better reflection of major and minor. Dorian, not Aeolian, was the model for the minor mode in many late seventeenth-century and early eighteenth- century writings, including even Rameau's *Traité* of 1722.[18] This choice was probably influenced by the relative ease of cadencing on the dominant in Dorian as opposed to Aeolian. In Dorian, an authentic cadence on the dominant requires only a raised fourth scale step. In Aeolian, an authentic cadence on the dominant requires chromatic alteration of two scale degrees: the raised fourth and sixth scale steps. See Example 1-3.

Example 1-3.

Dorian mode   Aeolian mode

This was probably a factor in the persistence of incomplete key signatures for minor keys well into the eighteenth century.[19] Finally, although some early seventeenth-century theorists adopted Zarlino's ordering, many theorists later in the seventeenth century and at the beginning of the next century when major-minor keys

---

[17]See p. xi, footnote 6.

[18]See Book III, chapter 22, article 2 of the *Traité* (pp. 264-265 of the English translation by Philip Gossett [New York: Dover, 1971]). In a footnote to p. 264, Gossett points out that in the supplement issued along with the *Traité*, Rameau changed his mind and argued for the Aeolian mode as the model for minor.

[19]See the arguments of Janowka concerning why Aeolian is the proper model for the minor mode in appendix I of the present study. The number of accidentals that have to be added during a piece is a criterion he uses.

were becoming widely recognized returned to Glarean's ordering and maintained Dorian in first place.[20]

The second essential difference between Glarean's and Zarlino's theories on mode concerns the latter's differentiation of the affect of the modes according to the major and minor imperfect consonances. This issue arises not in the formal presentation of mode in Part IV of the *Istitutioni*, but in two widely separated passages in Part III on composition. The first is in chapter 10: "On the property or nature of the imperfect consonances."

> The property or nature of the imperfect consonances is that some of them are lively and cheerful, accompanied by much sonority, and some, although they are sweet and smooth, tend somewhat toward sadness or languor. The first are the major thirds and sixths and their compounds: and the others are the minor [thirds and sixths]... There are some songs which are lively and full of cheer; and some others on the contrary which are rather sad and languid. The reason is that in the first the major imperfect consonances are often heard above the final or mediant notes of the modes or tones, which are the first, second, seventh, eighth, ninth, and tenth, as we shall see elsewhere. These modes are very cheerful and lively because in them we often hear the consonances placed according to the nature of the sonorous number: that is, the fifth divided harmonically into a major third and a minor third, which gives much pleasure to the ear.[21]

In the continuation, Zarlino notes that the other modes are characterized by the minor imperfect consonances above the final and mediant. It is important to examine carefully the choice of words in

---

[20]See especially Johann Crüger (footnote 12 p. 55), including the works listed in Table 4-1 (pp. 71-75). See also Johann Mattheson, whose *Das neu- eröffnete Orchestre* (Hamburg, 1713), pp. 60–63, lists D minor as the first of the twenty-four keys. See Chapter 6.

[21]"Della Propietà, o natura delle consonanze Imperfette. Cap. 10. Il propio, o Natura delle Consonanze imperfette è, che alcune di loro sono vive & allegre, accompagnate da molta sonorità; & alcune, quantunque siano dolci & soavi, declinano alquanto al mesto, overo languido. Le prime sono le Terze & le Seste maggiori & le Replicate: & le altre sono le minori...sono alcune Cantilene, le quali sono vive & piene di allegrezza; & alcune altre per il contrario, sono alquanto meste, over languide. La cagione è, che nelle prime, spesso si odono le Maggiori consonanze imperfette sopra le chorde estreme finali, o mezane de i Modi, o Tuoni, che sono il Primo, il Secondo, il Settimo, l'Ottavo, il Nono, & il Decimo; come vederemo altrove: i quali Modi sono molto allegri & vivi: conciosia che in essi udimo spesse fiate le Consonanze collocate secondo la natura del Numero sonoro: cioè la Quinta tramezata, o divisa harmonicamente in una Terza maggiore & in una minor; il he diletta all'Udito" (*Istitutioni*, p. 182).

this passage. Zarlino writes that "the major imperfect consonances [not only the major thirds] are often [not always] heard above the final or mediant notes [not only above the final: note that mediant here refers to the note which divides the octave of the mode, i.e., the fifth]...we often [not always] hear the consonances [note the plural] placed according to the nature of the sonorous number [not merely according to the sonorous number]." For Zarlino, the perfect fifth and fourth are generated by the harmonic and arithmetic division of the octave. Similarly, the major and minor thirds arise from the divisions of the perfect fifth. But the major sixth arises from the addition of a major third to the perfect fourth, and the minor sixth from the addition of the minor third to the perfect fourth.[22] Thus, the consonances which are arranged according to the nature of the sonorous number are the sixth and third.[23]

The disposition of these intervals (thirds and sixths) over the final and fifth in each mode are shown in Figure 1-2 (opposite). Note that the quality of the intervals corresponds in most cases, but not all, hence the modifier "often" in Zarlino's passage.

This differentiation of the affects of the modes is harmonic, not melodic. The intervals are heard "above the final or mediant notes." Earlier theorists, as well as many later ones, used the semitone placement as the sole criterion to differentiate modes. Zarlino himself uses this in all other aspects of mode in the formal presentation in Part IV. All modes have the same number of tones and semitones, major and minor thirds, etc. The crucial factor in Zarlino's differentiation of affect lies in the harmonic intervals that arise over certain important tones in the different octave species.

The *Istitutioni* also contains some of the first statements concerning the fundamental harmony with a fifth and third over the bass and its differentiation into major and minor according to the quality of the third.[24] This discussion appears twenty-one chapters

[22]"L'hexachordo maggiore, anco il minore, nascono della congiuntione della Diatessaron col Ditono, o Semiditono," (*Istitutioni*, Part I, chapter 13, "The major sixth, as well as the minor, arise from the conjunction of the perfect fourth with the major third, or the minor third").

[23]See Matthew Shirlaw, *The Theory of Harmony*, chapter 2, for a study of Zarlino's generation of intervals.

[24]Benito V. Rivera, in "Harmonic Theory in Musical Treatises of the Late Fifteenth and Early Sixteenth Centuries," in *Music Theory Spectrum*, 1 (1979): 93-95, cites the discussion of harmonies with more than two notes in works by Franchino Gafori (Milan,

Figure 1-2

Mode	Quality of thirds and sixths over final		Quality of thirds and sixths over fifth	
Ionian	M 3	M 6	M 3	M 6
Lydian	M 3	M 6	M 3	M 6
Mixolydian	M 3	M 6	(m 3)	M 6
Aeolian	m 3	m 6	m 3	m 6
Phrygian	m 3	m 3	m 3	m 6
Dorian	m 3	(M 6)	m 3	m 6

after the sole mention of the major-minor differentiation of the affect of the modes. It arises more or less as a rule of thumb for avoiding problematic harmonic intervals. Zarlino is a contrapuntal theorist. In dealing with textures containing three or more voices, he maintains the age-old tradition of calculating each voice separately from the tenor.[25] This can lead to problems when two voices are consonant with the tenor but dissonant with each other. For instance, if the tenor is on D and the bass is on B, an F in the alto creates a diminished

---

'1496) and Guillermus de Podio (Valencia, 1495). Despite his enumeration of numerous possible doublings, Gafori clearly considers the resulting "triad" to be combination of individual intervals, not a harmony in and of itself. De Podio's discussion is similar in nature, even though it does make clear the difference between a perfect fifth divided by a major third and minor third, and perfect fifth divided by a minor third and major third. Comparison of these passages with those by Zarlino, and especially that by Avianius (who recognizes a complete triadic harmony in 1581 even when only two notes are sounding; see pp. 28-31), make it clear that these two earlier theorists did not offer "triads as unified entities," as Rivera asserts on p. 93.

[25]"Dobbiamo etiandio sempre osservare, di far le Cadenze principalmente nel Tenore: essendo questa parte la Guida principale di ciaschedun Modo; sopra il quale si compone la Cantilena: & de esso deboe il Compositore pigliar la inventione dell' altre parti" (Istitutioni, p. 394: "We should always take care to make the cadence principally in the tenor, this part being the principal guide of each mode, over which the song is composed; and from this the composer should take the invention of the other parts").

15

fifth, but only against the bass. Or if the tenor is on D, a B-flat and B-natural are both consonant with it, but clash with each other.

In chapter 30 of Part III, Zarlino discusses problematic harmonic intervals ("*Intervalli relati*"[26]) such as the tritone, diminished fifth, and diminished and augmented octave. The discussion continues in Chapter 31 concerning the presence of such intervals in counterpoint with more than two voices.[27] In the midst of this discussion, Zarlino notes that something other than a composite of intervals is involved when there are more than two voices:

> ...The variety of the harmony in such situations does not consist solely in the variety of the consonances that are found between two voices, but also in the variety of the harmonies—which [variety] is determined by the position of the note that makes a third or tenth above the lowest voice of the composition. Either these [intervals] are minor, and the harmony that arises is determined by or corresponds to the arithmetical proportion or division, or they are major, and such a harmony is determined by or corresponds to the harmonic mean. On this variety depends all the diversity and perfection of harmonies...For as I have said elsewhere, when the major third is below, the harmony is cheerful, and when it is placed above, the harmony is sad."[28]

"Elsewhere" refers to the passage in chapter 10 differentiating the affects of the modes.

Inversions of this fundamental harmony are not mentioned as such by Zarlino. What we refer to today as the triad of the first inversion is mentioned in Chapter 59 of Part III: "many times

[26]"Nonharmonic relations," as translated by Guy Marco and Claude Palisca, *op. cit.*, p. 68.

[27]"Che rispetto si de havere a gli Intervalli relati nelle compositioni di piu voci" (chapter heading of chapter 31, "Concerning Nonharmonic Relations in Compositions of More [than Two] Voices."

[28]...Conciosia che la varietà dell' Harmonia in simili accompagnamenti non consiste solamente nella varietà delle Consonanze, che si trova tra due parti; ma nella varietà anco delle Harmonie, la quale consiste nella positione della chorda, che fà la Terza, over la Decima sopra la parte grave della cantilena. Onde, overo che sono minori & l'Harmonia che nasce, è ordinata, ò si assimiglia alla proportionalità, o mediatione Arithmetica; overo sono maggiori & tale Harmonia è ordinata, over si assimiglia alla mediocrità Harmonica: & da questa varietà dipende tutta la diversità & la perfettione delle Harmonie...percioche (como hò detto altrove) quando si pone la Terza maggiore nella parte grave, l'Harmonia si f àallegra; & quando si pone nell' acuto si fà mesta" (*Istitutioni*, pp. 210ff).

musicians place the sixth in the position of the fifth."[29] What we refer to today as the second inversion triad is referred to in chapter 60, on how to use the fourth. Any systematic treatment of harmony according to intervals over the bass would be alien to Zarlino's theories. The tenor is still the central voice of a composition for him—the voice that determines the mode and the first to be composed. As noted above, Zarlino generates the sixth by adding a third to the perfect fourth. Thus, the thirds are related to sixths of like quality (the major third to the major sixth), which contradicts the inversional relationship in which thirds are related to sixths of opposite quality (the major third to the minor sixth). In chapter 58, a table lists fifty-four different consonant arrangements of four voices. In all cases, the chord is constructed from the tenor. There is no differentiation according to the modern classification into triads and their inversions, or into major and minor. Indeed, some combinations are a single interval with multiple doublings. See Figure 1-3, next page.

That is the extent of the direct discussion of what we call the triad and of the relationship between the distinction of mode and the major-minor consonances. This was evidently a new area for theory, and its relationship to traditional contrapuntal and modal theory was not recognized in all its ramifications. The incorporation of a harmonic unit of more than two notes as a fundamental of compositional theory would require a thorough revision of contrapuntal/harmonic theory. And the harmonic differentiation of modes according to certain harmonic intervals over crucial scale degrees would require a revision of the very nature of mode. These transformations of traditional theory began to appear in the writings of other theorists during Zarlino's own lifetime, and were fully developed by the early years of the next century. But they are not a part of Zarlino's own work. Zarlino was the first to articulate that much consonant harmony is dependent on the major and minor triads and that there is a fundamental difference between those modes with a major third over the final and those with a minor third. But, in neither case was the differentiation stated as the modern musician (continued, p. 20)

---

[29]"molte volte li Prattici pongono la Sesta in luogo della Quinta" (p. 287).

Figure 1-3. Types of Chords Listed by Zarlino on pp. 284-285 of the *Istitutioni* **(1573)**

Interval Between Soprano and Tenor	*Interval Between Bass and Tenor*	*Interval Between Alto and Bass*
Unison	Third below	Fifth or Sixth above
	Fifth below	Third or Tenth above
	Sixth below	Third or Tenth above
	Octave below	Third, Fifth, Sixth, Tenth, or Twelfth above
	Tenth below	Fifth or Twelfth above
	Twelfth below	Third or Tenth above
	Two Octaves below	Third, Fifth, Sixth, Tenth, Twelfth, or Thirteenth above
Third above	Third below	Unison or Octave above
	Sixth below	Third or Tenth above
	Octave below	Fifth or Sixth above
	Tenth below	Unison or Octave above
Fourth above	Fifth below	Third or Tenth above
	Twelfth below	Tenth above
Fifth above	Octave below	Third or Tenth above
	Sixth below	Unison or Octave above
Sixth above	Fifth below	Unison or Octave above
	Third below	Fifth above
	Tenth below	Fifth or Twelfth above

Fig.1-3 cont.

Interval Between Soprano and Tenor	Interval Between Bass and Tenor	Interval Between Alto and Bass Octave above
Octave above	Third below	Third, Fifth, Sixth, Tenth, Twelfth, or Thirteenth above
	Fifth below	Third above
	Octave below	Third, Fifth, Tenth, or Twelfth above
	Twelfth below	Tenth or Two Octaves and a Third above

[Zarlino does not present examples. The following all start from a tenor on C. The dotted and solid barlines correspond to the dotted and solid lines in the chart above.]

would state it, and—more importantly—in neither case did Zarlino intend many of the implications that the modern musician tends to add automatically.[30] In short, Zarlino did not present a completed theory of major-minor polarity.Both the mention of the "triad" and this differentiation of the modes appear only in Part III of the *Istitutioni*—the practical section on composition. They are in effect rules of thumb useful in composing, but not yet sufficiently considered to be incorporated into formal theory. Indeed, this major-minor differentiation of the affect of the modes is the only important aspect of mode not presented in Part IV. The only systematic differentiation of the modes in Part IV is that by the placement of their semitones.

The passage on the major and minor consonances and their relation to modes is essentially unchanged from the 1558 edition to the complete edition of Zarlino's works in 1589, prepared under his supervision. In other areas of theory, he made substantial changes during this period, and he engaged in extensive disputes with other theorists. Zarlino died in 1590, not having changed in print his concepts of the "triad" or major and minor, both of which had appeared thirty-two years earlier.

---

[30]Hermann Gehrmann, "Johann Gottfried Walther als Theoretiker," in *Vierteljahrsschrift für Musikwissenschaft*, 7 (1891): 469: "Es ist dies derselbe Unterschied, den wir heute zwischen einer Dur- und Mollskala wahrnehmen..." The same viewpoint is presented in a study of Zarlino by Robert Wienpahl, "Zarlino, the Senario, and Tonality," in *Journal of the American Musicological Society* 12 (1959):27–41. On p. 29, he mistranslates the sentence beginning "La cagione" (see footnote 21 in the present chapter) of the *Istitutioni* (chapter 10 of Part III) to read: "The reason is that in the first [case] the Major imperfect consonances frequently appear above the final note, as in the case of the Modes, or Tones, such as the First, Second, Seventh, Eighth, Ninth, and the Tenth..." But Zarlino writes that the major imperfect consonances appear "above the final or mediant notes of the modes." The same mistranslation appears in Mr. Wienpahl's "English Theorists and Evolving Tonality," in *Music and Letters* 36 (1955):377.

Walter Atcherson ("Key and Mode in 17th Century Music Theory Books," in *Journal of Music Theory* 17 [1973]:207) notes that Lippius differentiates modes into two types "according to the quality of third above the final; Zarlino had already done this before him"[!].

Cf. also footnote 6 on p. xi.

Chapter 2

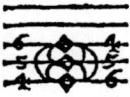

German Theorists Before Lippius

Johann Lippius, in several works published at the end of the first decade of the seventeenth century, for the first time presented a unified harmonic conception of music, in which the triad was the basis of counterpoint as well as of the modes. The writings of Lippius are the subject matter of chapter 3. The present chapter discusses the generation of German theorists that preceded these works of Lippius's. This generation introduced Zarlino's theories to a German audience and greatly deepened the understanding of triadic structures. Indeed, the first complete theory of inverted triads appears in German theory before 1610. None of these theorists was able to come up with the unified conception of musical structure that Lippius offered. But each played a role in introducing or refining concepts that were important to Lippius. In addition, each theorist demonstrates by other aspects of his writings how far the pre-Lippius generation remained from Lippius's unified harmonic perspective of music.

Sethus Calvisius (Seth Kalwitz) (1556-1615)

Zarlino's theoretical writings became the foundation of early seventeenth-century theory largely through the works of Calvisius, cantor at the Thomasschule in Leipzig from 1594 until his death in 1615, and known as "a most learned man...an outstanding musician as a theorist, as well as a composer and performer."[1] He wrote the

---

[1] Wolfgang Caspar Printz, *Historische Beschreibung der edelen Sing- und Klingkunst* (Dresden, 1690; facsimile edition Graz: Akademische Druck- und Verlagsanstalt, 1964), p. 132: "ein sehr gelahrter Mann...fürtrefflicher Musicus so wohl Theoreticus als Poëticus und Modulatorius." Kurt Benndorf's "Sethus Calvisius als Musiktheoretiker," in *Vierteljahrsschrift für Musikwissenschaft* 10 (1894):411–470, remains, despite some errors, the most comprehensive survey of his life and work.

first true history of music, "De origine et progressu musices," as the second of his *Exercitationes musicae duae* (Leipzig, 1600) and was also known as an expert on such nonmusical subjects as philology and chronology (history). Calvisius did not directly translate Zarlino's works from Italian, but reorganized the material in pedagogical publications, omitting much of the speculative material.[2]

Discussions of the modes appear in the *Melopoeia sive melodiae condendae ratio* (Erfurt, 1592),[3] *Exercitationes musicae duae* (Leipzig, 1600),[4] and the *Exercitatio musica tertia* (Leipzig, 1611).[5] With few exceptions, Calvisius's treatment of the modes is similar or identical to Zarlino's. Thus, modes are held to be "...certain harmonic genera that arise from the seven octave species by the varied joinings of the fifths and fourths."[6] There is a reference to the ordering of the modes starting with Dorian, but Ionian is placed first. "If that mode which arises from the first species of octave and which is composed from the first species of fifth and the first species of fourth should be placed first in order, Ionian with its plagal will be the first."[7] As with Zarlino, the differentiation of the modes according to the major and minor imperfect consonances does not appear along with the formal presentation of the modes. Calvisius places the discussion in Chapter 18 of the *Melopoeia*, the chapter on text setting ("De oratione sive

---

[2] A lost German manuscript translation of Zarlino's *Istitutioni* by Johann Caspar Trost, Sr. (an organist at Halberstadt whose birthdate is unknown and who died before 1645) was located by Martin Gerber through an entry in a Leipzig catalogue of 1673. The date of the translation is unknown, but considering the date of Trost's death, it is improbable that the translation was done before 1592, the date of Calvisius's *Melopoeia*. The translation apparently did not receive a wide circulation. See Michel Brenet, "Deux traductions françaises inédites des *Institutions harmoniques* de Zarlino," in *L'Année musicale* 1 (1911):125–144.

[3] Second edition edited by Heinrich Grimm (Magdeburg, 1630).

[4] "...Quarum prior est, de Modis Musicis, quos vulgò Tonos vocant, rectècognoscendis, & dijudicandis..." ("Two essays on music, of which the first concerns the musical modes, which are commonly called tones, how to properly understand them and differentiate them").

[5] Written in answer to Rektor Hubmeier's *Disputationes quaestionum illustrium* (Jena, 1609).

[6] *Exercitatio musica tertia*, p. 76: "Modi sunt certa Harmoniae genera, quae ex septem diapason speciebus, seu octavis pro varimâ quintarum & quartarum connexione oriuntur."

[7] *Melopoeia*, fol. H2r- H2v: "Si is modus in ordine primus collocari debet, qui oritur ex prima specie diapason, & componitur ex prima specie diapente, et ex prima diatessaron, Ionicus cum suo remisso, primus erit."

textu"). After discussing the different intervals used to express various emotions, Calvisius notes that

> the more joyful modes are Ionian, Lydian, and Mixolydian, because the fifth is divided harmonically. The sadder and more languid [modes], on the other hand, [are] Dorian, Phrygian, and Aeolian because of the arithmetic division of the same interval. For everywhere the harmonic division expresses a smoother sound than the arithmetic.[8]

This differentiation of modes does not appear elsewhere in Calvisius's works.

Calvisius treats the differences between authentic and plagal modes with somewhat less emphasis than Zarlino (or, indeed, than most sixteenth-century theorists). Although Calvisius cites the difference between authentic and plagal modes (referring to them as *contentus* and *remissus* in the *Melopoeia*, fol. H2r), less emphasis is given throughout to the plagal forms. Thus, in the *Exercitationes musicae duae*, he notes that "there are six principal modes."[9] Only after each is discussed separately are the plagal modes introduced. In the *Melopoeia*, cadences are discussed solely for the authentic modes, with a note explaining that "modes of the same name, authentic as well as plagal, form the same cadences."[10] The plagal form is treated independently in the *Exercitationes musicae duae* only in the course of discussing the combinations of modes and different forms of the same mode in polyphonic music.[11] The reduced emphasis on plagal modes is part of a long-range trend that saw mode change from the specific characteristic of a single part (a monophonic composition or

---

[8] *Melopoeia*, fol. I3r: "Modi etiam laetiores sunt Ionicus, Lydius, Mixolydius propter diapente quod Harmonica dividitur. Tristiores contra & languidiores Dorius, Phrygius, & Aeolius, propter ejusdem intervallis Arithmeticam divisionem ubiq[ue] enim suaviorem sonum exprimit Harmonica, quam Arithmetica divisio."

[9] P. 11: "Modi principales Sex sunt."

[10] Fol. H3v: "Clausulas autem formant ejusdem nominis Modi, tam Contentus quam Remissus."

[11] "De variatione Modorum in cantu figurato" ("On the varieties of modes in figured song"). *Cantus figuratus* refers to music with different rhythmic values, i.e., all polyphonic music, as opposed to chant, which has only one rhythmic value; chant is called *cantus choralis*. See, for example Christoph Demant, *Isagoge artis musicae* (Onoldsbachi, 1611), fol. A4r: *Choralis* "in welcher eine Nota nicht mehr gilt als die ander" ("in which a given note does not have a greater rhythmic value than any other); *Figuralis* "in welcher eine Nota mehr gilt als die ander" ("in which a given note [may] have a greater rhythmic value than another").

a single voice in a polyphonic composition) to a property of the piece as a whole.

Transposition is discussed much more fully by Calvisius than by earlier theorists. Almost all musical examples in the *Exercitationes musicae duae* are presented in one-flat signature in addition to their untransposed form. Thus, the listing of cadences for each species of fifth on pages 10–11 recurs on page 11 in the one-flat signature. The third part of the discussion of mode in this work extensively treats the use of transposition when singing with instruments.

In summary, Calvisius's modal theory is basically a restatement of that of Zarlino. In some areas, notably the differentiation of the modes into *laetiores* and *tristiores*, Calvisius is somewhat less assertive than Zarlino had been. It was on this foundation that Lippius and others of his generation built in the early seventeenth century.

German Modal Theory Around 1600

German writers around 1600 either adopted the modal theories of Glarean and Zarlino (as did Calvisius) or adapted these theories to their own ideas. The new ideas concerning mode introduced by these theorists as a rule had little to do with the development of major-minor thinking, even when the same theorists contributed to the growing awareness of triadic structures. Both Johann Magirus and Joachim Burmeister, for instance, were among the first theorists to present the triad and its inversions. Yet in the works of both writers, mode remains a purely melodic concept. Both even extended the role of semitone placement to modal aspects unaffected by this criterion in earlier writings.

The *Artis musicae* of Johann Magirus (ca. 1557-1631) appeared in two editions (Frankfurt, 1596 and 1611).[12] Each orders the modes differently. In 1596, Magirus divides the modes into even modes (*pari*, those which have the semitones on the same degree of the species of

---

[12] See Eckhard Nolte, *Johannes Magirus (1558-1631) und seine Musiktraktate* (Marburg: Görich & Weiershäser, 1971), for new information on Magirus's birthdate (pp. 6-7), and for the correct identification of Frankfurt as the place of publication for the second edition of the *Artis musicae* (p. 58); previous lists, including the RISM *Écrits imprimés* (apparently working from an erroneous library card), give Braunschweig as the publication site. Nolte's study includes a reprint of the 1596 edition (pp. 192–311). The preface to the 1596 edition carries a date of 1592; thus the work was probably completed before the publication of Calvisius's *Melopoeia*.

fourth and fifth) and odd (*impari*, those in which the semitones appear on different degrees within these species). Within each grouping, those modes which have the semitone in the lowest position are placed first, those which have the semitone in the second lowest position are placed second, and so forth. Thus, the even modes are ordered Phrygian (with the semitones above the first note in the fifth-species on E and the fourth-species on B), Dorian (with the semitones above the second note in the fifth-species on D and the fourth-species on A), and Ionian (with the semitones above the third note of the fifth-species on C and the fourth-species on G); the odd modes Aeolian, Mixolydian (here referred to as Mixoaeolian), and Lydian. Plagal forms are placed along with their corresponding authentic forms.[13]

Part I of the 1611 edition orders the species of all intervals from the fourth to the octave according to the lowest placement of the semitone. In Part II, the authentic modes are similarly ordered Phrygian, Aeolian, Dorian, Mixolydian, Ionian, and Lydian. The plagal modes are coupled with the corresponding authentic ones. The modes are differentiated into two general categories.[14] In the first category, the semitone is in the lower part of the fifth and fourth (Phrygian, Aeolian, and Dorian); in the second cagetory, the semitone is placed in the upper half of these intervals (Mixolydian, Ionian, and Lydian).[15] The resulting groups contain the same modes as in the major-minor differentiations of Zarlino, Calvisius, and Lippius, but the quality of the third is not the criterion, and the major-minor characteristic is not mentioned. In both editions of Magirus's work, Glarean's numbering appears as the common ordering (*volgaris*). The remainder of the discussion of mode is traditional.

Magirus's work was influential on a number of other German writers. Maternus Beringer (1580-1632) published a free translation into German of the 1596 edition under the title *Musicae, der Freyen lieblichen Singkunst* (Nürnberg, 1610). It includes various tables and charts on the modes (pp. 51-56). Magirus's ordering is "the proper natural order of the modes" ("Ordinem modorum naturalem rectum"); Glarean's ordering is "the common ordering" ("Vulgarem

---

[13] Book II, chapters 5–23 (pp. 42–98); pp. 232–270 of the 1971 reprint.

[14] The table appearing on page 51 is reproduced in facsimile in Nolte, *op. cit.*, p. 136.

[15] Although Magirus claims to use the species of both fourths and fifths in his differentiation, the placement of Dorian and Mixolydian makes it clear that the species of fifth is the principal criterion.

ordinem modorum"); Zarlino's ordering appears twice, first labeled "the inverted natural ordering of the modes" ("Ordinem modorum naturalem inversum"), and then in the ordering according to solmization syllables. Erasmus Sartorius (1577–1637) uses Magirus's 1596 division into even and odd modes in his elementary manual, *Institutionum musicarum...verum etiam pulcherrima modorum musicorum doctrina exhibetur* (Hamburg, 1635).[16]

Joachim Burmeister (ca. 1566–1629), cantor in Rostock from 1586, discusses modes in three of his works:[17]

1. *Hypomnematum musicae poeticae* (Rostock, 1599). Of the thirteen chapters (numbered 1–14, there is no number 7) the sixth is on the modes and the eighth on cadences.

2. *Musica autoschediastike...* (Rostock, 1601). Section 1 of *Accessio III* is on the modes.

3. *Musica poetica* (Rostock, 1606).[18] Chapter 6 deals with the modes, and Chapter 7 with their transpositions.

The most extensive treatment is in the *Musica autoschediastike*. The material in *Musica poetica* is essentially the same but more concentrated. In the *Hypomnematum*, only the essentials for the recognition of modes are treated. Burmeister, like Magirus, differentiates the modes according to the placement of the semitone. As in the works of Magirus, there is no hint of major-minor thinking in these differentiations or in the discussion of the affects of the modes. The ordering used is either Glarean's (in the *Musica autoschediastike*) or alphabetical according to the final (in the *Musica poetica*). In terms of affect, however, the modes are listed according to where the semitone is placed: whether it is next to the final of the mode, the fifth of the mode, or the third of the mode. The first group contains those modes which do not have a semitone adjacent to the final or fifth of the mode. This includes those with a semitone below the third (Dorian and Hypodorian, which are for *graves* and *seriae* subjects) and those which have a semitone above the third (Mixolydian and Hypomixolydian, which are for *laetae* and *incitantes* subjects). Next are mentioned those modes with a semitone below both the final and

---

[16] See the discussion of elementary manuals on pp. 68-75 for more information on this work, and on this genre of writing.

[17] For a complete biography and study of his works, see Martin Ruhnke, *Joachim Burmeister: Ein Beitrag zur Musiklehre um 1600* (Kassel: Bärenreiter, 1955).

[18] Facsimile edition, edited by Martin Ruhnke (Kassel: Bärenreiter, 1955).

fifth (Lydian and Hypolydian, for *tragicae* and *turbulentae* subjects). Those modes with a semitone above both the fifth and final are Phrygian and Hypophrygian, used for *lamentosae* and *flebiles* subjects. Those with a semitone below the final and a major second around the fifth are more *mediae res* (Ionian and Hypoionian). Aeolian is not listed in this manner but is placed between Dorian and Phrygian; it has a semitone above the fifth but whole tones around the final.

The encyclopedic *Syntagma musicum* (Wolfenbüttel, 1619)[19] of Michael Praetorius (1571–1621) lists the modes in several charts in the third volume. The first series (pp. 36–40) presents each mode in the ranges of discant and bass, in regular and transposed system (with no signature, and with one flat in the signature), and with both Glarean's and Zarlino's orderings ("Series modorum juxta vulgatem opinionem" and "Series modorum juxta Italorum opinionem"). The repercussio of each mode is indicated by black noteheads. The second series (pp. 40–45) presents each pair of authentic and plagal modes in bass, tenor, alto, and cantus registers. A third series (pp. 46–47) repeats the second series in organ tablature in both regular and transposed systems. The remaining aspects of modal theory presented are traditional, including the range of an octave as the limit of the ambitus. Praetorius discusses neither the application of the modes to composition, nor any major-minor differentiation. Perhaps the projected fourth volume of the *Syntagma*, which was to have dealt with composition,[20] would have included a fuller discussion. Praetorius refers the reader to many other works, including those of Calvisius, Glarean, and Magirus, for further information.

None of the works just enumerated shows the influence of Zarlino's differentiation of the modes into two categories, or even of Calvisius's more ambiguous presentation of that differentiation. Indeed, neither Magirus nor Burmeister even refers to Zarlino's ordering of the modes, and Praetorius, twenty-seven years after Calvisius's *Melopoeia*, still considers Zarlino's ordering of the modes an Italian phenomenon.

---

[19]Facsimile edition (Kassel: Bärenreiter, 1958).

[20]Apparently, Heinrich Baryphonus was to have written this volume, a plan probably aborted by Praetorius's death in 1621.

Growing Recognition of the Triad

During the half-century following Zarlino's *Istitutioni* of 1558, a small but growing number of German theorists expanded recognition of the triad, leading eventually to the central placement of harmonic structures in the works of Lippius. Benito Rivera has discovered the earliest known such discussion in the *Isagoge in libros musicae poëticae* (Erfurt, 1581) of Johannes Avianius (?–1617).[21] Perhaps for the first time in print, Avianius stresses right from Chapter 1 the importance of the lowest voice in a harmony, differentiating *basis* (the foundation of a harmony) from *bassus* (the lowest voice part in a composition): "We call the *basis* of the harmony that voice which at a given moment contains the lowest note...since the bass voice can sometimes be silent, it follows that the *basis* is not always to be found in the same voice, but is sometimes even in the highest voice."[22] Avianius proceeds to build a "perfect harmony" ("Harmonia perfecta," chapter 3) by adding a third and fifth to a given *basis*. An "imperfect harmony ("Harmonia imperfecta, chapter 3) contains a third and sixth over the *basis*. Zarlino had also made the distinction between a harmony with a third and fifth over the lowest voice and a harmony with a third and sixth, but only in widely separated passages, and not with the clarity of Avianius. So Avianius clearly advanced a step beyond Zarlino in recognition of the triad. Nonetheless, Avianius does not yet arrive at the modern understanding of the triad. His *basis* is not the root of a chord in the modern sense, for Avianius names the three notes of both perfect and imperfect harmonies *basis* (the lowest note), *media* (the third over the *basis*), and *summa* (the fifth or sixth over the *basis*).

Perhaps most significant in Avianius's theory is his recognition that harmonies with only two pitch-classes can be understood as incomplete versions of the perfect and imperfect harmonies. In his example of perfect harmonies, part of which appears in example 2-1, he comments on the asterisked chord: "one finds the same notes as

---

[21] See Benito V. Rivera, *German Music Theory in the Early 17th Century* (Ann Arbor: UMI, 1980), pp. 132–137 for a full discussion of the *Isagoge's* treatment of triads, including translations and transcripts of important passages. The present discussion is based on Rivera, but some of the translations differ in details from Rivera's.

[22] Chapter 1: "Basin vocamus Harmoniae eam vocem, quae in momento considerando habet Clavem gravissimam. Quoniam...Bassus interdum tacere potest, consequens est, non modo Basin in eadem voce non semper reperiri, verum etiam aliquando ad acutissimam pertinere." See Rivera, *op. cit.*, p. 132.

were on the first [tactus], but all voices except the discant have changed positions."[23]

Example 2-1. Avianius, *Isagoge*, Chapter 2

[Perfect Harmonies]

In his example of imperfect harmonies, part of which appears in example 2-2, Avianius comments on the asterisked chord: "The first part of the fourth [tactus] is an imperfect [harmony], because to the *basis* C[-sharp] is added A in the altus and discant; the *media, which would have been E*, is missing" [emphasis added].[24]

Example 2-2. Avianius, *Isagoge*, Chapter 3

[Imperfect Harmonies]

---

[23] Chapter 2: "...eaedem sunt claves quae erant in primo sed mutatis locis omnium vocum, si Discantum excipias." See Rivera, *op. cit.*, p. 135. The complete example appears in Rivera on p. 134.

[24] Chapter 3: "...prior pars quarti imperfecta: Quoniam ibi ad Basin C annectuntur A in Alto & Discanto media clave, qua erat E futura, omissa." See Rivera *op. cit.*, p. 137. The complete example appears in Rivera, p. 136.

Avianius here and elsewhere seems to assume that it is common knowledge that harmonies have three pitch-classes. Right in chapter 2 he casually begins discussing the construction of harmonies by writing of "the three notes" that can be arranged.

Very little is known of Avianius's life. He apparently wrote thirteen manuscript treatises in addition to the *Isagoge*, but all are lost.[25] Perhaps most tantalizing about his ideas on harmony is that they seem to derive from an oral tradition—both because of the assumption that three notes constitute a harmony, and because of the matter-of-fact presentation of ideas that have no precedent in print. But at our present state of knowledge, we can only guess at the extent or nature of such an oral tradition.

Joachim Burmeister follows Avianius in his approach to harmony, but expands some notions. His *Musica autoschediastike* (Rostock, 1601) begins with a discussion similar to that of Avianius, differentiating perfect and imperfect harmonies (chapter 3). As in Avianius, tables are presented with the possible chords: what we call root-position and first inversion triads. In Burmeister's *Hypomnematum musicae poeticae* (Rostock, 1599), the tables include only those root-position and first-inversion triads that are built on the notes of the diatonic scale and that require the fewest accidentals.[26] The tables in the *Musica poetica* (Rostock, 1606) are more comprehensive than those in the earlier work, including at least one form of all major and minor triads (either root position, first inversion, or both) with the sole exception of E-flat minor.[27] But Burmeister does not

[25] A list of Avianius's unpublished theoretical works appears in Johann Gottfried Walther, *Musicalisches Lexicon* (Leipzig, 1732), facsimile edition (Kassel: Bärenreiter, 1953), pp. 58–59.

[26] See Martin Ruhnke, *op. cit.*, p. 108 for the tables. Their content agrees with tables in Avianius.

[27] Three "schemae" appear on pp. 19–21. Burmeister differentiates between chords that are commonly used and those that are rarely used, and lists separately those chords with chromatic bass pitches other than B-flat. There are several errors in the *schemae*: in the *Schema Secundum*, the chords on the left should be entitled *Purè semi-imperfecti*; in addition there are some errors in accidentals. Burmeister uses organ tablature notation, resulting in chord spellings such as B, E-flat, F-sharp and B-flat. C-sharp, F-sharp.

formally relate the root-position and inverted triads in any way, and does not explicitly differentiate major and minor triads on the basis of their quality.

A true theory of triadic inversion arises for the first time in the *Artis musicae* (Frankfurt, 1608) of Otto Siegfried Harnish (ca. 1568–1623).[28] Harnish differentiates the *basis* from the lowest voice. But Harnish, unlike Avianius, goes on to note that the *basis* of a harmony can appear above the other notes in that harmony and still be the *basis*. The discussion of harmonic intervals begins on page 54, under the title "De symphonia." After treating intervals of two notes, Harnish turns to what he calls compound consonance ("consonantia composita").

> A compound consonance is that which is composed of more than two notes. It arises either from only consonances or even from dissonances.
> [A consonance] compounded from only consonances is that which consists of three constituent notes [in the relationship of] a fifth with a third in between—which [intervals] are, as it were, the roots of all consonances in song. The lower [note] is as a foundation of the entire consonance, whence it can rightly be called the proper *basis*.

> This first consonance is either simple, consisting of only three notes in this manner, or it is varied and augmented by octaves. The fourth attains the strength of a consonance when the lower note of the fifth is [also] expressed an octave higher, and thus constitutes a fourth with the upper note of the fifth.

> This compound concordance, varied by the addition of the octave, is either perfect or imperfect. Perfect [is that] in which the *basis* or the lower note of the fifth is expressed in its own position or an octave lower. Imperfect [is that] in which the *basis* is expressed only an octave higher, and the lower voice or note of the concordance is relinquished. That [note] which is the mediant between the upper and lower [notes] of the fifth (that is, the third) is now [the lowest note]. Where it is

---

[28] The remarkable triadic theories of Harnish escaped the notice of modern scholars until 1971. See Eckhard Nolte, *op. cit.*, pp. 146–147, and Joel Lester, "Root-Position and Inverted Triads in Theory around 1600," in *Journal of the American Musicological Society* 27 (1974): 113–114, 119.

observed that the lower third be absent, the fourth which is left in the lower position is considered a dissonance.[29] [example 2-3]

Example 2-3[30]**. Harnish,** *Artis musicae*

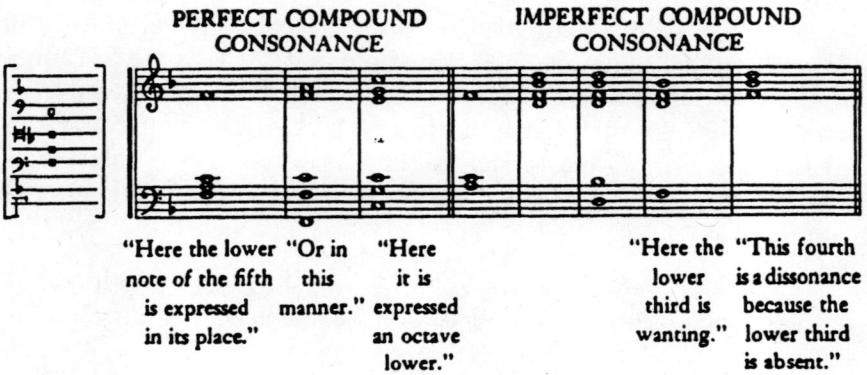

| **PERFECT COMPOUND CONSONANCE** | **IMPERFECT COMPOUND CONSONANCE** |

"Here the lower note of the fifth is expressed in its place." "Or in this manner." "Here it is expressed an octave lower."   "Here the lower third is wanting." "This fourth is a dissonance because the lower third is absent."

This is a clear presentation of the identity relationship between root position and inverted triads, including both a differentiation between the lowest note of a triad and the root of a triad, and the rationale for the fourth being a consonance or a dissonance depending on the circumstances.

[29] "Composita consonantia est, quae e pluribus quam duobus sonis componitur. Est que vel ex solis consonantiis vel etiam ex dissonantiis.

E solis consonantiis composita est, quae constat tribus sonis, in quinta & tertia interiecta, consistentibus, qui quasi radices sunt omnium in cantu consonantiarum, & inferior est tan quam fundamentum totius consonantiae; unde & basis recte vocari potest.

Haec prima consonantia aut simplex est e tribus tantum sonis eius modi constans, aut per octavas variata & aucta: unde & quarta consonantiae vim consequitur, quando nempe inferior quintae sonus per octavam superiorem exprimitur, & sic cum sono quintae superiori quartam constituit.

Composita haec & per octavae additionem variata concordantia, aut perfecta est, aut imperfecta.

Perfecta, in qua Basis vel inferior quintae sonus suo loco aut per octavam inferiorem exprimitur.

Imperfecta, in qua basis tantum per octavam superiorem exprimitur, & inferior concordantiae vox sive sonus relinquitur, ille, qui est inter quintae superiorem & inferiorem medius, hoc est, qui est tertiae: ubi observetur, si tertia inferior absit, quartam, quae inferiori loco relinquitur, pro dissonantia haberi."

[30] "Hic suo loco exprimitur inferior 5 sonus. Vel sic. Hic per 8. infer. exprimitur. Hic 3 infer. deest. Haec 4. est dissonantia, quia tertia inferior abest."

Harnish's explicit discussion of triadic inversion precedes what had hitherto been considered the first such reference—the somewhat parenthetical remark in *A New Way of Making Fowre Parts in Counterpoint* (London, 1613– 18[31]) by Thomas Campion (1567–1620). Campion shows how to compose four parts with a root position triad over the bass. But when a sixth is used over the bass instead of a fifth, he notes that "such Bases are not true Bases, for where a sixt is to be taken, either in F sharpe, or in E sharpe [i.e., natural], or in B or in A the true Base is a third lower, F sharpe in D, E in C, B in G, A in F, as for example:"[32]

Example 2-4. Campion, *A New Way...*

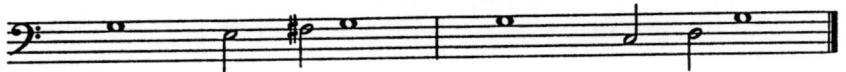

The parallels between Campion's presentation and earlier works of Burmeister and Harnish, and, perhaps, Lippius, suggest that he might have received his ideas from one of these German works. Since all were published in Latin, the language would not have been a barrier to Campion.[33]

Johann Magirus, in the second edition of his *Artis musicae* (Frankfurt, 1611), presents a discussion of triads similar to Harnish's, but insists on calculating intervals from the tenor. As a result, Magirus does not explicitly recognize the relationship between root-position and inverted triads. His discussion is quite roundabout because he calculates intervals from the tenor. A root-position triad, for instance, arises when a fifth below the tenor appears in the bass. To this is added a third below the tenor, and then doublings of various notes.

[31] The work was first published without a date by Thomas Snodham for John Browne. These publishers worked together beginning in 1613. See Charles Humphries and William Smith, *Music Publishing in the British Isles*, second ed. (Oxford: B. Blackwell, 1970), p. 90. Thurston Dart, in the *MGG* article on Campion, dates the work as late as 1618.

[32] Percival Vivian, *Campion's Works* (Oxford: Clarendon Press, 1909), p. 204.

[33] That Campion was aware of at least one German work is clear from the beginning of his chapter on counterpoint ("Of the taking of all Concords"), where Campion announces that this section is a free translation of the work of "Zethus Calvisius." See Vivian, *op. cit.*, p. 219.

A compound consonance is a conjunction of simple [consonances] in order by means of many notes to make a symphony.

A perfect compound [consonance] is that which has a fifth at the bottom in the ordinary range of the bass, to which, in order to make more notes in the symphony, the third can be added below [i.e., below the tenor]; and from there by an octave the tenth can be derived in the second stage [i.e., the second octave range], and the seventeenth in the third stage. Even higher, to complete the third-stage octave, the fourth can be added on [example 2-5].

An imperfect compound [consonance] is that which in the ordinary range of the bass has a fourth at the bottom, which, since its nature is dissonant, cannot be placed along and exposed at the bottom. In a constitution of several voices it takes a third below itself in order to mitigate its dissonance, thus going outside the ordinary range of an octave.

This new imperfect consonance of nine notes and therefore [nine] voices (without the lower third) is arranged on the large staff in this manner [example 2-6].[34]

This then was the situation that faced Lippius when he published his works. Earlier theorists had suggested as individual tenets a major-minor differentiation of the affects of the modes and a triadic basis for harmony. But no theorist had shown the connection between harmonic structures and the nature of mode. And no theorist had demonstrated how the new harmonic ideas might be related to the traditional intervallic understanding of counterpoint and the modes.

---

[34] Part. II, chapter 27: "Consonantia Composita est simplicium ad Symphoniam pluribus vocibus constituendam conjunctio. Composita perfecta est, quae in ordinario Bassi ambitu inferius Quintam habet: cui ad plures Symphoniae voces constituendum inferius Tertia inferi: & inde per octavam in secundum Gradum Decima & in tertium, Decima-Septima, deduci: Superius etiam, ad tertij gradus octavam complendam, Quarta assumi potest.

Composita Imperfecta est, quae in Ordinario Bassi ambitu inferius Quartam habet: Quae cum natura sua sit Dissonantia, indeq[ue]: inferius natura nuda vel sola collocari non possit: ideo in plurium vocum constitutione ad Dissonantiam suam vel mitigandam, tertiam, vel prorsus tollendam, Quintam inferius, extra tamen octavae ordinarium ambitum assumit. Haec (infima tertia dempta) novem sonorum, & ita vocum consonantia Imperfecta in systemate majore collocatur hoc modo."

Example 2-5. Magirus, *Artis musicae* **(1611), Part 2, Chapter 27**

[Perfect Consonance]

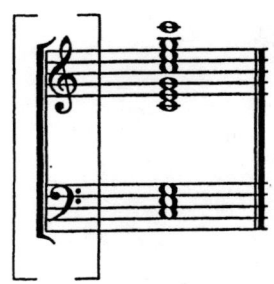

Example 2-6. Magirus, *Artis musicae* **(1611), Part 2, Chapter 27**

[Imperfect Compound Consonance]

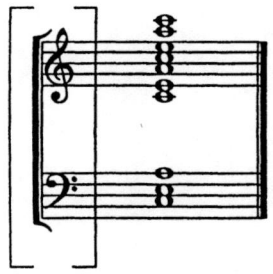

Chapter 3

Johannes Lippius

By the end of the first decade of the seventeenth century, all the ingredients of a fully harmonic approach to composition and modes had appeared in published form: the primacy of the bass in determining harmonic combinations, the difference between the bass of a harmony and the bass voice of a composition, the fundamental nature of what we call the triad, the fact that the triad has a root that may or may not be the lowest sounding note, the fact that major and minor forms of the triad are fundamentally different from one another in quality, and the fact that crucial harmonic intervals determine the quality of modes. It was left to Johannes Lippius (1585–1612) to organize all these disparate tenets into a unified theory—a harmonic approach whose resulting power changed many theoretical focuses. Among other achievements, Lippius recognized all inversional relationships between intervals, including those between thirds and sixths and seconds and sevenths; he suggested that music be composed from the bass, not the tenor; he coined a term for the triad (*trias harmonica*); he differentiated the modes by the major and minor tonic triad; and, finally, he replaced the study of counterpoint with a study of harmony based on the triad.

Perhaps most remarkable about Lippius's achievements is that he accomplished so much before his death at the age of twenty-seven. A theologian as well as a music theorist, Lippius drew upon his detailed knowledge of Christian theology for models for some of his music-theoretical innovations. Lippius traveled throughout Germany from 1609 until his death in 1612, visiting Leipzig (where he met Calvisius[1]), Wittenberg, Jena, Erfurt, Frankfurt, Ingolstadt, and Tübingen, presenting lectures and disputations at several univer-

[1] A poem by Calvisius praising Lippius appears at the end of both the *Disputatio musica secunda* (Wittenberg, 1609) and the *Synopsis musicae* (Strasbourg, 1612).

sities. His principal work, and that by which he was best known to later theorists, is his *Synopsis musicae novae*, published in Strasbourg in 1612.[2] The *Synopsis* was preceded by six *Disputationes*, of which the third (Wittenberg, 1610) treats intervals, triads, and some aspects of mode more extensively than does the *Synopsis*.[3]

After defining music as a mathematical science, the *Synopsis* turns to a systematic treatment of harmonic structures of one, two, and three pitches: monads, dyads, and triads. Under monads, melodic intervals and rhythmic and pitch notation are discussed.[4] In the discussion of dyads, Lippius uses the fifth and third to generate all consonances and the second to generate all dissonances. This is the first recognition of octave inversion as used to generate all intervals.[5]

> It is advantageous and most fundamental in music theory and practice to consider simple dyads, both consonant and dissonant, within a single octave, and to judge similarly their repetitions and multiplications by octaves, whether higher or lower... Moreover, it is still more advantageous and more fundamental in composition to observe the fewest [possible] roots for all the dyads used in harmonic song. The root of every consonant dyad is the fifth and both kinds of third. Indeed, the fifth [is the root] of perfect consonance: that is, of the octave and the fourth. The third [is] truly [the root of all] imperfect [consonance]: that is, of both kinds of sixth. The root of dissonance is the second... The octave or compound unison is identical with the simple unison or prime with which the fifth harmonizes so perfectly, as was stated above. Hence, indeed, the meaning of all intervals joined to the compound unison, whether above, below, or within, is the same as that of the intervals joined to the simple unison, as the repetitions

---

[2] English translation by Benito V. Rivera (Colorado Springs: Colorado College Music Press, 1977). A second edition appeared in 1614.

[3] For the most complete biography to date of Lippius and a thorough study of his theories (especially on triads and the inversion of intervals) and their relation to contemporary theory, see Benito V. Rivera, *German Music Theory in the Early 17th Century: The Treatises of Johannes Lippius* (Ann Arbor: UMI, 1980), a revision of the author's 1974 Rutgers University dissertation.

[4] See fols. B7v-E1v. Several folios in this section appear in the wrong order. They should read as follows: B7r, B8r, B7v, B8v, C1r; the folios then continue correctly.

[5] Rivera, *op. cit.*, pp. 95–98, locates discussions of interval inversion in treatises by Zarlino and Salinas. Both these sixteenth-century theorists introduce such discussions to argue for the consonance of either a fourth or a minor sixth. In the works of neither author is invertibility of intervals a subject treated for its own sake, as it is in Lippius.

of the note names indicate. Thus, the fourth is associated with the fifth, for the same note, for example g, which makes a fifth with respect to the simple unison C, makes a fourth at the same time with respect to the compound unison c, and vice versa in the harmonic and arithmetic proportion. The sixth is reduced to the third, the major to minor, and the minor to major...[6]

The last sentence of the above quote is essential to the recognition of the major-minor differentiation of inverted triads. For when a major triad appears in first inversion, both the third and sixth over the bass are minor, yet the quality of the chord is major. Similarly, the first inversion of a minor triad gives rise to major imperfect consonances over the bass. Only if the third is the "root" of the sixth, and if the quality of the triad is determined by this "root" interval, can a theorist recognize triadic inversions retaining the major-minor differentiation.

The exposition of the triad in the *Synopsis* is bound in with the number 3. "The musical triad is composed of three notes and just as many root dyads... The simple and proper root harmonic triad is the true trinity of all harmony, even the most nearly perfect and full that can exist in the world."[7] Three different types of classifications are used. The triad is either consonant and harmonic, or dissonant and aharmonic. It is either simple or compound, and it is either "more

---

[6]*Disputatio musica tertia*, fol. B1v: "Compendiosum & fundamentale valde est in Theoria & praxi Musica respicere ad Dyades simplices consonas & dissonas in una diapason, similiterq[ue], judicare de earum repetitione & multiplicatione per Octavas sive inferas sive superas... Caeterum adhuc compendiosius & fundamentalius est Melopoëtae spectare pauculas Radices Dyadum omnium in Cantilena Harmonica ponendarum. Est autem Radix Dyadis omnis Consonantis, Quinta & Tertia utraq[ue]: Quinta quidem perfecte consonantis, Octavae, & Quartae: Tertia vero imperfecte, sextae utriusq[ue]: Dissonantis Radix est secunda... Octave seu Unisonus compositus idem est cum Unisono simplici seu prima qua quinta potissimum constat, ut hactenus declaratum. Hinc enim idem est sensus de omnibus Intervallis unisono composito adjunctis sive supra, sive infra, sive in medio, qui est de Unisono simplici additis, ut ipsae etiam iteratae claves significant. Ergo Quarta refertur ad Quintam: quia idem sonus verbi causa, g, qui facit Quintam respectu Unisoni simplicis, C, facit simul Quartam respectu Unisoni compositi, c, & contra in proportionalitate Harmonica & Arithmetica. Sexta redigitur ad Tertiam, major quidem ad minorem, minor vero ad majorem..."

[7]*Synopsis*, fol. F4r: "Trias Musica ex Tribus sonis, & totidem Dyadibus Radicalibus constat... Trias Harmonica Simplex & Recta Radix vera est Unitrisona omnis Harmoniae perfectissimae plenissimaeq[ue] quae dari in Mundo potest." See Rivera, *German Music Theory...*, pp. 113 and 120-127 concerning theological inspirations for Lippius's theories of the triad. Rivera discusses theological influences on other aspects of Lippius's theories throughout his study.

natural, more perfect, more noble, and sweeter" or "more imperfect, and softer"—the major and minor triads.[8] "The *aucta* triad is that whose parts (either some or all) are increased by the compound unison or octave to cause a more varied and fuller harmony."[9] "The *diffusa* [triad] is that whose parts or root voices, less mutually neighbors to one another, are dispersed or spread to diverse octaves."[10] It is not clear in the *Synopsis* whether the *diffusa* triad includes inversions of the root position form. This point is fully discussed in the *Disputatio musica tertia*.

> The *diffusa* [triad] is that whose parts or root voices, less mutually neighbors to one another, are dispersed to different octaves than that which their proper root requires. Indeed, either only one part may be transferred form the fundamental [position], the other two remaining the same; or two [parts can be transferred], one constant; or all three [can be transferred]. Yet all of these conjunctions sound together perfectly because of the direct root whence they arise according to elegant proportions... And, moreover, that triad is always sweeter, fuller, and more perfect, whose prime is firmly in place lowest and deepest, the remaining notes above...[example 3-1].[11]

---

[8]*Synopsis*, fol. F5v: "Naturalior, Perfectior, Nobilior & Suavior...Imperfectior & Mollior." Note the use of the term "mollior" (softer) to describe the quality of the minor third and minor sixth (see the *Synopsis*, fol. E7r). This terminology may be taken from Harnish's *Artis musicae*, where the same term is used for the minor thirds and sixths. Zarlino and his followers had used a different set of terms to describe the minor imperfect consonances. Zarlino used the terms "meste & languide" to describe the quality of the minor triad (see the *Istitutioni*, p. 183 of the 1573 edition). Calvisius translated these terms into Latin as "tristiores & languidiores" in his *Melopoeia*, fol. I3r. Lippius may well be the originator of the term *moll* used in the sense of minor. The antonym *dur*, which Lippius did not use, was not associated with the major triad until much later in the seventeenth century. See footnote 30 in chapter 5 for further on the term *dur*.

[9]*Synopsis*, fols. F6v- F7r: "Aucta Trias Harmonica est, cujus partes auctae sunt Unisono Composito seu Octava, & vel quaedam, vel omnes, ad variam magis & pleniorem Harmoniam excitandam."

[10]*Ibid.*, fol. F6v: "diffusa est, cujus partes seu voces Radicales minus sibi invicem vicinae dispersae sunt atque diffusae in diversas Octavas."

[11]*Disputatio musica tertia*, fol. B3v: "diffusa est cujus partes seu voces radicales minus sibi invicè vicinae dispersae sunt in diversas Octavas, quam requirit Radix Recta. Atqui aut una tantum pars, reliquis duabus manentibus: aut duae, una stante: aut omnes tres transferri ex fundamentali possunt sede: ita tamen, ut omnes istae Syzygia consonent perfecte ob Radicem Rectam unde germinát juxta elegantes proportiones... Ac semper suavior, plenior & perfectior est Trias, cujus prima basissimo & gravissimo substat loco, caeterae superiore."

Example 3-1. Lippius, *Disputatio musica tertia*, fol.B4v

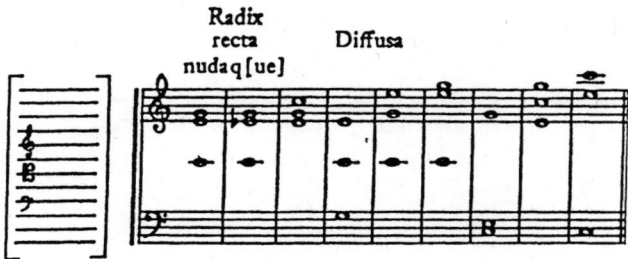

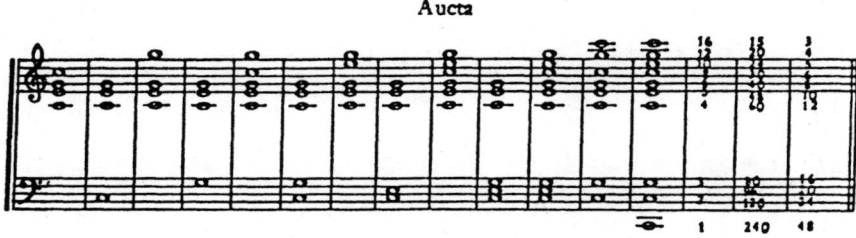

Modes

For the first time, Lippius's *Synopsis* links virtually the entire presentation of mode to the triad.[12] Mode for Lippius is that which controls melodies, keeping them within limits and preventing them from being vague in structure. Modes are not determined by octave species; rather the triad determines the range:

> Musical mode is either simple or compound; simple is that in which one triad dominates, along with the range of its octave... Compound mode is derived from the simpler modes: either from a related primary and secondary mode, such as Ionian and Hypoionian, which is common; or from wholly diverse modes, such as Ionian and Dorian, which is less common.[13]

---

[12]*Synopsis*, H8r-I4r.

[13]*Ibid.*, fols. H8v, I3v: "Modus Musicus est vel Simplex: vel Compositus. Simplex est, in quo una saltem dominatur Trias Harmonica cum suae Octavae Circulo... Compositus Modus ex Simplicioribus pronascitur: & vel ex cognatis Primario & Secundario, ut Jonico & Hypoionico, qui creber: vel ex planè diveris ut Jonico & Dorio,...quiminus consuetus."

The difference between authentic and plagal modes depends not on the disposition of a species of fourth above or below a species of fifth, but on the disposition of a fourth above or below the triad built on the final of the mode.

> [Mode] is also primary, that is authentic; or secondary [plagal]... [It is called secondary] because the harmonic division of the octave, which forms the primary mode, is changed into an arithmetic division by the inversion of the fourth below the fifth, which continues to contain the triad.[14] [See example 3-2]

Example 3-2. Lippius, *Synopsis*, fol. I1r

Cadences and points of imitation depend on the triad built on the final of the mode.

> Primary fugue and cadence is made on the prime of the mode's own triad, secondary on the highest note of the triad, tertiary on the mediant.[15] [See example 3-3]

Example 3-3. Lippius, *Synopsis*, fol. 13r

Propriae   Peregrina

Most significantly, modes are differentiated into major and minor according to the quality of the triad on the final—this *before* the individual modes are enumerated.

[14]*Ibid.*, fols. H8v- I1r: "Estque aut Primarius seu Authenticus: aut Secundarius..., quia Mediatio Octavae Harmonica quae Competit Primario mutatur in Arithmeticam inversione Quartae infrà Quintam manentem cum Triade."
[15]*Ibid.*, fol. I3r: "Primaria Fuga & Clausula est à Primâ Triadis Propriae: Secundaria à Supremâ: Tertiaria à Mediâ."

Primary mode is either legitimate or spurious: legitimate is either *naturalior* (which has the *naturalior* triad), or *mollior* (which has the *mollior* triad)... Spurious mode is based on the spurious triad b-d-f and is therefore rejected.[16]

Both species of legitimate modes are themselves trinities, the one—Ionian, Lydian, and Mixolydian; the other—Dorian, Phrygian, and Aeolian. And thus there are six simple primary legitimate modes. Counting their plagals...there are twelve modes.[17]

The discussion of each individual mode is summary in nature.

Ionian with its secondary, Hypoionian, having the triad c- e-g (bo, di, lo), is the most natural and primary of all in today's music (many past and present writers do not agree with this). Dorian is the triad d-f-a (ce, ga, ma) with Hypodorian. Phrygian is the triad e-g-b (di, lo, ni) with Hypophrygian...[18] [See example 3-4]

Example 3-4. Lippius,*Synopsis,* fols.I1v-L2r

Each mode is listed in the order Ionian-Aeolian. Scalar differences between the modes of the same type of triad are not even mentioned, although they are implied by the discussion of affects.

The presentation of the modes is similar in the *Disputatio musica tertia* (fols. D3r-D4r) but with some changes of emphasis and different examples. Glarean's generation of the modes is discussed first,

---

[16]*Ibid.*, fols. I1r, I2v: "Primarius ergo vel Legitimus est vel Spurius. Legitimus est alius Naturalior qui tenet Triadem Harmonicam Naturaliorem: alius Mollior, qui Triadem Molliorem obtinet... Spurius Modus est Triadis Spuriae ♮ . d. f...ideoque rejectus est."

[17]*Ibid.*, fol. I1r- I1v: "Uterque Trinus est juxta Species Triadum: ille Jonicus, Lydius, & Mixolydius: hic Dorius, Phrygius & Aeolius: ut ita 6. sint Simplices Modi Primarii Legitimi & 12, cum suis υποτζ'ποισ."

[18]*Ibid.*, fols. I1v- I2r: "Omnium Naturalissimus & Primus in hodiernâ Musicâ (contrà quàm plerique Veteres & Recentiores autumant) est Jonicus cum suo Secundario Hypoionico habens Triadem Harmonicam propriam. c. e. g. bo, di, lo.

2. Dorius est Triadis, d. f. a. ce, ga, ma, cum Hypodorio.

3. Phrygius cum Hypophrygio est Triadis e. g. ♮ di, lo, ni..."

Note the use of bodecization syllables, based on the octave.

after which Lippius reduces the number of modes to two, first noting that of the twelve modes, six are plagal.

> In every legitimate primary mode, the principal proper harmonic triad is that whose root is the same as the lowest note of the [modal] octave... Hence, we reduce these six modes to two: one, which has the *naturalis* triad, the other which has the *mollis*. The trinity [of modes] of each type is formed according to the same triad—from which the special ornaments, fugues, and cadences of harmonic song should be chosen and formed.[19]

Lippius's approach effects a thorough shift in modal theory. Each mode is no longer a separate entity, with properties dependent on its scalar construction. Rather, there are two types of mode: in modern terms, major and minor. This is virtually the modern position, where we accept major and minor and simply enumerate the locations of the tonic (C major, C-sharp major, D major...C minor, C-sharp minor, D minor...). To be sure, Lippius does not recognize all twenty-four keys. And Lippius does recognize, at least implicitly, differences among the modes within each category. Ironically, in Lippius's *Synopsis* it is only in the discussion of affect that differences arise between modes with the same quality of triad on their finals—remember that in Zarlino and Calvisius it was only in the discussion of affect that the modes were grouped according to major and minor. For Lippius, the nature of mode is harmonic. Review Glarean's discussion of the importance of semitone placement. Glarean argues

---

[19]*Disputatio musica tertia*, fol. D3v: "Est in omni Modo primario legitimo propria Trias Harmonica potissima cujus Basis eadem est cum voce Infimâ suae octavae... Hinc 6, Modos illos stringimus ad duos: unum, qui tenet Triadem Naturalem: alterum, qui Mollem: quorum uterq[ue] Trinus est juxta eandem Triadem, ex quâ, quod mirum, praecipua Cantilenae Harmonicae ornamenta Fuga, & Clausula sunt desumenda atq[ue] formanda."
Walter Atcherson ("Key and Mode in 17th Century Music Theory Books," in *Journal of Music Theory* 17 [1973]:207) totally misstates Lippius's position when he identifies him with Zarlino and notes that both theorists recognize two types of modes "...according to the quality of third above the final... The remainder of Lippius's discussion of the modes adheres faithfully to the tenets and procedures of Glarean's twelve-mode theory; that there are seven octave species, six of them capable of harmonic division and six of arithmetic division, and so on." A footnote refers to both the *Synopsis* and the *Disputatio musica tertia* but without folio numbers. No such discussion is to be found in either work. The *Disputatio musica tertia* presents Glarean's tenets only as a premise to be rebutted: "Modi simplices vulgò numerantur in Genere Diatonico, 14... Hinc 6, Modos illos stringimus ad duos" (fols. D3r-D3v: "Fourteen simple modes are commonly counted in the diatonic genus... We reduce these six legitimate primary modes to two").

for the integrity of his new modes by pointing out that if you drop the first semitone in Mixolydian a single step, the mode changes to Dorian; otherwise the two modes are identical. Such a discussion is inconceivable in Lippius—Mixolydian is a major mode, Dorian a minor one. Only the quality of the third scale degree matters for Lippius.

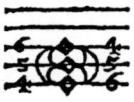

Chapter 4

The Mid-Seventeenth Century

The generation of German theory from Avianius's *Isagoge* (1581) to Lippius's *Synopsis* (1612) offered a remarkable series of developments unmatched anywhere else at that time. Discussions of the triad changed from parenthetical remarks in an otherwise intervallic harmonic theory to the centerpiece of compositional and modal instruction. The triad and its inversions received a full study in a manner until recently ascribed only to the early eighteenth century (Rameau's *Traité* of 1722). Twelve separate modes became incipient major and minor keys.

But despite these advances, German theory retained an extremely conservative strain for over another century and a half. It was only in German-speaking areas that vitriolic attacks on major and minor keys and only half-hearted acceptance of these keys persisted until the middle of the eighteenth century. As late as the generation of Haydn and Mozart, German theorists of the stature of Kirnberger were still insisting on the importance of knowledge of the modes for composers and performers alike.

In holding onto modal theory well into the eighteenth century, German theory was out of line with the evolution of major-minor thinking elsewhere on the continent. A dramatic illustration of the difference between the German attitude and beliefs elsewhere is furnished by the English historian John Hawkins. Writing in 1776, not for contemporary composers and performers, but in a history of music, Hawkins displayed a singular lack of interest in the modes. In his discussion of Zarlino, for instance, he noted that the Italian theorist "does not indeed profess to follow Glareanus in his division [of the modes], but whether he has so done or not is a matter in which the science of music is at this time so little interested, that it scarce deserves the pains of an enquiry[!]"[1] This in the same year that Kirnberger implored German performers and composers to study the modes for their use in contemporary music.

It is one of the ironies of music history that the same factors may well have been responsible both for the early and rapid development of triadic and major-minor modal theories and the later reluctance to abandon traditional modal theory. The ultimate cause of both developments may well have been religious. Consider the unique status of the chorale in the Protestant world. As part of Martin Luther's attempt to narrow the gap between clergy and laity, he insisted that the performance of church music be shared with the congregation. The organist playing a simple block-chord accompaniment to the chorale melody, or the composer writing a simple homophonic harmonization of the chorale melody could not help but become aware of the importance of what we call root-position and first-inversion triads, as did Avianius and Burmeister. The importance of the bass in determining the legitimacy and the sonority of such chords required the composer to shift attention from the tenor to the bass as the controlling voice in the composition, even when the tenor carried the chorale melody in chorale harmonizations. Avianius's unquestioning statements about the primacy of the bass and of chords as opposed to separate intervals may well reflect a whole generation of practical experience with such matters.

In the works of Lippius, chords built upon the bass become the foundation of a method of composition for both homophonic and polyphonic music. Lippius recommends beginning instruction in composition by learning to build chords on the bass. Example 4-1 (opposite) illustrates his method. Over the bass, he indicates by dots all the notes that belong to a root-position triad over each bass note. The voices are then selected from these possibilities, keeping in mind the principles of good voice-leading that he enumerates earlier. Once this technique has been mastered, a composer can take a melody to be harmonized, compose a bass to it, and then proceed as in example 4-1 to complete the other voices. More florid textures and first-inversion triads then arise from the embellishment of these voices.[2]

---

[1] John Hawkins, *A General History of the Science and Practice of Music* (London, 1776), I, p. 399.

[2] *Synopsis*, fols. G7v- H1r; *Disputatio musica tertia*, fol. C3v. See Benito V. Rivera, *German Music Theory in the Early 17th Century* (Ann Arbor: UMI, 1980), pp. 179-181 for a discussion of the differences between Lippius's approach and that of Avianius and

Example 4-1. Lippius, *Synopsis*, fols. G8r-H1r.

[Composing a texture from a bass part.]

Lau- da- te DO-MI-NUM

[The bracketed notes are printed erroneously in the *Synopsis*.]

Lau- da- te DO-MI-NUM

[The bracketed note is printed erroneously in the *Synopsis*.]

[Composing a texture from another part.]

Lau- da- te DO-MI-NUM

Lau- da- te DO-MI-NUM

Burmeister. Johannes Nucius (c. 1556-1620), in his *Musices poeticae* (Neisse, 1613), confirms that many composers work from the bass, even though he himself begins instruction in the traditional manner of starting with the tenor and soprano, then adding bass and alto. See Rivera, p. 179.

Religion was an influence on modal and harmonic developments not only through the role of the chorale, but also symbolically in Lippius's extension of harmonic ideas to the modes. The entire organization of Lippius's *Synopsis,* as well as many specific ideas on the triad (including, of course, its name) arose from his attempt to reflect in music theory the triune perfection of the Holy Trinity. Lippius attempted to create in modal theory that which worked so well in harmonic theory. Throughout his works he searched for the most "compendious" and unified approach: "Truly that which can be accomplished more easily by fewer means is ill done by more."[3] What better way to carry out this goal than to show the unity of conception among harmony and mode? Lippius's genius is that he was able through these theological analogies to sum up the individual achievements of a generation of theorists, thereby opening new vistas of insights into musical structure. The role of theology in his thinking cannot be underestimated. In the struggle between Reformation and Counter Reformation, and on the eve of the Thirty Years War that devastated Central Europe (1618-1648), religion was not a peripheral matter in any human affairs.

The position of the chorale in the Protestant liturgy may have stimulated a rapidly developing harmonic theory. But for several generations it also gave rise to considerable hesitancy in fully embracing major and minor keys. In the Catholic countries, modal plainchant was a body of centuries-old music increasingly divorced from contemporary compositional styles. The Council of Trent in 1565 had intensified this separation by expunging many of the more modern elements from the official body of chants. In both France and Italy, works appeared between 1610 and 1614 definitively separating the theoretical systems of ancient sacred music from contemporary compositional styles: Pierre Maillart's (1550-1622) *Les Tons, ou discours sur les modes de musique, et les tons de l'église et la distinction entre iceux* (Tournai, 1610), and Adriano Banchieri's (1568-1634) *Cartella musicale,* third edition (Venice, 1613/1614). These theorists stand in sharp contrast to Glarean, Zarlino, and other sixteenth- century theorists for whom mode in plainchant and contemporary polyphony could be treated together.

---

[3] *Synopsis,* fol. D8r: "Verum quod commodius fiere potest per pauciora, malè fit per plura." See Rivera, *op. cit.,* pp. 29, 63–64, *passim,* for many instances of the law of parsimony used as an argument by Lippius.

In the Protestant north no such development was possible. Modal chorales were a living musical force. The melodies were still being composed and adapted throughout the seventeenth century, and even into the eighteenth. There was a symbiotic relationship between the chorale melodies and the changes in musical styles. The older melodies may have evolved according to changes in compositional styles from generation to generation. And new harmonizations in each passing generation reflected new styles. But in addition, the structures of the melodies themselves affected the evolution of musical styles. Chorale preludes and a broad range of sacred music incorporated the modal chorale melodies in the harmonies, texture, and rhythms of contemporary musical styles. Even presumably secular music was infiltrated by chorale influences. To cite only two instances from the late Baroque, both written over a century after the death of Lippius, think of the fugue from J. S. Bach's *Sonata No. 3 for Violin Alone* (BWV 1005), whose subject is close to the chorale melodies *An Wasserflüssen Babylon* and *Komm, heiliger Geist, Herre Gott*, and Johann Gottfried Walther's trio sonatas using elaborated chorales for their themes.[4] At least some such compositional output continued into the latter part of the eighteenth century. From a purely practical point of view, German theorists could not ignore this strong modal influence. Later sections of this chapter explore treatises, practical manuals, and elementary instruction books that emphasize the traditional modes over newer conceptions.

A further influence on German theory and, indeed, on theory internationally, may be traced to the nature of Lippius's own works and to his early death at the age of twenty-seven. The *Synopsis*, because of its compendious nature, is not a practical manual for students or for other musicians. Many important tenets are stated only tersely. A contemporary musician may well have viewed these tenets as arbitrary without the more extensive explanations of these issues found in the *Disputationes*. The dearth of practical examples, and the many speculative passages relating musical issues to theology and numerology may well have frustrated a musician seeking practical advice.[5]

---

[4] See the article on Walther in *The New Grove* for references to these compositions.

[5] The combination of innovative ideas with an almost medieval preoccupation with other matters in Lippius's works was noted by Peter Benary in *Die Deutsche Kompositionslehre des 18. Jahrhunderts* (Leipzig: Breitkopf and Härtel, 1961), pp. 13-14. Lippius was not alone in his age with these preoccupations. Numerology, this (*cont.*)

Because of Lippius's early death, the *Synopsis* can hardly be considered his intentionally definitive work. Yet because of his death, the *Synopsis* attained that role. It was left to others to promulgate his theories. Lippius's ideas had their widest circulation in the more practical treatises and manuals of Johann Crüger. Crüger did not present these theories with the force, originality, and insights of Lippius's own writings, and Crüger retreated in later years from some of Lippius's innovations. As a result, Lippius's theories never had the opportunity to be expounded as they might have been by Lippius himself had he lived longer and attained the stature in the musical community that he had seemed destined to achieve.

Johann Crüger (1598-1662) as Transmitter of Lippius's Theories

Much as Calvisius was the author who presented Zarlino's teachings to a German audience in a pedagogical form, Johann Crüger presented the achievements of Lippius in a more practical form than that found in Lippius's own works. What is essential to this study is the manner in which these theories were transmitted. Many of Lippius's most radical advances do not appear at all in Crüger's works, and those points which are stated are often not presented as strongly as in Lippius's *Synopsis* and *Disputatio musica tertia*. The status of modal theory in Crüger's works was probably an influence on contemporary and later German theoretical works, especially since Crüger was prominent not only as a theorist but also as a composer, a pedagogue, and as a compiler and publisher of chorales.

Crüger's discussions of mode are found in two types of works:

1. instruction manuals designed for use in *Lateinschulen*: *Praecepta musicae practicae figuralis* (Berlin, 1625) *Quaestiones musicae practicae* (Berlin, 1650)[6]

---

time concerning the number 7, also provides the basis of organization and thought in the *Plejades musicae* (Halberstadt, 1615) by Lippius's contemporary Heinrich Baryphonus (1581-1655). See Martin Vogel, *Die Zahl Sieben in der Spekulativen Musiktheorie* (Ph. D. dissertation, Friedrich Wilhelms Universität, Bonn, 1954).

[6] In addition to what is presented here on these works, see the discussion of the *Lateinschul* manuals on pp. 68-75.

2. two editions of a composition manual: *Synopsis musica* (Berlin, 1630 and 1654),[7] modeled on Lippius's work of similar title.

Both the *Praecepta musicae* and the 1630 edition of the *Synopsis* draw heavily on Lippius, but they also contain much traditional modal theory. In chapter 7 of the first work ("De Modis musicis"), various aspects of mode are defined in terms of the triad.

> How does one recognize the modes? First, observe above all the final tone of the lowest voice or bass. Add above this 1. the diapente or perfect fifth and 2. the mediant, distant by a major third from one of the extreme tones [of the fifth] and distant by a minor third from the other, and you will have the triad, the root of all most perfect and fullest harmony which can exist in the world, and the root of thousands and thousands of thousands of sounds, all of which are led back to a part of the triad... If a fourth will be placed above the triad (harmonically), the concord will form the authentic and primary mode. If the same be placed below (arithmetically), [it forms] the plagal and secondary [mode].[8]

Finally, each mode is listed with its triad. But before this, Crüger opens the chapter by counting "fourteen modes [which] are born from the seven octave species."[9] The differentiation into major and minor is not made explicit in this work.[10]

A similar presentation occurs in chapter 11 of the *Synopsis*. Only after listing each mode does Crüger note that the modes are differentiated into two classes by virtue of the major or minor triad. This is a

---

[7] The two editions of Crüger's *Synopsis* have occasionally been confused because a broken numeral 5 in *1654* on the title page of the second edition can appear to be a 2. See Elisabeth Fischer- Krückeberg, "Johann Crüger als Musiktheoretiker," in *Zeitschrift für Musikwissenschaft* 12 (1930):612–614, concerning this. Her study is the most complete survey of Crüger's life and works.

[8] *Praecepta musicae*, fols. B6v-B7r: "Unde cognoscuntur Modi? Primum omnium respice vocis insimae sive Basis clavem finalem. Huic superadde 1. Diapente vel quintam perfectam, 2. Intermediam ab extremarum una per Ditonum, ab altera per Semiditonum distantem, & habebis Triadem omnis perfectissimae harmoniae, quae dari in mundo potest, radicem, sonorum etiam mille & millies mille, qui omnes ad unam hujus Triadis partem referri debent... Si quarta supra Triadem (harmonicè) fuerit locata, Authenticum modum & primarium concentus repraesentabit. Si verò infra eandem (Arithmeticè) locetur, Plagalem & secundarium."

[9] *Ibid.*, fol. B6v: "Ex septem diapason speciebus quatuordecim oriuntur Modi."

[10] Since the scales and semitone placements of each mode are not specifically mentioned by Crüger in this work, Fischer-Krückeberg (*op. cit.*, p. 618) argues that the only difference between modes is between major and minor. The double generation of the modes, however, makes it clear that Crüger is using the octave species as a determinant.

return to the position of Zarlino and Calvisius: the modes are octave species and are then differentiated into two classes. In Lippius, the qualities of the modes determined by the triads had been discussed first; only then were the names of the individual modes mentioned as subdivisions within major and minor.

In the study of harmonic intervals, Crüger presents a similar combination of Lippius's advances and traditional theory. Crüger generates the major and minor sixths both by the addition of a whole or half step to the perfect fifth (*Synopsis*, chapter 6) and by the addition of a third to the perfect fourth (chapter 7). In Lippius, the generation of the sixths by the addition of intervals is contradicted by other passages deriving them as inversions of thirds of opposite quality. In Crüger, the derivation as inversions of thirds does not appear at all. Without the derivation of sixths as inversions of thirds, the conceptual power of the harmonic focus on inverted triads is absent. Crüger's presentation of the triad (chapter 8) is based in large part on Lippius, but it omits some of the numerological and theological comments as well as any discussion of inversions. A new feature is the listing of possible triads of each type. The "native and ficta *naturaliores* triads" ("Naturaliores nativae & fictiles;" *native* refers to those triads with only naturals, *ficta* to those with accidentals) are C, D, E, F, G, and A major. The *molliores* are C, D, E, F, G, and A minor. Three examples are listed from B and B-flat: b–d-sharp–f (*sic*, probably an error for b–d–f-sharp), b–d–f, and b-flat–d–f. In *cantus mollis*, Crüger notes the triad e-flat–g–b-flat.

After the *Synopsis* (1630), Crüger's next extant theoretical work is the *Quaestiones* (1650), an elementary manual similar to the *Praecepta* of 1625.[11] Four years later the second edition of the *Synopsis* appeared. Some sections of the 1654 *Synopsis* are literal copies of the 1630 edition. But other sections are largely rewritten, and some new sections are added. These works present a changed view of some aspects of modal theory. Fischer-Krückeberg ascribes this to the fact that Crüger's duties in Berlin included teaching, and the changes represent what Crüger, through his teaching experience, had determined to be the best way of introducing the material.

---

[11] On the title page, Crüger labels the 1650 print "Editio Tertia. Auctior & Correctior." The 1625 *Praecepta* is presumably the first edition. Is there a lost second edition?

In some matters, Crüger returned to older theoretical positions. Thus, whereas the modes had been ordered as in Zarlino in the earlier works, Crüger returns to Glarean's ordering in the later ones:

> Although the most convenient and most natural ordering of the modes occurs if Ionian with its Hypoionian holds the first position, yet in order not to confuse young students, we want to retain that ordering of the ancients, in which Dorian and its Hypodorian take the first position.[12]

Also added is a listing of the *repercussio* of each mode, an archaism that had been dropped in his earlier works. In other matters, the changes represent accommodations to newer musical practices. Thus, in the *Synopsis* of 1654, Crüger added the B-flat-minor and B major triads to the list of possibilities.[13]

The most important change in the 1654 *Synopsis* concerns the thirteenth and fourteenth modes—Hyperaeolian (the authentic mode on B) and Hyperphrygian (for Crüger, the authentic mode on E in the transposed system with a one-flat signature).[14] In this discussion, Crüger betrays a fundamental contradiction in his concept of modes—a contradiction that was not be resolved until a later generation recognized twenty-four major and minor keys as equally original.

> These two modes [Hyperaeolian and Hyperphrygian] are rejected by most musicians and called spurious on account of the aharmonic triad. But truly the more reasonable musicians will decide, with me, that they not be done away with altogether and rejected on account of that. For these aharmonic triads can easily be turned into harmonic triads with the help of semitones: namely in B *cantus durus*, the uppermost

---

[12] *Quaestiones*, fol. C5v: "Licet convenientissimus & omnium naturalissimus sit Modorum ordo, si primum locum obtineat Jonicus cum suo HypoJonico: Attamen, ne confundantur ingenia discentium, veterum illum, quo primo loco collocant Dorium cum Hypodorio suo retinere voluimus ordinem." Crüger's reasoning seems to point elsewhere for the cause of his return to the older ordering. Young students presumably would not be confused by either ordering if that were the only one that they were taught. The confusion would arise if different teachers of theirs (perhaps different choirmasters?) used different orderings. Had the young Crüger of the *Praecepta* and the 1630 *Synopsis* been willing to champion a newer idea, while the older Crüger of the *Quaestiones* despaired of convincing the more entrenched of his colleagues?

[13] Fischer-Krückeberg (*op. cit.*, p. 619) writes that the E-flat-minor, A-minor, and B-flat-major triads are also added here. But they were already present in the 1630 edition.

[14] Crüger gives no reason for this last name. Hyperphrygian had meant the rejected plagal mode with a final on B for all theorists from Glarean up to this point.

tone of the triad, F, changed to F-sharp (*fis*, as the instrumentalists call it) by the addition of a semitone. Hence, out of the false fifth the true disposition of the same triad will arise in this manner:

Example 4-2. Crüger, *Synopsis* **(1654), p.123**

Trias anarmonica   Trias harmonica

On the other hand, in *cantus mollis*, E, the lowest tone of the aharmonic triad having been changed to E-flat [*sic*: d-sharp],[15] that diminished and false fifth is changed to the pure fifth:

Example 4-3. Crüger, *Synopsis* **(1654), p.123**

Trias anarmonica   Trias harmonica

And thus all aharmony is removed. Accordingly, the thirteenth and fourteenth modes have the harmonic triads: b–d–f-sharp in *cantus durus*, e-flat–g–b-flat in *cantus mollis*.[16]

---

[15] *Dis* (D-sharp) was used to refer to the semitone between D and E well into the eighteenth century, no matter what the function. In staff notation, of course, the pitch referred to here would be notated E-flat, but organ tablatures in German used *dis* exclusively. See Willi Apel, *The Notation of Polyphonic Music 900-1600* (Cambridge: Mediaeval·Academy of America, 1953), pp. 24-26, *passim*. A number of later writers complained about this usage, but it apparently persisted at least through 1789, when Daniel Türk argued against it in his *Klavierschule* (Leipzig & Halle; facsimile edition Marburg: Bärenreiter, 1962), pp. 58–59.

[16] *Synopsis*, 1654, p. 123: "Rejiciuntur hi duo Modi a plerisq[ue] Musicis, & Spurii propter Triadem anarmonicam vocantur. Verum non omnino istos esse abolendos & rejiciendos mecum saniores: Musici statuent, propter ea, quod Triades istae anarmonicae beneficio Semitonii in harmonicas apte verti queant, mutata nimirum, in [natural] cantu duro, suprema Triadis clave F addito Semitonio minor in Fis, (ut a Musicis Instrumentalibus appellatur). Hunc enim in modum ex quinta ista falsa vera ejusdem dispositio pronascetur... Sic in cantu molli versa infima Triadis anarmonicae clave E in

This presentation is either borrowed from another theorist, or was presented by Crüger in an earlier work now lost (c.f. footnote 11). Conrad Matthaei argues against this type of mode generation in his *Bericht von den Modis Musicis*, a work published in 1652, but possibly written before 1637.[17] In the preface, Matthaei credits his teacher Heinrich Grimm (1593-1637) with writing the book: "this entire treatise is not mine but the work of the late Grimm; I have not changed so much as a single letter in it."[18] See pp. 59-60 for more information on Matthaei's work.

In any event, Crüger's formulation is the earliest extant attempt to introduce into the formal presentation of the modes transpositions other than those down a fifth or up a fourth; and it is also the first attempt to introduce transposed modes as "original" modes. Zarlino had already noted in 1558 that modes could be transposed to any pitch if necessary. Crüger's own *Quaestiones* of 1650 contains similar statements (fols. D3r-D4r). But any octave species other than the original twelve or fourteen was always regarded as a transposition, not an original mode.

Dis, Quinta ista diminuta & falsa in veram mutatur... & ita omnis anarmonia tollitur ut: Sunt igitur decimus tertius, & decimus quartus Modus Triadis harmonicae H D Fis in Cantu duro Dis G B in Cantu molli."

A similar classification of modes is found in Wolfgang Mylius's *Rudimenta musices, Das ist: Eine kurtze und Grundrichtige Anweisung zur Singe-Kunst* (Gotha, 1686). Mylius first lists all the diatonic octaves between c and a, divided both arithmetically and harmonically (with the F–f octave divided arithmetically by B-flat). His second grouping of modes includes the octave B–b divided arithmetically (the traditional Hypophrygian), and then harmonically with F-sharp (Crüger's thirteenth mode); and two divisions on e-flat (*dis*). The third grouping includes various ficta triads: D, E, A, and B majors, and F-sharp and B minors. The separation of modes on B and E-flat from the other modes probably derives from Crüger. See fols. G4r-G5r in Mylius.

[17] *Kurtzer doch ausführlicher Bericht von den Modis Musicis, welchen aus den besten, aeltesten, berühmtesten und bewerthesten Autoribus der Music zusammen getragen*...([Königsberg], 1652).

[18] Fol. B1v: "...dieser gantze Tractat sey nicht meine sondern des sehl: Grymmi Arbeit und dass ich auch keinen eintzigen Buchstaben daran verändert hatte." But Grimm's name does not appear on the title page, and later writers refer to the work solely under Matthaei's name. If Grimm is indeed the author, then the work must date from 1637 or earlier. Grimm published the second edition of Calvisius's *Melopoeia* and Baryphonus's *Plejades* in 1630. In addition to Matthaei, he was the teacher of Otto Gibel (1612-1682), the author of works on mathematical aspects of music, including temperament.

Of great interest is the manner in which these modes are presented. No scale is given, and they are not likened to any other mode. If the thirteenth mode is understood as a white-note scale on B with an F-sharp instead of F, then is it a transposition of Phrygian? Both Conrad Matthaei[19] and Christoph Bernhard[20] used this very argument to reject this mode. Similarly, if the fourteenth mode is understood with a two-flat signature, it is a transposition of Lydian to E-flat. But if this were the case, there would be no reason to present these two new modes. Certainly there would be no cause to add a new form of Lydian, which even Glarean had noted was long out of common use. But if other sharps and flats are implied, this would contradict Crüger's own statements of 1650: "Whence arise the modes? From the seven notes c d e f g a b, on which the entire doctrine of the modes depends."[21]

There is inherent here a confusion about the nature of mode and the criteria by which one mode is differentiated from another. Before Lippius, theory had accepted mode in terms of octave species divisible harmonically and arithmetically. There were twelve modes, each of which had a different octave species. In order to identify the mode of a melody with an accidental throughout, the octave species was compared to the twelve modes, and the correct mode was located. Such a discussion is found in Zarlino's *Istitutioni* (Part IV, chapter 16). Lippius no longer viewed mode as the combination of a species of fourth and a species of fifth making an octave species. Rather, there was a fourth added to a major or minor triad. Scalar criteria were not necessarily implied here. According to his system of classification, there were three authentic major modes and three authentic minor modes. It was not explicitly stated that the modes of similar quality were interchangeable (i.e., that Mixolydian and Ionian were one). But the implication is that they were variants of the same type.

In order to present a consistent view of mode, contemporary theorists had two choices. Either there were two modes, major and minor, which could begin on any note. Or there were twelve different modes because of the structure of the white-note scale. In that

---

[19] *Op. cit.*, p. 22.

[20] *Tractatus compositionis augmentatus*, chapter 45. See footnote 30 in this chapter for more information on Bernhard's treatise.

[21] *Quaestiones*, fol. C5v: "Unde oriuntur Modi? Ex septem Clavibus c d e f g a h, a quibus tota Modorum doctrina dependet."

case, any transposition of a mode removed it from its original locus. In Crüger's works, elements of both solutions can be found. He differentiated modes both by octave species and by major-minor triads. Some modes, which had the common quality of "tonic triads" (e.g., Ionian, Mixolydian, Lydian), had different octave species and were separate modes. Other modes, which had a similar quality of "tonic triads" and the same octave species, were transpositions of these original modes. But some modes, which were transpositions of other modes, were considered original, independent modes. This conflict was not resolved until all the twenty-four major and minor keys were recognized as equally original. And it would have been a rash theorist indeed to suggest such an idea in the mid-seventeenth century, when, except for a handful of special cases, most chromatic keys had not yet appeared in any compositions. The recognition of all twenty-four keys as equally original did not arise until the early eighteenth century.

The Maintenance of Traditional Modal Theory

During the mid-seventeenth century, German writings offering a traditional view of modes fall into three groups. There are treatises that derive from a purely German tradition, those that derive from an Italian tradition, and the elementary manuals for use in the *Lateinschulen*.

The German Tradition. The *Bericht von den Modis Musicis* of Conrad Matthaei (1619-1667?) has already been mentioned (see footnote 17 on p. 57). Matthaei was a cantor in Königsberg after 1654. The *Bericht* is the first of a number of German treatises published between 1650 and 1750 in which the authors attempted to restore the old teaching of the modes to its supposedly rightful place. Other such works are by Johann Buttstett (in 1715?), Franz Murschhauser (in 1721), and Meinrad Spiess (in 1745). In all these works, the author bemoans the current state of ignorance and cites various authorities to restore the modes. The authorities are often several decades old, sometimes even more than a century old. Yet the teachings of the old authorities are interspersed with contemporary practice. Thus, in some respects, Matthaei's *Bericht* is more progressive than some other contemporary treatises. Matthaei studied music with Heinrich Grimm (1593–1637), himself a student of Michael Praetorius and a musician and publisher in Magdeburg and Braunschweig.

Most of the *Bericht* is paraphrased from earlier authors. Seventy writers are listed in the preface, ranging from ancient Greek and medieval theorists to a larger number of sixteenth and seventeenth-century writers and composers. Glarean and Michael Praetorius are quoted often in the course of the text. Matthaei complains in the preface that students sometimes never even hear about the modes because cantors know little about them.[22] Composers ignore them and make foreign cadences. Organists who do not know them cannot improvise preludes and fantasies correctly. Some even mix ("das grösseste Elend!") different transpositions. This last is an essential point. One of the principal differences between sixteenth-century *prima-prattica* and tonal compositions concerns the type of scale used in "nontonic" portions of the piece. In sixteenth-century *prima-prattica* music, the same diatonic scale is often used for the entire composition. In tonal music, each new key area uses "transpositions" of the tonic scale.

Matthaei notes that his book is written in German so as to reach a wider audience. The thorough discussions in each chapter cover all the aspects of traditional modal theory. Glarean's and Zarlino's theories form the basis of many points. And even Lippius's triad of each mode appears, but not as a harmonic entity—only as a term for the three important notes of each mode. There is no hint of a major-minor differentiation. Lippius's *trias harmonica*, a revolutionary innovation only a generation earlier, had now joined the teachings of the ancients in venerability.

Wolfgang Caspar Printz (1641–1717) is one of the most important writers on music in Germany in the seventeenth century. His works, printed between 1668 and 1690, include several singing manuals, theoretical essays, an extensive and important history of music, and *Phrynis (Mytilenaeus) oder Satyrischer Componist* (Quedlinburg, 1676–77), of which the Erste Theil is, in part, a composition treatise. Only in the last-named work is there a full discussion of mode.[23] In most details, Printz is conservative. Modes arise from the harmonic and arithmetic divisions of the octave, differentiating them into authentic and plagal. The fifth of each mode can also be divided

---

[22] See pp. 68-75 concerning the elementary manuals used by young students at the time. About two-thirds of these manuals do not even mention the modes.

[23] The work was published in three parts and later in complete edition (1696). Part I, in which mode is discussed, was first published in 1676. Mode is discussed in chapters 9 and 10.

harmonically and arithmetically, resulting in the *trias harmonica*, but Printz does not use this to differentiate modes. The only relationships between modes that he discusses are between authentic and plagal modes of the same name.

Only in two matters does Printz's treatment differ significantly from traditional modal theory. The first concerns cadences, in which area Printz retreats from standard practice of the previous century. He lists primary, secondary, and tertiary cadences on the final, fifth, and third of each mode, as many other writers do. But when these fall on B, they are not listed at all. Thus Phrygian has no secondary cadence and Mixolydian no tertiary. One of the progressive features in Zarlino's *Istitutioni* of 1558 had been to standardize the cadences of all modes on scale degrees 1, 5, and 3. This was another step that minimized the individual differences between the separate octave species. Over a century later, Printz is still troubled by the problems of a cadence on B, thereby re-emphasizing the special characteristics of the individual octave species.

The other significant change concerns the term *repercussio*, now defined to conform with more contemporary practice. Printz rejects the ancient opinion that *repercussio* is the repeated note of a mode, for that would hinder variety. "The *repercussio* of each mode is best taken into account when the discant and bass travel, for the most part in accented notes, through the harmonic triads whose lowest notes are the notes of the harmonic triad of the mode in use. The harmonic triad of the lowest note is used the most, that of the uppermost is used often, and that of the mediant more rarely."[24] A rudimentary theory of harmonic progression has now joined the notion of mode.

The Italian Tradition. The emergence of a new style in Italy around the turn of the seventeenth century is a signal event in the history of music. The Monteverdi-Artusi controversy (1600–1608) definitively established the split between the traditional *prima prattica* and the new *seconda prattica*. Many German musicians, most prominent among them Heinrich Schütz (1585–1672), studied in Italy

---

[24]*Satyrischer Componist*, p. 37: "Die Repercussion eines ieden Modi wird am besten in acht genommen wenn Discant und Bass am meisten Notis Quantitate Intrinseca longis durch die Triades Harmonicas, deren unterste Soni von denen Sonis Triadis Harmonicae des gebrauchten Modi seyn schweiffen; Doch das Trias Harmonica Soni infimi am meisten supremi offt und medii seltener gebraucht werde." I am indebted to Ms. Susan Jackson for pointing out that the term *Notis Quantitate Intrinseca longis* refers to accentuation in Printz.

in the early years of the seventeenth century and then returned north, bringing the new style with them.

The *seconda prattica* opened new vistas in terms of texture, dissonance treatment, harmonic/melodic interaction in general, continuity, and open expressiveness. The treatises that arose later to demonstrate that the newer practice was built on the foundation of the *prima prattica* are among the most important theoretical writings of any era—most notably the *Tractatus compositionis augmentatus* (ms. ca. 1655) of Christoph Bernhard (1627–1692) and the *Gradus ad parnassum* (Vienna, 1725) of Johann Joseph Fux (1660–1741).

Whatever the importance of the *seconda prattica* to the theory of counterpoint and the increased understanding of harmony and voice leading, the theoretical treatises associated with this tradition brought no new insights into developing consciousness of major and minor. In the late sixteenth century, Italian practice had developed a listing of eight commonly used modes arranged in a series with their finals and signature. As early as 1605 (that is, before Lippius's treatises), Adriano Banchieri (1567–1634) enumerated these as the "eight tones of ecclesiastical chant"[25] (to be discussed fully in chapter 5). This convenient system of enumerating the possible finals and scales most commonly used bypassed the need for speculative discussions on the nature of mode, the systematic differentiation of original and transposed modes, and even the differentiation of major and minor. These "church keys," with various modifications, remained a standard codification in Italy throughout the seventeenth century, often appearing along with discussions of traditional modal theory. The *Musico prattico* (Bologna, 1673)[26] of Giovanni Maria Bononcini (1642–1678), an important counterpoint treatise reprinted in 1678 and 1688, and translated into German in 1701, contains a long discussion of modes (chapters 15–21, pp. 121–161), largely derived from Glarean and Zarlino. Chapter 17 (pp. 137–147) refers to one version of the church keys. As a composer, Bononcini wrote secular instrumental music, and was one of those who explored the new virtuosity of violinists. But his treatise reflects only a traditional view of modes. As late as a generation after Bononcini's treatise, the

---

[25] *L'Organo suonarino* (Venice, 1605; facsimile editions [Amsterdam: Knuf, 1969; Bologna: Forni, 1969]), Part II: "sopra gli Otto Tuoni spettanti al Canto fermo Ecclesiastico."

[26] Facsimile edition (New York: Broude, 1969). All references are to the 1673 edition.

church keys remained a well-known Italian codification. In 1713, Johann Mattheson begins his listing of twenty-four major and minor keys with the church keys, referring to them as an Italian phenomenon. These developments are fully treated in chapters 5 and 6. What concerns the present discussion is how German writings on modes that derive from the Italian styles do not treat major and minor at all.

The first such treatises are by Johann Andreas Herbst (1588–1666). Although he lived and worked in Germany for his entire adult life (in Darmstadt, Nürnberg, and Frankfurt), Herbst was best known as a musician versed in the contemporary Italian vocal styles. There are extensive discussions on the Italian manner of vocal embellishments in his *Musica practica sive instructio pro symphoniacis...auff jetzige Italienische Manier* (Nürnberg, 1642) and *Musica moderna prattica, overo maniera del buon canto* (Frankfurt, 1653 and 1658). Herbst's *Arte prattica et poëtica* is a translation of the counterpoint text, *Arte pratica latina et volgare di far contrapunto* (Venice, 1610) by Giovanni Chiodino. Herbst's composition treatise, *Musica poëtica* (Nürnberg, 1643),[27] presumably represents the outlook of mid-century musicians active in contemporary styles. The treatise is a compilation from many different sources, as is noted in the subtitle: "collected for the most part from the foremost Latin and Italian authors and musicians, old as well as new, and presented briefly in this compendium."[28] But Herbst failed to digest much of the material, giving rise to a confusing organization of data and contradictions between different presentations of the same material only a few pages apart.

Mode is discussed in four of the twelve chapters: chapter 6 on the modes proper (pp. 45–48), chapter 7 on cadences (pp. 58–80), chapter 8 on the beginning, middle, and end of songs (pp. 81–88), and chapter 11 on text, which consists of a discussion of the affect of each mode (pp. 101–112).

---

[27] Herbst believed this to be the first composition treatise ever published in German: "...in Teutscher Sprach/der gleichen zuvor niemals also gesehen worden..." But in 1610, Maternus Beringer had published a free translation into German of Magirus's *Artis musicae* of 1596. (see p. 25). The choice of language was not an inconsequential decision among German writers of the period. Conrad Matthaei consciously chose German for his *Bericht*, blaming some of the ignorance of modal theory among musicians on the use of Latin in many earlier treatises.

[28] Title page: "...So mehrentheils auss den fürnembsten/so wol Alten als Newen/Lateinischen und Italienischen Authoribus und Musicis, mit besonderm Fleiss zusammen getragen/und in dieses Compendium kürtzlich verfasset..."

Eleven points on modes are listed at the beginning of chapter 6: (1) whether to refer to the modes with the term *tonus* or *modus*; (2) the definition of mode; (3) the fundamental intervals of a mode; (4) the ambitus; (5) freedom in the ambitus; (6) the division of the octave; (7) the placement of cadences; (8) the final; (9) the *repercussio*; (10) the intonation in psalms and antiphons; and (11) the use of the modes. The list is apparently taken from a work on the Gregorian modes. Thus the *repercussio* is listed for only eight modes (p. 50, point 9). Yet only two pages later, the number of modes is established at fourteen with two rejected.

In point 3, the modes are generated as octave species differentiated by semitone placement and arising from addition of species of fifth and fourth. The important intervals are named as the semitone, the whole tone, the fourth, the fifth, and the octave; conspicuously absent are thirds and sixths.

According to point 8, the modes are recognized from the tenor or discant. The tenor is still the center of the composition for Herbst. As its name implies, this voice "maintains the melody of the chorale and the ambitus of the mode."[29] Similarly, in chapter 5 ("De harmoniae partibus und vermischung der Consonantien"), treating counterpoint in four voices, which Herbst recommends as the first composition exercise, he suggests successive composition of the voices: first the tenor with the chorale; then the discant, the bass, and finally the altus (pp. 32–33). Yet in line with the confused nature of the work, he then begins exercises with the bass only two pages later!

The *principalis* cadence of Phrygian (on the final) can end on an A-major triad, with only the tenor on E, while the *minus principalis* (on the fifth of the mode) ends on an E-major chord. See example 4-4 (opposite). Thus, in Phrygian a separate *finalis* cadence must be added.

Several important subjects, such as the number of modes and their ordering, transposition, and affects, are not mentioned among the eleven points, but are treated separately later in chapter 6 or elsewhere. Different orderings of the modes are treated in chapter 6. Some writers begin with A because it is the first letter of the alphabet; some begin with D in agreement with common usage; others start with C because it is the lowest note on the organ, and the hexachord

---

[29]P. 32: "...weil er die Melodiam und gemeiniglich den Choral, und dess Modi ambitum oder Lauff in sich begreifft und hält..."

Example 4-4. Herbst, *Musica pöetica,* **p.71**

Cadences for the Phrygian mode

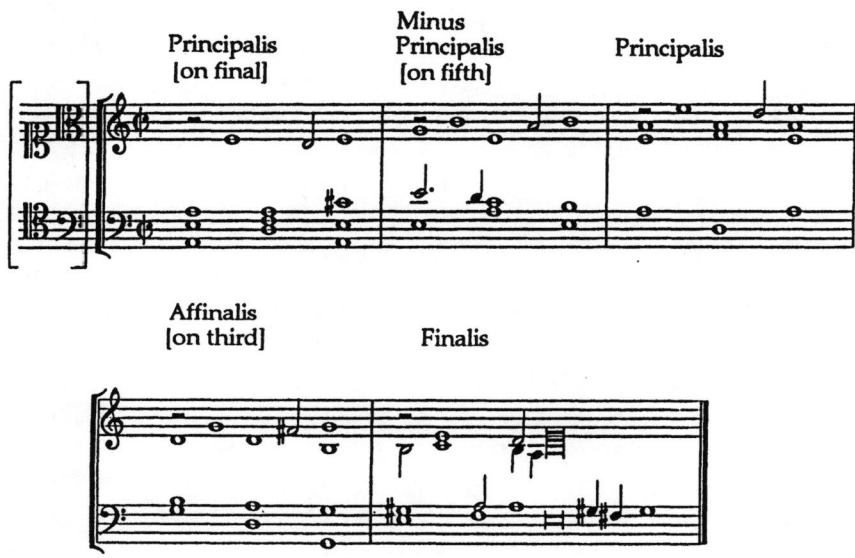

begins with *ut.* Herbst opts for beginning on D to avoid confusion. But different systems of ordering appear in later sections. Ionian assumes prime position when the modes are first discussed (p. 53) and in the discussion of notes on which cadences are to be made (pp. 67–68). Yet in the fuller discussion of cadences (pp. 69–80) and the listing of affects in chapters 8 and 11, Dorian is discussed first.

In chapter 8, a *Verselein* borrowed from the singing manuals is presented as a mnemonic device for the affect of each mode. Included in each line is the name, the affect, the *repercussio*, and the order. The line for Dorian reads: "Dorius est hilaris: Re La sonat: ordine Primus." The affects are taken from Adam Gumpelzhaimer's elementary manual (concerning which, see pp. 69–70), but Herbst makes some larger groupings, including the cheerful (*fröhlich*) modes (Dorian, *hilaris*; Aeolian, *suaviter*; and Ionian, *jucundus*) and the sad and gentle (*traurig und gelind*) modes (Hypophrygian, *blandi*; Hypolydian, *lenis*; and Hypoaeolian, *tristis*). Lydian is hard and angry (*hart und zornig*). The plagal forms are often different from their corresponding authentics. Clearly there is no differentiation according to major and minor.

Based on the remarkably poor editing of the work, it might be argued that Herbst merely patched it together without much care, possibly as a purely commercial venture, and did not necessarily believe the contents. But surely it would have cost him just as little effort to write his own thoughts from scratch as it would have taken him to collect all the different sections that appear in this work. Additional evidence that the attitudes expressed in this treatise were his own is found in the treatment of mode in Lorenz Erhard's *Harmonisches Chor- und Figural Gesang- Buch* (Frankfurt, 1659), an elementary manual discussed in the next subdivision of this chapter (see p. 75). Erhard worked with Herbst in Frankfurt during several periods after 1625. The conservative treatment of mode in the *Gesangbuch* agrees with Herbst's own presentations.

Herbst's work, though of poor quality in itself, may be indicative of a more general situation of mid-seventeenth-century German theory. The lack of new light on major and minor from the then-ascendent Italian tradition may have influenced even those German theorists who were earlier aware of the German major-minor theories of earlier in the century. On pp. 54-55 we took note of Johann Crüger's retreat to more conservative traditions in a number of aspects of modal theory in his later publications. Crüger's last published work, his *Musicae practicae* (Berlin, 1660), incorporated a section on the popular vocal embellishments similar in presentation to the same material found in Herbst's works. Perhaps some of Crüger's growing conservatism may derive from the Italian tradition.

Christoph Bernhard's *Tractatus compositionis augmentatus* is one of the best-known treatises of the second half of the century. The treatise, apparently written after 1655, was not published until the twentieth century, but it circulated widely in manuscript until well into the eighteenth century.[30] Bernhard (1627-1692) was a student of Paul Siefert (himself a student of Sweelinck), Heinrich Schütz, and

---

[30] See Josef Maria Müller-Blattau, *Die Kompositionslehre Heinrich Schützens in der Fassung seines Schülers Christoph Bernhard* (Leipzig, 1926; reprinted Kassel: Bärenreiter, 1953). This contains the first publication of the treatise. See also Helmut Federhofer, "Der Gradus ad Parnassum von Fux und seine Vorläufer in Österreich," in *Musikerziehung* (1957):31-35, in which it is shown that Bernhard's treatise circulated in manuscript copies in southern Germany and Austria as well as in the north. An English translation of the *Tractatus* by Walter Hilse appears in *The Music Forum* 3 (1973):1-196.

Giacomo Carissimi. It was formerly thought that the *Tractatus* was based solely on Schütz's teachings, but it now appears that it might be derived from other sources as well.[31] The study of composition is approached through a solid grounding in the strict style of the *prima prattica*. Contemporary usages are then explained as modifications and combinations of this strict practice. If this approach had been extended to the modes, a traditional approach might have been followed by a discussion of modern usages. But such is not the case. Instead, the presentation of mode is largely traditional.

The discussion of mode covers ten brief chapters (chapters 44-53). Zarlino's ordering is followed: "...the mode on C must be the first because all the remaining modes arrange the perfection of their cadences according to this one."[32] There is no formal distinction made between modes with major and minor thirds over the final. Various statements in the chapters on the individual modes relate those with minor thirds to one another. But the modes with major thirds over the final are not related in any special ways. Among the minor modes, Dorian is "quite closely related to the eleventh [Aeolian] because it often changes the B above the fifth to B- flat..."[33] Similarly, Phrygian "also has a great kinship with the above-mentioned eleventh, especially if the cadence on A is often heard in it, considering that the cadence on B is not at all acceptable..."[34] The Hypophrygian "is mixed with the twelfth [Hypoaeolian] quite a bit, as its authentic is mixed with the eleventh, so that they can hardly be differentiated from one another except by their endings."[35] But the irregular cadences are not the same in all minor modes. In Dorian and Phrygian they are on the fourth and sixth degrees (in Dorian on B-flat!), in Aeolian on the

---

[31] See the preface to Walter Hilse's translation cited in footnote 30.

[32] *Tractatus*, chapter 45: "...der Modus aus dem C. der erste seyn müsse, weilen die übrigen alle ihrer Schlüsse Perfection nach diesem richten..." Walter Hilse, *loc. cit.*, interprets this to mean that all final cadences end with a major third. But such a criterion would allow Mixolydian or even Lydian in first position. It seems more likely that Bernhard is referring to the entire cadential progression with the raised leading tone in the penultimate chord. See chapter 12 of the *Tractatus* concerning the "bass cadence."

[33] *Tractatus*, chapter 47: "Dieser modus ist gar nahe verwandt mit dem undecimo, weil er über die Quinte das ♮ offt in b molle verändert."

[34] *Ibid.*, chapter 48: "Auch dieser hat grosse Verwandschafft mit dem vorigen gemeldeten eilften, zumahl wenn die Cadenz des a offt darinnen gehöret wird, angesehen die ins ♮ nicht gar annehmlich ist..."

[35] *Ibid.*, chapter 48: "Er wird gar sehr mit dem 12ten Modo vermenget, wie sein Authenticus mit dem 11ten, so dass sie kaum von einander als am Ende unterscheiden."

fourth and seventh. The modes with major thirds above the final are not so closely related except for the customary statements that Lydian modes are changed to Ionian. Mixolydian is treated independently.

The Elementary Manuals. Music held an important position in the curriculum of the German *Lateinschulen*. Handbooks containing the elements of notation, solmization, some rudimentary theory, and many singing exercises were published by a broad spectrum of authors, including music teachers, headmasters, pastors, well-known composers, and theorists.[36] Among prominent musicians discussed elsewhere in this study who wrote such works are Calvisius, Crüger, and Printz. The aim of the manuals was primarily to teach schoolboys to sing religious music. The repertoire of musical examples is generally limited to chant or chorales with the possible addition of some polyphonic sacred music or secular didactic exercises. Since texts for general educational purposes often present the lowest common denominator of accepted musical pedagogy, these works are, virtually without exception, rather conservative in their treatment of mode. It is precisely for this reason that they are important to the present study. Well into the eighteenth century, the premise that the quality of the tonic triad should be the principal differentiating factor between modes was highly controversial in Germany. Of the works of more than thirty-five authors surveyed, about one third contain discussions of the modes. These works help fill in the complete picture of the acceptance of new theoretical ideas on the modes by the general musical audience of the seventeenth century. The manuals of Faber and Gumpelzhaimer, which were the two most widely circulated works, are cited in theoretical literature into the eighteenth century. Some works listed below appeared virtually unchanged in many editions over the period of a century or more, even though they became increasingly alienated from contemporary developments with each new edition.

One of the earliest German manuals, and the one which appeared in the most editions, was written by Heinrich Faber (Magister Heinricus Faber), about whose life little is known. He died in 1552,

---

[36] The most thorough surveys of these works are Eberhard Preussner, *Die Methodik im Schulgesang der evangelischen Lateinschulen des 17. Jahrhunderts*, unpublished dissertation (University of Berlin, 1924), and Albert Allerup, *Die "Musica Practica" des Johann Andreas Herbst und ihre entwicklungsgeschichtliche Bedeutung: Ein Beitrag zur Geschichte der deutschen Schulmusik* (Kassel: Bärenreiter, 1931).

leaving his *Compendiolum musicae pro incipientibus* in one Latin edition, that printed in Braunschweig in 1548. As many as forty-six subsequent prints through 1617 are extant, published in numerous places, the most common of which are Leipzig, Nürnberg, Hantzch, Frankfurt, Erfurt, Goslar, and Augsburg.[37] There were several German translations:

1. by Christoph Rid: *Musica. Kurtzer Innhalt der Singkunst, auss M. Heinrich Fabri lateinischem Compendio Musicae...*(Nürnberg, 1572 and 1586).

2. by Johann Colhardt: *Musica. Kurtze und einfeltige Anleitung der Singkunst für...Lehrschüler. Anfänglichen durch M. Heinricum Fabrum in Latein beschrieben. Jetzo aber...in Deutsch vertiret...*(Leipzig, 1605).

3. A bilingual version (Latin and German) by Melchior Vulpius containing additions borrowed from Michael Praetorius: *Musicae compendiolum latino germanicum M. Heinrici Fabri...*(nine editions from 1608–1665).

Christoph Rid's translation appeared in a new bilingual format in 1591 published by Adam Gumpelzhaimer (1559–1625), a composer who may have studied with Lassus. This *Compendium musicae latinogermanicum* appeared in thirteen editions through 1681. Its contents will be presented here as representative of other manuals of the time. (See table 4-1 on pp. 72-75 for information on other works.) The editions of 1616 and 1632 were compared; both are virtually identical in contents except for the edition number on the title page and the introductory notes. There are ten chapters:

Chapter	Musica	folio	Singekunst
1	Musica	4	der Singekunst
2	Clavibus	4	den Schlüsseln
3	Vocibus	7	den Stimmen
4	Cantu	7	dem Gesang
5	Mutatione	8	der veränderung der Stim
6	Figura & Signis	10	gestalt der Noten und Zaiche
7	Ligatura	12	Zusamen bindung der Note
8	Pausis & Punctis	14	den Pausen und Puncten
9	Proportionibus	15	der Proportion
10	Tonis seu Modis	17	dem Thon

[37] RISM, *Écrits imprimés* lists these forty-six prints. For all the elementary manuals discussed in this section, the number of prints agrees with the library holdings *(cont.)*

69

Chapters 1–9 are bilingual with Latin and German on opposite sides of each page. Chapter 10 on the modes appears in Latin only. The work was probably used as a Latin text as well. By the time the student was ready for chapter 10, he had presumably mastered Latin sufficiently to allow him to understand the discussion without German. The end of the book (fols. 23v-78v) contains canons for singing practice. The material is presented in the form of catechisms. The first chapter, for instance, opens: "What is music? It is an art of singing properly and well."[38]

Chapter 10 on the modes covers folios 17–23, nearly one-third the length of the text. Fourteen modes are listed in Glarean's ordering in a table presenting the number, name, and affect of each. Hyperaeolian and Hyperphrygian are listed last and are rejected as spurious because they lack a proper division. The range and *repercussio* of each authentic and plagal mode, in its original position and transposed down a fifth to a one- flat signature, are presented in musical examples. Each mode is then discussed briefly, as:

> Dorian is the first mode or tone. The first tone is used in *cantus* { $\frac{durus}{mollis}$ } between { $\frac{d}{g}$ } & { $\frac{d}{g}$ } through an octave. It has two intervals. The first from { $\frac{d}{g}$ } to { $\frac{a,\ durus}{d,\ mollis}$ } by the fifth *re, la*. The second from { $\frac{a}{d}$ } to { $\frac{d,\ durus}{g,\ mollis}$ } by the fourth *re, sol*. It has a final in D, *durus* and G, *mollis*.[39]

This is followed by three examples: one presenting the range in original and one-flat transposition; one with a composition in four voices; and one containing a *tropus* in chant notation. The same format is used for all the modes.

---

[38] "Was is die Music? Sie ist ein Kunst recht und wol zu singen."

[39] Fol. 17v: "Dorius, id est, tonis sive modus primus. Primus tonus versatur in cantu { $\frac{duro}{molli}$ } inter { $\frac{D}{G}$ } & { $\frac{D}{G}$ } per octavam. Intervalle habet duo. Primum ex { $\frac{D}{G}$ } in { $\frac{A, durum}{D, mollem}$ } per quintam Re, La. Alterum ex { $\frac{A}{D}$ } in { $\frac{D;\ durum}{G,\ mollem}$ } per quartam Re, Sol. Finem habet in D, duro & G, molli."

Table 4-1 (pp. 72-75) indicates some features of the discussion of mode in singing manuals after Gumpelzhaimer. Note that most follow Glarean in ordering, and only Crüger's and Mylius's works introduce the concept of the triad.

NOTES FOR TABLE 4-1

[1]The discussion of modes is in Latin only.

[2]This is probably the earliest published discussion of mode in German.

[3]Authentic modes appear alphabetically, plagal modes according to solmization syllables *ut-si.* But the numbering in each list follows Glarean.

[4]Kretzschmar discusses transpositions via solmization, moving *ut* to d, e, f, g, a, and b-flat, with signatures of 1-4 sharps and 1-2 flats.

[5]The work appeared in several editions (1602-71). Only the 1617 edition discusses mode in a section borrowed from the *Musicae practicae* (four editions, 1566-96) by Nicolaus Roggius, cantor in Braunschweig from 1551 to his death in 1567.

[6]The twelve modes are listed along with twelve (*sic!*) tones.

[7]The 1649 edition appears in a reprint in Ernst Langlütge's *Die Musica Figuralis des Magister Daniel Friderici* (Berlin, 1901). The modes are presented on pp. 51-95, nearly half the length of the entire work.

[8]Glarean's ordering is the basis of the examples, following an earlier rejection of modes 11 and 12 with finals on B (pp. 53 and 92 of the 1901 reprint).

[9]The treatise on mode is appended to the 1619 edition, but not to the other two prints (1617 and 1624).

[10]The manual is in two parts, the first one in Latin. The following part in German only summarizes the opening portions for students not yet proficient in Latin.

[11]Sartorius divides the modes into "even" and "odd" in agreement with Magirus (see pp. 24-26 of the present study), but the ordering is Glarean's.

[12]A single transposition is listed as the norm, but more transpositions can be used with instruments.

[13]Zarlino's ordering is the most natural, but Glarean's is better for pedagogical purposes (see p. 13 of the present study).

[14]The twelve modes are ordered as in Zarlino; the eight tones follow the traditional ordering.

[15]The *Gesang-Buch* contains 811 pages of songs in 2-6 voices. An appendix with separate signatures discusses "necessary musical subjects and also shows clearly the *toni* of every song in a new manner." The modes are discussed in a second appendix (fols. C3r-C8v).

[16]There is no formal derivation of the modes. Examples are given for twelve of them.

[17]Mylius was a pupil of Christoph Bernhard.

[18]No names, orderings, affects, etc., are given. The modes of the ancients appear first as six octave species from C to A divided arithmetically and harmonically. Then the tones used by more recent musicians appear: a B octave divided both ways with a one-sharp signature and an E-flat octave divided both ways with a one-flat signature. (Cf. Crüger's *Synopsis* of 1654; see pp. 55-57 of the present study.) Finally, various triads appear: D, E, A, and B major, and B and F-sharp minor.

Table 4-1. Treatment of Mode in Singing Manuals

Work (In the case of works which appeared in more than one edition, the date of the edition (or editions) consulted appears in italics.)	Language: German	Language: Latin	Language: Latin-German	No. of modes: 12 modes and 8 tones	No. of modes: 14 modes with 2 rejected	Ordering: Zarlino	Ordering: Glarean	Concepts: Affects	Concepts: Repercussio	Concepts: Mode is Fifth + fourth	Concepts: Mode is Triad + fourth	Transpositions: Terms *dur* and *moll* used for transposition	Transpositions: One transposition	Transpositions: Several transpositions
1. Adam Gumpelzhaimer, *Compendium musicae* ... (Augsburg, 1591). In many editions in various cities to 1681.			X[1]		X		X	X	X	X		X	X	
2. Peter Eichmann, *Praecepta musicae practicae sive elementa artis canendi, modorumque musicorum doctrina* ... (Stettin, 1604).		X		X			X	X	X	X		X	X	
3. Johann Kretzschmar, *Musica latino-germanica* ... (Leipzig, 1605).			X[2]		X		X[3]			X				X[4]

Table 4.1 (*continued*)

Work	Language			No. of modes		Ordering		Concepts				Transpositions		
In the case of works which appeared in more than one edition, the date of the edition (or editions) consulted appears in italics.	Latin-German	Latin	German	14 modes with 2 rejected	12 modes and 8 tones	Glarean	Zarlino	Affects	Repercussio	Mode is: Fifth + fourth	Mode is: Triad + fourth	Terms *dur* and *moll* used for transposition	One transposition	Several transpositions
4. Bartholomäus Gesius, *Synopsis musicae practicae . . . et exercitiis ad 12. modos in utroque cantu . . .* (Frankfurt, *1609*, 1615).		X		X		X		X	X	X		X	X	
5. Christoph Demantius, *Isagoge artis musicae . . . cui additus est Nicolai Roggii gottingensis tractatus de intervallis & modis . . .* (Nürnberg, 1617).[8]		X			X[6]	X				X		X		X

Table 4.1 (*continued*)

Work	Language: Latin-German	Language: Latin	Language: German	No. of modes: 14 modes with 2 rejected	No. of modes: 12 modes and 8 tones	Ordering: Glarean	Ordering: Zarlino	Concepts: Affects	Concepts: Repercussio	Concepts: Mode is Fifth + fourth	Concepts: Mode is Triad + fourth	Transpositions: Terms *dur* and *moll* used for transposition	Transpositions: One transposition	Transpositions: Several transpositions
6. Daniel Friderici, *Musica figuralis . . . neben vollkommener Erklärung der modorum. . .* (Rostock, 1618, 1619, 1624, *1649*, 1660, 1671).[7]			X	X		X[8]		X		X		X	X	
7. Heinrich Elsmann, *Compendium musicae latino-germanicum . . . cum brevi tractatu de modis* (Wolfenbüttel, 1619).[9]	X[1]			X		X			X	X		X	X	
8. Johann Crüger, *Praecepta . . .* (Berlin, 1625).	X[10]			X			X				X	X	X	

Table 4.1 *(continued)*

Group	Category	9. Nicolaus Gengenbach, *Musica nova*... (Leipzig, 1626).	10. Erasmus Sartorius, *Institutionum musicarum... verum etiam pulcherrima modorum musicorum doctrina exhibetur...* (Hamburg, 1635).	11. Johann Crüger, *Quaestiones...* (Berlin, 1650).	12. Wolfgang Hase, *Gründliche Einführung...* (Gosslar, 1657).
Transpositions	Several transpositions		X[18]	X	
	One transposition				
	Terms *dur* and *moll* used for transposition	X	X	X	
Concepts	Mode: Triad + fourth			X	
	Mode: Fifth + fourth		X		
	Repercussio	X	X	X	X
	Affects	X	X	X	
Ordering	Zarlino				X[14]
	Glarean	X	X[11]	X[18]	
No. of modes	12 modes and 8 tones	X		X	
	14 modes with 2 rejected		X	X	
Language	German	X			X
	Latin		X		
	Latin-German			X[10]	

Table 4.1 (continued)

Work	Transpositions			Concepts				Ordering		No. of modes		Language		
	Several transpositions	One transposition	Terms *dur* and *moll* used for transposition	Mode: Triad + fourth	Mode: Fifth + fourth	Repercussio	Affects	Zarlino	Glarean	12 modes and 8 tones	14 modes with 2 rejected	German	Latin	Latin-German
13. Laurentius Erhardi, *Harmonisches Chor- und Figural Gesang-Buch* (Frankfurt, 1659).[16]		X	X			X		X			X[18]	X		
14. Johann Quirsfeld, *Breviarum musicum ... Nebenst einem Anhange unterschiedenen Deductionen und Fugen, nach den zwölff Modis Musicis ...* (Dresden, several editions, 1675–1717. 1683).		X	X		X	X	X		X		X	X		
15. Wolfgang Mylius,[17] *Rudimenta musices ....*			X	X	X[18]						X[18]	X		

Chapter 5

Toward Twenty-Four Keys

Along with the persistence of the modal tradition during the later seventeenth and the early eighteenth centuries, two other traditions in German theory led toward recognition of more and more keys and toward a major-minor differentiation of those keys. These two traditions were first, the various listings of finals and key signatures known as the church keys, and second, the gradual recognition of larger numbers of the twenty- four keys. Many theorists who wrote on the subject of modes or keys in this period came up with a new combination of aspects drawn from each of these traditions; hence the diverse presentations of keys around the turn of the eighteenth century. This chapter traces these traditions and diverse presentations. It concludes with a consideration of the works of Andreas Werckmeister, who came close to recognizing twenty-four major and minor keys, and whose thoughtful comments on the contemporary situation give us insights into the change from modal to major- minor thinking around 1700.

The Church Keys

Italian musicians during the latter part of the sixteenth century began to organize the commonly used modal finals and key signatures into a list that was at first related to the eight psalm tones. By simply listing the possible finals along with the key signature or triad on the modal final, this system allowed theorists and composers alike to use various of the major-minor keys without having to ponder the nature of mode or to explain how the modes differed from one another. The more speculative and analytical theorists, from Lippius

77

at the beginning of the seventeenth century through Werckmeister at the beginning of the eighteenth, avoided such listings. But the lists are common in instrumental collections and treatises from the late sixteenth century through the mid eighteenth century.[1]

The origins of this practice remain obscure. Their earliest appearance in a treatise seems to be in L'Organo suonarino (Venice, 1605)[2] by Adriano Banchieri (1567–1634), who, in addition to being a theorist, was an important composer of sacred and secular music. Part II of L'Organo discusses "the eight tones of ecclesiastical plainchant,"[3] introducing the following list on page 41:

Tone Number	Final Pitch	Signature
1	D	none
2	G	one flat
3	A	none
4	E	none
5	C	none
6	F	one flat
7	D	one flat
8	G	none

The fourth register of the same work contains compositions on the Magnificat in these eight tones. But tones 3 and 8 are one step lower with a flat in the signature "to accommodate the chorus."[4]

The present study refers to this organization of tones as the church keys. This term is a close translation of the name given them in several languages by seventeenth-century theorists: Banchieri's "tones of ecclesiastical plainchant," Choral-Töne in a German treatise

---

[1] Walter Atcherson errs in calling them a "strictly seventeenth-century phenomenon," for they are used from the late sixteenth century well into the eighteenth century, and are even cited in Koch's Musikalisches Lexikon of 1802 (article Kirchentöne, pp. 833–834). See Atcherson, "Key and Mode in 17th Century Music Theory Books," in Journal of Music Theory 17 (1973):216. See also the various listings below.

[2] Facsimile edition (Bologna: Forni, 1969).

[3] P. 39: "sopra gli Otto Tuoni spettanti al Canto fermo Ecclesiastico."

[4] Pp. 94 and 104: "Una voce bassa per comodita del Choro."

by Poglietti (see below), and *acht tonos ecclesiasticos oder Kirchen Thon* in a keyboard collection by Fischer (see below), among others.[5]

Banchieri's *Cartella musicale* (third edition, Venice, 1613–1614) contains a fuller description of the church keys than his *L'Organo suonarino*. The *Cartella* first introduces the eight traditional modes on pages 68–71 and then offers duos set in the church keys. On page 73, introducing the duo of the second "ecclesiastical tone," Banchieri notes: "The second tone is plagal as we have said, contrary to the first authentic [tone]; it has as its limits the octave from the note g to g...[!]"[6] When he reaches the seventh mode, Banchieri describes the difference between it and the first, since both share the same final (D) and differ only in the presence or absence of a flat in the signature:

> This seventh tone has the same overall structure as the first: it has cadences in the same positions, similar fugues; only in this is it different: that it is more languid, since the first possesses a B natural, and this seventh has a B flat...[7]

Banchieri offers no explanation of the origin of these church keys, nor of their relation to either the traditional modes or the psalm tones. But various comments make it clear that the church keys arise from common modal transpositions. For several of the church keys, Banchieri explains the level of transposition for the convenience of singers or instrumentalists. Thus the transposition of Dorian to a one-flat signature explains tones 1 and 2. The same transposition of Phrygian results in tones 4 and 5, but the ordering is reversed, and there is no flat in the signature of the A mode. In this way, there is no need for Glarean's Aeolian as an added mode. Lydian was often changed to Ionian; here tone 5 is Ionian, tone 6 its transposition. Tone 8 is Mixolydian; tone 7 the ambitus of Hypomixolydian, but with D as final.

Though Banchieri's presentation may be the earliest in a treatise, a number of earlier keyboard collections contain a similar presentation:

---

[5] Walter Atcherson, *op. cit.*, calls them *pitch-key modes*.

[6] "Il secondo Tuono è Plagale come detto habbiamo contrario al primo Autentico, hà per suo termine l'Ottava dalla corda G. alla G..."

[7] P. 82: "Questo Settimo Tuono hà l'istessa corrispondenza del Primo, hà le cadenze ne gli stessi luoghi, fuga simile, solo in questo è differente, che si rendo più lãguido, perche il primo fa modulare le parti per quadro, & questo Settimo per b. molle..."

1. The anonymous *Intavolatura d'organo facilissima accomodata in versetti sopra gli otto tuoni ecclesiastici* (Venice, 1598)[8] uses the eight church keys as presented by Banchieri.

2. Part I of *Il Transilvano* (Venice, 1593)[9] by Girolamo Diruta (1557–1612) contains a number of toccatas and other keyboard compositions in various of the twelve modes. Not all the first eight are included, but those that are (numbers 1, 2, 3, 6, and 8) agree with Banchieri's presentation.

3. In the *Intonationi d'Organo...composte sopra tutti li dodeci toni della musica* (Venice, 1593),[10] which contains compositions by both Gabrielis, the first eight modes are similar to those of Banchieri. They differ only in number 3, which is here on E, and number 7, which is here on G. Is this listing, with "untransposed" modes 3 and 7, an earlier form of the church keys?

At some point later in the seventeenth century the seventh mode was changed from D with one flat in the signature to D with one sharp in the signature, probably either to differentiate it more clearly from the first mode, or to present a true transposition of Mixolydian. With this change, the first four modes contain a minor triad on the final, and the last four a major triad on the final. This listing of the church keys found its way into many later treatises, some as late as the early nineteenth century, among which the following are German:

1. *Compendium oder Kurtzer Begriff und Einführung zur Musica sonderlich einem Organisten dienlich*, a manuscript treatise by Allessandro Poglietti (d. 1683)[11] dating from before 1676, lists these as the *acht Choraltöne*.[12]

2. *Instructio musicalis Domini Antonii Berthali* (1676), a manuscript treatise, cites these as the *8 Toni* which are now (*aniezo*) in use.[13]

---

[8]Transcribed by Macario Santiago Kastner, and published as *Altitalienische Versetten für Orgel oder andere Tasteninstrumente* (Mainz: B. Schott, 1957).

[9]Facsimile edition (Bologna: Forni, 1969).

[10]Reprinted as *Composizioni per organo*, edited by Dalla Libera (Milan: Ricordi, 1957).

[11]According to Johann Gottfried Walther's *Lexicon* (Leipzig, 1732; facsimile edition Kassel: Bärenreiter, 1953), Poglietti was a German (article *Polietti*, p. 486).

[12] See Helmut Federhofer, "Zur handschriftlichen Überlieferung der Musiktheorie inÖsterreich in der zweiten Hälfte des 17. Jahrhunderts," in *Die Musikforschung* 11 (1958):275.

[13] Ibid., p. 274.

3. *Idea boni cantoris* (Nürnberg, 1688), by Georg Falck (1630–1689), cites these as the regular tones or modes in his listing of sixteen keys. (See p. 83, below.)

4. *Clavis ad thesaurum magnae artis musicae* (Prague, 1701) by Thomas Balthasar Janowka, which otherwise lists only the twenty-four major and minor keys, refers to these as the eight tones or modes of chant in the article *Cantus*. (See pp. 105-6 below for further information on Janowka's work, and see Appendix 1 for a translation of this article.)

5. *Das neu-eröffnete Orchestre* (Hamburg, 1713), by Johann Mattheson, cites these as the first eight of the twenty- four keys, and refers to them as the Italian manner of differentiating the keys (see p. 114).

6. *Der wohl unterweisene General-Basse-Schüler* (Augsburg, 1751; second edition, 1768), by Georg Joachim Joseph Hahn (c. 1690-after 1769), lists all the major and minor keys (chapters 2 and 3). He also includes the church keys (the "8 keys observed in chorale singing;" "8. Töne bey dem Choral-Gesang beobachtet," p. 62) in the discussion of chorales at the end of a general chapter on thoroughbass, following discussion of the Rule of the Octave, quick bass notes, and recitatives.

7. *Die Kunst des reinen Satzes* (Berlin, 1771–1779), by Johann Philipp Kirnberger, suggests that these keys were probably the first to be listed since they were the ones most easily performable on organs tuned in meantone temperament.[14]

8. *Musikalisches Lexikon* (Frankfurt, 1802),[15] by Heinrich Christoph Koch, treats the traditional church modes under the title *Tonart*, but lists these church keys under *Kirchentöne* after having noted the deterioration of the traditional modes since the time of Pope Gregory.[16]

A number of German keyboard works used these church keys well into the eighteenth century:

---

[14] Part II, p. 66; Kirnberger lists tones 7 and 8 as G major and A major.

[15] Facsimile (Hildesheim: Olms, 1964).

[16] Pp. 833–834. See Herbert Schneider, *Die Französische Kompositionslehre in der ersten Hälfte des 17. Jahrhunderts* (Tutzing: H. Schneider, 1972), pp. 271–273, for a listing of French treatises of the early seventeenth century mentioning the church keys.

1. *Blumen Strauss...in acht tonos ecclesiasticos oder Kirchen Thon eingetheilet* (Augsburg, c. 1702),[17] by Johann Caspar Ferdinand Fischer (c. 1670–1746), includes one prelude and six fugues in each of the church keys. Tones 7 and 8 differ from the above listings only in that they have the modern key signatures for D major and G major.

2. *72. Versetl sammt 12 Toccaten* (Vienna, 1726),[18] by Gottfried Muffat (1690–1770), contains settings in the "12 more usable tones." The first eight agree with the church keys, although all keys except Phrygian use the modern signatures.

3. *Certamen aonium...ab octo tonis* (Augsburg, 1733),[19] by Carlmann Kolb (1703–1765), contains settings in the eight church keys, with the following differences in signatures from the older listings: tone 1 has one flat, tone 4 appears both with and without one sharp, and tones 7 and 8 have the modern signatures.

4. *Toccate e fughe per l'organo* (Augsburg, 1747),[20] by Johann Ernst Eberlin (1702–1762), orders the toccatas and fugues according to the eight church keys.

None of the theorists who worked with church keys prior to Mattheson in 1713 distinguishes major keys from minor. This is in line with the more practical and descriptive nature of the church keys going back to their initial appearance in Banchieri. Indeed, as suggested above, the origin and the continued use of the church keys during the seventeenth century and the early eighteeenth century may well have been motivated by the desire to simply list the modes in use without having to explain what was to the musicians of that time the complicated question of modal structure and differentiation. By contrast, the more speculative and analytical treatises, such as those by Lippius and Crüger, do not mention the church keys at all.

---

[17] Published undated. Walther's *Lexicon* dates it about the same time as Fischer's *Ariadne* (1702). See also Lothar Hoffmann-Erbrecht in *Die Musikforschung* 5 (1952):349. The collection is reprinted, edited by Rudolf Walter (Altötting: A. Coppenrath, 1956).
[18] Facsimile edition (New York: Broude, 1967). Reprinted, edited by Guido Adler (Vienna, 1922).
[19] Reprinted, edited by Rudolf Walter (Altötting: A. Coppenrath, 1957).
[20] Reprinted, edited by Rudolf Walter (Altötting: A. Coppenrath, 1958).

Expanded Listings of Keys

Working either from the basis of the church keys, or from other bases, several German theorists between 1685 and 1710 gradually expanded the number of possible keys. As with listings of the church keys, most of these listings of modes or keys contain no explicit differentiation of major and minor and no systematic comments on the nature or meaning of mode.

Wolfgang Mylius's elementary manual, *Rudimenta musices* (Gotha, 1685, 1686; see table 4–1, p. 75), lists twelve modes, then modes on B and E-flat (as Crüger did in 1654), and then various triads as modal finals: D major, E major, F-sharp minor, A major, B major, and B minor. Georg Falck (1630–1689) begins the listing of keys in his 1688 singing manual (*Idea boni cantoris* listed in the previous section of this chapter) with the eight church keys (called the "regular tones or modes").[21] He then adds to this listing another eight "transposed or ficta tones or modes:"

According to A *dur* by the major third	a c-sharp e
According to B-flat by the major third	b-flat d f
According to B by the minor third	b d f-sharp
According to C *moll* by the same	c e-flat g
According to E-flat by the major third	e-flat g b-flat
According to E by the same	e g-sharp b
According to F by the minor third	f a-flat c
According to F-sharp by the minor third	f-sharp a c-sharp

No scale or signature is presented for these keys; nor is any major-minor differentiation cited for the first eight.

Note Falck's use of the terms *dur* and *moll* in the listing of the *ficta* modes. Although *dur* is used for A major and *moll* for C minor, Falck does not intend the terms as "major and minor." Later, in the discussion of key signatures, he uses *dur* for signatures with no

---

[21] Tone 7 is listed with f-sharp (pp. 85–86). P. 86: "...den Tonis oder Modis Regularibus."

accidentals or with sharps, and *moll* for signatures with flats. Thus, B-flat and E-flat major would theoretically be *moll* triads for Falck had he wished to list them that way.[22]

The *Unterricht der musicalischen Kunst* (Ulm, 1687; second edition, 1697)[23] of Daniel Speer (1636–1707) also lists keys by the tonic triad, dividing them into three categories:

1. the natural keys, of which there are six: a c e, c e g, d f a, e g b, f a c, and g b d.

2. the hard or sharp keys (*dur, hart, scharffen*), of which there are five: a c-sharp e, b d-sharp f-sharp, d f-sharp a, e g-sharp b, g b d.

3. the soft (*mol, weich*), of which there are five: f a-flat c, g b-flat d, b-flat d f, c e-flat g, e-flat g b-flat.[24]

Discounting the repetition of G major in the natural and sharp categories, fifteen keys are listed here. B minor and F- sharp minor, which were listed by Falck, are not here, but B major is added. As in Falck, *dur* and *moll* refer to the presence of sharps or flats in the signature. Thus, B-flat major and E-flat major are listed among the *moll* keys.

In Part II, on thorough-bass, Speer presents intonations, preludes, and *toccatinas* in thirteen of these keys, beginning with two sharps and ending with two flats. Those keys with two sharps, one sharp, no accidentals, and one flat are given modern major and minor key signatures (that is, Ionian and Aeolian signatures). A major is notated with a Mixolydian signature (two sharps), G and C minor have Dorian signatures (one flat, two flats), and B-flat and E-flat major have Lydian signatures (one flat, and two flats). Once again, as in Falck, there is no differentiation into major and minor, and, except for the examples in Part II, no scale or signature is presented.

---

[22]P. 38. Note that similar or identical meanings of *dur* and *moll* are found in Daniel Speer's *Unterricht* (p. 84 below) and in Janowka's *Clavis* (discussed on pp. 105-6). See also Johann Philipp Eisel's *Musicus autodidaktos* (Erfurt, 1738), p. 15. Jacob Adlung comments on this usage in his bibliographical *Anleitung zu der musikalischen Gelahrtheit* (Erfurt, 1758; facsimile edition Kassel: Bärenreiter, 1953), p. 218. Carl Dahlhaus lists nine distinct meanings of *dur* and *moll* from antiquity to the seventeenth century, but omits this usage in "Die Termini Dur und Moll," in *Archiv für Musikwissenschaft* 12 (1955):280–296.

[23] Facsimile edition (Leipzig, 1974).

[24] Second edition, p. 20.

Friderich Erhard Niedt (1674–1708) lists sixteen keys in his *Musicalische Handleitung* (Hamburg, 1710),[25] so that an organist playing in any one of these keys would know the correct pitches even if the signature were lacking. He lists the major and minor forms on all the white keys and on B-flat. For a number of these an incomplete signature is noted: C minor with two flats (although a note points out that A-flat is usually added), G minor with either one or two flats, and A major with two or three sharps. Because of the rationale of his selection, Niedt includes two keys with five accidentals (B major and B-flat minor), while omitting several keys with only three or four accidentals (F-sharp and C-sharp minor, and E-flat and A-flat major).

In 1704, Johann Phillip Treiber (1675–1727) published a novel approach to thorough-bass instruction. Instead of rules and examples, *Der accurate Organist* (Jena, 1704) uses two chorales, one in major and one in minor, which are presented in twenty out of the twenty-four keys. Only the major keys of F-sharp/G-flat and C-sharp/D-flat and their relative minors are absent. The key signatures are divided into those with flats and those with sharps, but apparently no explicit differentiation is made between major and minor keys.[26]

It is not without interest that Treiber and Niedt, both musical amateurs, presented several keys earlier than many of their professional colleagues. As musical amateurs, they were less burdened by theoretical tradition than professionally trained musicians. But the depth of their understanding of modes or keys is not on the level demonstrated by their contemporary, the organist and theorist Andreas Werckmeister, who struggled to understand the evolution of modes into major and minor keys.

---

[25]Facsimile edition (Buren: Frits Knuf, 1976). The first edition was published in 1700. Although Niedt planned a three-part work, only the first two parts appeared in his lifetime. The remaining part and the second edition of the second part were published posthumously, edited by Johann Mattheson. Since it is unclear to what extent Mattheson may have altered Niedt's work, only the first part is treated here as Niedt's own. (The second part, on variation, contains no discussion of the modes.)

[26] I have not seen a copy of *Der accurate Organist*, and have taken the information presented here from Frank Thomas Arnold's *The Art of Accompaniment from a Thorough-Bass* (London: Oxford University Press, 1931; reprinted New York: Dover, 1965), pp. 243–247. Arnold does not state categorically whether or not Treiber makes explicit the differentiation between major and minor. The two chorales are *Was Gott thut, das ist wohlgethan* (Hypoionian), and *Wer nun den lieben Gott läst walten* (Hypoaeolian).

Andreas Werckmeister

The works of Andreas Werckmeister (1645–1706) differ from those discussed earlier in this chapter. Werckmeister basically continues the line of theorists that includes Zarlino and Lippius. He fully understands the traditional modes, yet he recognizes the need for accommodations to newer musical practices. He recognizes that most contemporary music is written in major and minor keys, yet he believes that many concepts associated with the modes remain useful. As a result, Werckmeister actually understands the nature of the new major and minor keys better than those theorists who merely recognized a number of keys. Yet because he insisted on continuing knowledge of the modes in order to understand the major-minor keys, Werckmeister was an anathema to the very next generation of theorists. His works were ridiculed by Heinichen and others who recognized twenty-four major and minor keys as the sole basis of contemporary music.

Werckmeister's theories on mode are presented in six treatises published between 1687 and 1707. Since most of his views did not change substantially over these twenty years, the six works will be discussed together:

1. *Musicae mathematicae* (Frankfurt and Leipzig, 1687), on the derivation of rules of composition from calculations and the monochord.

2. *Hypomnemata musica* (Quedlinburg, 1697), "musical notebook...in particular on composition and temperament."

3. *Erweiterte und verbesserte Orgel-Probe* (Quedlinburg, 1698). Referred to hereafter as *Orgel-Probe*.

4. *Die nothwendigsten Anmerckungen und Regeln wie der Bassus Continuus oder General-Bass wol könne tractiret werden* (Aschersleben, [1698][27]). Referred to hereafter as *General-Bass*.

5. *Harmonologia musica* (Frankfurt and Leipzig, 1702), "or brief introduction to musical composition."

---

[27] Published undated. The date is found in the introduction to the *Harmonologia musica* (1702).

6. *Musicalische Paradoxal-Discourse* (Quedlinburg, 1707), "or special presentation on how Music has a high and holy origin, and how to the contrary it is so misused."[28]

As a traditionalist and a church musician, Werckmeister saw much of value in modal theory. And even though he recognized that only two (possibly four) modes were still in contemporary use, he argued that only a solid foundation in modal theory allowed one truly to understand the use of the new keys.

> We only want to discuss here something of the twelve modes because our chorales, and, still from time to time, other musical pieces are based on them. Nowadays one could well make do with two modes; but because of the chorales we will discuss the twelve modes a little. For one so often hears some organists who do not know the least of this subject debase themselves: for example, when they prelude to the German *Hr. Gott dich loben wir* (which was considered and sung by the ancients as a humble prayer), they take the transposed Aeolian in the range of e f-sharp g a b c d e; yet it is regular Hypophrygian. Also, to *Erbarm dich mein O Herre Gott*, the same. When they would play *Ach Herr mich armen Sünder*, they make a prelude in C and take the Ionian mode for Phrygian, yet these two modes are quite different...[29]
>
> Thus only a few of today's musicians understand the above-mentioned modes, and many fewer know how to use them. What will we do? Will we discard them or the diatonic scale from which they have their origin? Not at all, for the foundation must remain... For if a fully experienced composer hits on a foreign cadence by degrees now and then, an inexperienced one does not know that it is done by degrees, and cites this as a precedent that the modes are no longer in use,

---

[28] Title page: "Oder Ungemeine Vorstellungen/ Wie Die Musica einen Hohen und Göttlichen Uhrsprung habe/ und wie hingegen dieselbe so sehr gemissbrauchet wird." Items 2, 3, 5, and 6 on this list of Werckmeister's works are in facsimile edition (Hildesheim: Olms, 1970).

[29] *Harmonologia musica*, p. 56: "Wir wollen allhier nur etwas von den 12. modis handeln/ weil unsere Choral-Lieder/ und noch unterweilen andere Musicalische Stücke darauff gerichtet werden: man könte heutiges Tages wohl mit zween modis auskommen/ allein/ um der Choral-Lieder/ wollen wir etwas weniges von den 12. modis handeln/ denn man höret ja wie so offte einige Organisten die noch nicht geringe seyn wollen hierinnen sich prostituiren: Zum Exempel/ wenn sie auff das teutsche *Hr. GOtt dich loben wir* (welches als ein demüthiges Gebeth von den Alten ist consideriret und gesungen worden) praeambuliren/ so nehmen sie den AEolium fictum in seinen ambitu e. fis. g. a. h. c. d. e. da es doch der Hypophrygius regularis ist; Auch zu dem/ *Erbarm dich mein O HErre GOtt*: item, wann sie/ *Ach HErr mich armen Sünder*/ spielen wollen/ machen sie ein Praeambulum aus den C. und nehmen Jonicum vor den Phrygium, da doch diese beyden Modis sehr weit differiren..."

claiming that the most eminent composers have seen the modes decline, and therefore proceed from one cadence to another, now major, now minor, now diatonic, now chromatic, and so forth...[30]

Although similar sentiments are expressed in all his works, Werckmeister is less insistent on knowledge of the modes in later treatises. For contemporary music, Werckmeister recognized that only two principal modes remained in use:

Today's music is entirely different (as noted above), and only some four modes are in use: Ionian mixed with Mixolydian and Dorian mixed with Aeolian, mostly in the range of the fourth [that is, these modes differ only in the semitone placement within the upper fourth of the modal octave]. Thus no more than two modes can now be established. And that is not so unnatural if we use them with the proper order. If we take Lydian, on account of the tritone or *falsette* there is such an unnatural progression in it that even the ancients themselves never or hardly ever used it. Who uses Phrygian in today's music? Nobody. Who Mixolydian? Hardly any. Therefore on behalf of a better order according to today's style of composition, we want to maintain only two modes. But because these can take their names neither from the Dorians, the Ionians, nor from any other nations (because they did not have our present style of music), therefore we want to name them according to their nature and character, so that they can be differentiated. The first can be named the natural mode, because it always maintains the major third in the beginning over the fundamental note, according to the natural order of the proportional numbers 4, 5, 6, 8 as in the notes c e g c or d f-sharp a d, etc. The second can be named the less natural mode, because the root numbers in its natural progression are further removed from perfection, and therefore do not establish such a happy harmony as the preceding. The natural progression of this mode is 10, 12, 15, 20, which is further from unity than the first... We can also name one mode perfect and the other

---

[30] *Musicae mathematicae*, p. 123: "...die wenigsten von den heutigen Musicis die oberrührten modos verstehen/ viel weniger dieselben zugebrauchen wissen. Was wollen wir nun thun? Wollen wir dieselben oder die Scalam Diatonicam, aus welcher sie ihren Ursprung haben/ verwerffen? Nein gar nicht; denn das Fundament muss bleiben..." p. 112: "Denn wenn ein wohl erfahrner Componist zuweilen per Gradus zu einer frembden Clausul geräth/ so weiss ein unerfahrner nicht/ dass es per grado geschehen sey/ berufft sich darauff/ dass die modi gar nichtmehr im Gebrauch wären/ denn die bewehrtesten Componisten achteten dieselbe fallen desswegen von einer Clausul zur andern/ bald dur bald moll, bald Diatonisch, bald Chromatisch/ und so weiter."

less perfect. Some performers name them *dur* and *moll*; e.g., C E G is C *dur*, C E-flat G is C *moll*, D F-sharp A is D *dur*, D F A is D *moll*. We are not happy with these names, because the word *dur* does not correspond with the harmony; for when something is sad, one says "that is rather *dur*," yet this triad is more joyful and perfect than anything else. Nevertheless, because these terms are now used so commonly, they will probably persist.[31]

This may be the first printed usage of both *dur* and *moll* meaning major and minor in the modern sense. Werckmeister seemingly accepts the terms grudgingly because they are used so commonly. But no publication earlier than Werckmeister's has been discovered with this usage.[32]

[31] *Musicae mathematicae*, pp. 124–125: "Weil aber die Music (wie schon gedacht) heutiges Tages gantz anders/ und nur etwa 4. modi im Gebrauch sind/ als Jonicus, mit dem Mixolydio, und Dorius mit dem AEolio, mehrentheils in dem ambitu der quartae vermischet/ so können dannenhero nicht mehr als 2 modi anjetzo statuiret worden/ und ist auch so gar unnatürlich nicht/ wenn wir fein ordentlich damit verfahren. Sehen wir an den Lydium, so ist ja wegen des Tritoni oder falsette ein solcher unnatürlicher Gang darinnen/ dass denselben die Alten selber nicht oder gar wenig gebrauchet haben. Wer brauchet in heutiger Music den Phrygium? Niemand: wer Mixolydium? gar wenig. Dannenhero wollen wir nun besserer Ordnung halben nach heutiger compositions-Arth nur 2. modos behalten; Weil aber dieselbe weder von den Doriis, Jonicus, noch von andern Nationen (weil Sie unsere jetzige Manier von Music nicht gehabt) ihren Namen haben können; So wollen wir dieselben nach ihrer Natur und Eigenschafft/ damit sie können unterschieden werden/ benahmen: Der erste kan genennet werden modus naturalis, weil er die Tertiam majorem allemahl im Anfange nechst dem Fundament clave, nach der naturlichen Ordnung der proportional-Zahlen 4. 5. 6. 8. behält/ als in clavibus c e g —oder d fis a d etc. Der andere kan genennet werden minus naturalis, weil die radical-Zahlen in ihrem natürlichem progressu, weiter à perfectione, und daher eine solche freudige Harmoniam nicht verursachen als die vorigen: der natürliche progress dieses modi ist: 10. 12. 15. 20. welcher da weiter ab unitate, als der erste...wir können auch einen modum nennen/ perfectum, denn andern minus perfectum: etliche practici nennen dieses dur, und moll. als c e g. is c. dur. c e moll. ist c. moll. d fis a ist d dur. d f a ist d moll. Weil aber das Wort durus mit der Harmonia nicht überein kommt/ also dass/ wenn was traurigs gemacht wird/ man also saget: das ist ganz dur; da hingegen diese Trias so freudig und perfect, das nichts drüber/ so haben wir denselben Namen nicht gern behalten wollen: allein weil diese Termini nun so in Gewohnheit bracht/ wird wohl dieser Name bleiben."

[32] But the usage does appear in a manuscript treatise from 1676. See footnote 18 on p. 105. A similar complaint against the terms *dur* and *moll* appears in Georg Andreas Sorge's *Vorgemach der musicalischen Composition (Lobenstein, 1745)*, p. 47.
In Karl Geiringer's *Bach* (New York: Oxford University Press, 1966, p. 278) and in *The Bach Reader*, edited by Hans David and Arthur Mendel (New York: Norton, 1966, p. 85) the authors assert that terms for major and minor were not yet in general use in 1722 when J. S. Bach worded his elaborate reference to them on the title page of the *Well-Tempered Clavier*: "preludes and fugues through all the tones and semitones both as regards the *tertia major* or Ut Re Mi and as concerns the *tertia minor* or Re Mi (cont.)

In his earlier works, Werckmeister accepts Dorian as the model for the minor mode. Only in his *Paradoxal-Discourse*, published posthumously in 1707, is Aeolian cited as the model.[33]

Werckmeister recognized all twelve possible transpositions, discussed harmonic progressions around the circle of fifths, and argued for an approximation of equal temperament to allow the use of these harmonies and transposed modes on the keyboard. But he never explicitly recognized twenty-four major and minor keys. The *Musicae mathematicae* discusses transposition only with the twelve modes. If each mode is transposed to all twelve pitches, and there are twelve modes, then theoretically 144 forms arise. But Werckmeister rejects a fuller discussion of this point as unnecessary.[34] After the reduction of the number of modes to two, Werckmeister does not again discuss transposition. Similar situations exist in his *Musicalische Temperatur* (Frankfurt and Leipzig, 1691) and *Harmonologia musica* (1702). In the introduction to the former, tempered intonation is considered necessary "because nowadays people want to play all songs on all the keys."[35] In the latter, Werckmeister states that the organist who does not know how to transpose to any of the twelve notes does not know the keyboard well enough.[36] But in neither work does he specify whether he is talking about twenty-four keys or 144 modal transpositions.

Fa." This in spite of Werckmeister's complaint of 1687 that *dur* and *moll* were in such common use that he would accept them even though he did not approve of them. Indeed, Bach's own *Gründlicher Unterricht des General-Basses*, (published in Philipp Spitta, *Bach*, second edition [Leipzig, 1916], vol. 2, pp. 915–950) uses *dur* and *moll* to mean major and minor in at least two passages (pp. 917 and 920). Bach's title to the *Well-Tempered* was possibly so worded in order to surpass Johann Kuhnau's two collections of seven partitas each on "UT, RE, MI or the major third of each tone" and "on RE, MI, FA or the minor third of each tone" (*Neuer Clavier-Übung*, 1689, 1692; reprinted with original title pages in *Denkmäler deutscher Tonkunst*, 4 [Leipzig, 1901]). Bach's compositions are on all the tones *and semitones*, in contrast to Kuhnau's partitas written only on the tones (C, D, E, F, G, A, and B-flat or B). Bach wrote the title page the year the Kuhnau died after a long illness, vacating the prestigious post at the Leipzig Thomaskirche for which Bach applied.

[33] Pp. 85–89.

[34] P. 123. In 1605, Johann Kretzschmar had already implied 72 possible modal transpositions in his singing manual. See table 4-1.

[35] Fol. A3r: "weil man heutiges Tages alle Lieder aus allen Clavibus spielen will."

[36] P. 69.

Example 5-1· Werckmeister, Paradoxal-Discourse, pp. 50-51

Similarly, Werckmeister discusses a "musical circle." But the circle refers to harmonic progressions that return to their chord of origin, not directly to modes or keys. Thus, in both the *Hypomnemata musica* (1697) and the *Orgel-Probe* (1698), the musical circle is mentioned as one argument for equal temperament, but is not described.[37] In the *General-Bass* (1698) a sequence of triads is presented both ascending and descending. Major and minor triads alternate in each direction: C e G b D, etc.; and C a F d B-flat, etc.[38] The same example recurs in the *Paradoxal-Discourse* (1707) along with the harmonic progression of a major triad around the circle of fifths through both the sharp and flat keys. See example 5–1.[39]

Werckmeister also argues for modern key signatures, complaining about those who set incorrect signatures to transposed compositions. Thus, in Ionian on A, f-sharp, c-sharp, and g-sharp all belong in the signature. Those who write only c-sharp or g-sharp write in no mode (*nullius modi*).[40]

In summary, Werckmeister comes across in these treatises as a thoughtful, practical theorist, ready to accommodate himself to contemporary practice and even to advocate new teachings (arguing that when God has revealed something new, we should accept it and discard the obsolete and imperfect teaching[41]), but also recognizing the problems in the newer theories and desiring to retain those aspects of the modes that are still valuable. He seems to speak from personal experience when he tells of musicians who regard g-sharp

---

[37] *Orgel-Probe*, p. 79. On p. 37 of the *Hypomnemata musica*, Werckmeister refers to a (lost?) *Canzona* by Froberger composed some 30 years ago, in which the theme is transposed "through the entire keyboard on all twelve keys...through the circle of fifths or fourths." ("Es hat der Weltberühmte Froberger schon vor etlichen 30. Jahren eine Canzon gesetzet/ da er algemach das thema durch das gantze Clavier in all 12. Claves transponiret, variiret/ und artig hindurch führet/ und also durch den Circul der quinten oder quarten gebet/ biss er wieder in den Clavem kömmt darinnen er angefangen hat..."). Apparently there was a tradition of transpositions of a subject around the circle of fifths or fourths as one way of elaborating or extending a composition. Claudia Jensen, in a presentation at the AMS National Conference in Vancouver (November, 1985), presented a paper on such progressions, one in a major mode, and one in a minor mode, written out around a graphic circle in manuscript treatises of Diletskii that circulated in the Ukraine and Muscovy around 1670.

[38] Pp. 20–22.

[39] Note that some letter spellings do not agree with the staff notations. Although Werckmeister eschews traditional organ tablature letter spellings (concerning which, see note 15 in chapter 4), he does not write double flats or double sharps or B-sharp.

[40] *Harmonologia musica*, p. 58.

[41] *Paradoxal-Discourse*, p. 85.

as a regular note in Aeolian mode and who proceed to build a minor triad over a g-sharp in the bass in compositions in that mode because they do not understand the modal ambitus.[42] For him, only knowledge of the modes will prevent this type of error. Remember that at that time there still was no recognized theory of a single model for major and minor scales, no theory of diatonic and chromatic chords, of function in harmony, of cadence points outside of modal goals, and so forth. Witness the confusion over key signatures (indicating a confusion over the proper diatonic notes in many keys) and over different types of classifications of keys side by side in the works of Mylius, Falck, Speer, and others of his contemporaries. For Werckmeister, only by knowledge of the modes could such confusion be avoided.

Werckmeister's moderate and reasoned stance is in sharp contrast to writers in the 1710s and later, when sharp polemic barbs flew between the defenders of antiquity and the proponents of the new keys, leaving little room for one who wished the best of both.

Werckmeister received some harsh criticism from Heinichen, for example, who argued that all facets of composition could be adequately treated under the major and minor keys and that there was therefore no cause to retain the modes. But the fact is that no theorist had done so during Werckmeister's lifetime. Perhaps what is most remarkable about Werckmeister's position on modes and keys is that he was a church organist. In the next decades, church musicians were to be among the most outspoken opponents of the twenty-four keys.

If the presentations of Werckmeister are compared with those of Falck, Speer, Niedt, and Treiber, it is clear that Werckmeister shows a much more profound understanding of the keys and their use. By basing the use of keys on aspects of traditional modal theory (cadence structure, modulatory possibilities, melodic structure, etc.), he fills a void found in the works of those theorists who merely recognized the new keys. Hence Werckmeister's above-mentioned arguments for maintaining the old modal theory even if only two modes remain in use. In addition, he explicitly discusses the major-minor dichotomy, which is not even mentioned in some of these other works. Not until Heinichen's treatise of 1711 is there a full discussion in German of the usage of the major and minor keys.

---

[42] *Ibid.*, p. 86.

Evolution from the Modes

Walter Atcherson has argued that major and minor did not in fact descend from Ionian and Aeolian for three reasons:

1) Those [theorists] who dealt with two modes and treated them as "modes," i.e., subjected them to transposition, generally chose Ionian and Dorian.

2) Those who dealt with two modes, one on C and one on A, treated them as keys from the start and ignored their fortuitous similarity to Ionian and Aeolian respectively.

3) Meanwhile there existed other groping attempts to arrive at the concept of key, notably on the part of theorists of the pitch-key modes [church keys], which, however, proved fruitless.[43]

The first two numbered assertions are contradicted by Werckmeister, surely the most important and learned German theorist of the end of the seventeenth century. Furthermore, the theorists of the church keys did indeed gradually increase the number of keys formally recognized (review the discussion of Falck, above). In fact, Mattheson stands as the culmination of this process, using the church keys as the first eight in his complete listing of the twenty-four keys (see p. 114-15).

There is a difference between the evolution of major and minor keys in music and the recognition of that new development by theorists. No historian will ever make the definitive assertions of the history of major and minor keys, for such assertions will always depend on analysis of the music and hence be subject to the biases, personal as well as generational, of historians and their era. What is major-minor to one analyst may be modal to another. The very definitions of these terms and whether they are defined according to the era under study or according to the era of the historian, will tend to precondition the answer.

The history of the recognition of major and minor keys is a different matter altogether. Here a definitive history is possible, but only by surveying the entire range of theoretical literature of the era. For the later seventeenth century, distinctions must be drawn among (1) those theorists who merely enumerated finals and scales in use

---

[43] Atcherson, *op. cit.*, p. 228.

(whether as church keys or otherwise) without attempting to relate these keys to the modes or to major and minor keys, (2) those theorists who continued to describe the old modes without attempting to relate them to contemporary practices, and (3) those theorists who understood that the teaching of the old modes contained valuable truths, but had to be modified to meet the needs of contemporary music.

The theorists in the first two groups may well have regarded the new keys as a phenomenon unrelated to the modes of the past, as Atcherson argues. But theorists in the last category, including Zarlino, Lippius, and Werckmeister, certainly viewed mode as an evolving concept, one that had to be modified with each passing generation. And since they understood both the past and the present (to the extent to which any theorists can understand their present), they were able to offer a more comprehensive view of the present than theorists who lacked this perspective. To them, the music of the present was not a wholly new phenomenon, but one that grew on the basis of the past. This was certainly true of Werckmeister, standing as he did at the threshold of a new era in music and in theory. For him, major and minor were indeed the product of a line of evolution beginning with the traditional modes.

Perhaps most interesting in the mid and late seventeenth century is that an understanding, by a theorist, of connections between new and old in one area of musical structure did not necessarily lead to the same understanding in other areas. Consider Christoph Bernhard as one example. His teaching of counterpoint and composition relates the most extreme dissonances and voice leadings of the new music to what he regarded as the eternal verities of strict *stile antico* counterpoint. Yet in terms of modes, Bernhard retains a mid-sixteenth century perspective, seemingly unaware of the application of his Italianate ideas to contemporary music.

Chapter 6

Twenty-Four Keys

Twenty-four major and minor keys first appeared in print toward the end of the seventeenth century. By the early years of the eighteenth century, recognition of twenty-four keys had become a common phenomenon in several different countries. In Central Europe, the earliest publication presenting the twenty- four keys is Janowka's *Clavis ad thesaurum magnae artis musicae* (Prague, 1701), written in Latin; the earliest publication written in German to do so is Heinichen's thorough- bass manual of 1711. A number of French and English theorists preceded Janowka and Heinichen in recognizing major and minor as the sole basis of music and, in some instances, in explicit recognition of twenty-four keys. Understanding these non-German works places Janowka's and Heinichen's achievements in the context of their contemporaries, and also demonstrates the gulf separating German ideas on the keys and modes from those in France and England. For it was only in German-speaking areas that controversies over the new keys continued for decades into the eighteenth century. This chapter surveys the early recognition of twenty-four keys in French, English, and German theory. Chapters 7 and 8 cover the controversies over modes and keys that continued in German theory for much of the eighteenth century.

French and English Presentations of the Keys

French Works. By the late seventeenth century, French works routinely differentiated keys solely on the basis of major and minor. The *Methode claire...* (Paris, 1683) of Jean Rousseau (1644-c.1700) and the *Pieces de clavecin...* (Paris, 1689) of Jean Henri d'Anglebert (c.1628-1691), for instance, both differentiate mode solely by the quality of third over the final. *L'Art d'accompagner sur la basse continue* (Paris,

1689) of Guillaume Nivers (1632-1714) also recognizes major and minor, but still includes Phrygian as a possibility for cadential progressions:

> The first type [of mode] is reduced to C; it is the type called sharp that proceeds by the major third over the final. The second type is reduced to D; it is the type called flat that proceeds by the minor third over the final. Thus, to name the tone one says *C sol ut sharp*, or *C sol ut flat*. There is a third type of song particularly at cadences which end on *mi* descending through *fa*.[1]

One has only to compare these presentations of keys with their contemporary presentations in the works of Falck, Niedt, Printz, Speer, and Werckmeister to see the gulf separating German and French theory concerning modes and keys at that time.[2]

The earliest listing of all twenty-four keys apparently is that of the French mathematician Ozanam (1640-1717) in his *Dictionaire mathematique* (Amsterdam, 1691) "in which are contained the terms of that science [that is, mathematics], and in addition some terms from the arts and from other sciences..."[3] Music is the last subject of study (pp. 640-672). Ozanam divides the modes into two classes: *de b quarre* and *de b mol*. "There are twice as many modes as there are notes in an octave: each of these notes gives its name to two modes, of which one proceeds by the major third and the other by the minor. Since the octave contains twelve notes, there are twenty-four modes."[4]

---

[1]p. 150: "La lere maniere se traite et se reduit par l'ut, c'est le chant qu'on appelle Becarre qui procede par Tierce maieure sur la Note finale. La 2e maniere se traite et se reduit par le re, c'est le chant qu'on appelle Bemol qui procede par la Tierce mineure sur la Note finale. De sorte que pour exprimer le Ton l'on dit C sol ut Becarre, ou C sol ut Bemol. Il y a une 3e maniere de chant et particuliere aux cadences qui se font en mi en descendant par le fa."

[2]Herbert Schneider, in "Charles Masson und sein *Nouveau traité*" (*Archiv für Musikwissenschaft* 30 [1973]:245-74), lists fourteen authors between 1669-1719 who cite a major-minor differentiation of keys (pp. 251-54). All but one (Bertali, who refers to the "French opinion" in discussing major and minor; see. p. 105 below) are French. Schneider does not include Janowka, Mattheson, Heinichen, and English theorists in his list.

[3]Title page: "DANS LEQUEL SONT CONTENUS LES TERMES de cette science, outre plusieurs termes des Arts & des autres sciences..."

[4]P. 659: "Il y a deux fois autant de Modes que de cordes dans l'entendue d'une Octave: chacune de ces cordes donne le nom a deux Modes, dont l'un procede par la Tierce Majeure & l'autre par la Mineure. Ainsi comme l'octave contient douze cordes, il y a vingt-quatres Modes."

The directness and clarity of this presentation is remarkable for its time, and one might imagine that this explanation could appear in a modern theory book. But Ozanam betrays his seventeenth-century origins on the very next page. He is not quite ready to accept all the keys as equally original, and divides the twenty-four modes into three categories: the modes on white notes or on B-flat with white notes or B-flat in their triad (*Les Modes Naturels au Naturel*), the modes on white notes or B-flat with black notes in their triad (*Les Modes Naturels par les chromatiques*), and the transposed modes with finals on black notes (*Les Modes Transposez*).

Other French publications after that date cite only major and minor keys. The important *Dictionaire de musique* (Paris, 1703)[5] of Sébastien de Brossard (1655-1730) demonstrates the contemporary French attitude toward the major and minor keys and the traditional modes. It is especially important to the present study because of the contrast between Brossard's treatment and that of Johann Gottfried Walther in his comparable German dictionary published nearly three decades later, the *Lexicon* of 1732, to be discussed in chapter 8. Brossard discusses the Gregorian modes in the article *Tuono*. The modes of polyphonic music and the major-minor keys are treated in the article *Modo*. Brossard begins the article *Modo* by noting that there have been many disputes concerning the names, ordering, number, affects, and nature of the modes, as well as the relation between the traditional and modern modes. He declines to enter into any of these disputes, promising only an objective account of the basic terms and concepts.

Throughout the following discussion, Brossard demonstrates a thorough familiarity with major and minor keys, but a somewhat more hesitant understanding of the traditional modes. After a brief summary of modal theory as in Glarean and Zarlino, Brossard explains that these modes would be sufficient if music used only diatonic notes. Since the advent of chromatic notes, the distinction between authentic and plagal modes has been rejected. But Brossard does not explain how the presence of chromatics bears on the issue of authentic and plagal modes.

---

[5]Facsimile edition (Amsterdam: Antiqua, 1964). The article *Modo* is on pp. 52-57.

There is a new system of modes "accepted nowadays by all people of good taste." The *trio harmonique* with a major or minor third over the final of each mode gives rise to the major and minor modes. With twelve notes in an octave, there are twelve of each type. Brossard then goes on to fix the other scale degrees, setting as the standards what we know as the major scale and the harmonic minor. In the following discussion, Brossard stresses the importance of using the notes of the mode, calling special attention to the lowered sixth scale step and raised seventh scale step in minor. Brossard also discusses how pieces may leave a mode for another, so long as the piece returns to its original mode at the end. Brossard's discussion, demonstrating such a thorough understanding of major and minor, and avoiding all traces of modal influence, stands in sharp contrast to the contemporary German publications discussed in chapter 5.

Within a decade after Brossard's *Dictionaire*, two other French publications introduced further important aspects of major and minor keys. The *Transpositions de musique* (Paris, 1706) by Alexandre Frère is largely concerned with setting the proper key signatures for each of the twenty-four keys. Even though Frère argues for the white-note scale on D, not on A, as the model for the minor mode, his work is important in that it reinforces the notion of twenty-four usable keys.

The *Nouveau traite de l'accompagnement* (Amsterdam, [c.1710]) of Saint Lambert (fl.c.1700) introduces the term *tonic* into the theoretical vocabulary, and differentiates the terms key and mode in their modern senses:

> The key of an air is the note on which it ends, and that note is called the *final*... This final is always the fundamental note of an air, and for that reason is called the *tonic note*... *Mode* is the determination of the path that the melody of an air should take...it is the particular system [that is, scale] on which a piece of music is built.[6]

Saint Lambert actually writes out the scales for forty-two different major and minor keys: a major and minor scale on all seven white

---

[6]P. 51: "Le ton d'un Air est la note sur laquelle il se termine; & cette note s'appelle aussi la *finale*... Cette final est toujours la note fondamentale de l'Air, & pour ainsi dire la note Tonique... Le Mode est la determination du chemin que doit tenir le chant d'un Air... C'est le sisteme particulier sur lequel une Piece de Musique est batie."

notes, on all seven flat notes, and on all seven sharp notes. Each scale has the proper key signature, including double sharps and double flats, with the white-note scale on A as the model for minor. Saint Lambert notes that all the scales on sharp and flat notes are uncommon except for B-flat and E-flat major.

English Works. Although English works do not explicitly cite twenty-four keys until well into the eighteenth century, a number of seventeenth-century works are clearly based on major and minor keys. English theorists in general had never gotten involved in the intricacies of Continental modal theory, and the political and religious upheavals in England of the sixteenth and seventeenth centuries certainly did not encourage scholarship into the modes associated with Catholic music. As a result, English theorists did not have to overcome entrenched habits of modal thinking, as did their Continental counterparts. For much of the early seventeenth century, little of any nature was written about the modes in English works.

A useful chronicle for charting modal and key theory in England in the later seventeenth century is that remarkable publication, one of the more long-lived music publications in any language, the *Breefe Introduction to the Skill of Musick* first published by John Playford in 1654. From then until 1730, this work appeared in numerous editions and reprints, with later generations of Playfords taking over the editorship. Various sections in the different editions are borrowed or adapted from other works. Other sections were commissioned from prominent contemporary musicians.

The 1654 edition is but 34 pages long (some later editions exceed 200 pages), and borrows from Thomas Campion's work of the 1610s. A peculiar discussion of five Greek *Moods* appears on pages 17-18, beginning with Dorian: "The Dorick Mood consists of sober slow timed Notes (or counterpoint) which in composition of parts goes Note for Note, be they of two, three, or four parts, as is usuall in Church Tunes to the usuall Psalms...and this Dorick had his name from Doria, a civill part in Greece near Athens." Later, in a discussion of various terms (pp. 23-29), amid other meanings of *tone*, Campion writes "by Tone wee intend the Key [that is, the note on the keyboard] which guides and ends the whole Song." That is the sole appearance of the concept.

The next edition of Playford, in 1655, repeats much of the 1654 edition, with additions by Christopher Simpson (c.1605-1669). The added discussion on modes is rather conservative. The octave is divided authentically and plagally; the resulting fifth is divided into a major and minor third. But this division of the octave and fifth is merely for the purpose of locating the proper notes for cadences.[7] There is no mention of major and minor. This passage is maintained through the 1679 edition.

Simpson published his own treatise in the 1660s: *A Compendium of Practical Musick* (London, 1665; second edition London, 1667).[8] In this work, Simpson discusses keys in chapter 5 of Part 2:

> Every composition of music, be it long or short, is (or ought to be) designed to some one key or tone in which the bass doth always conclude. This key is said to be either Flat or Sharp, not in respect of itself, but in relation to the flat or sharp 3rd which is joined to it. To distinguish this you are first to consider its 5th which consists always of a lesser and a greater 3rd, as you see in these two instances, the key being in G. [An example follows of a G-minor and a G-major triad.] If the lesser 3rd be in the lower place next to the key, then is the music said to be set in a flat key. But if the greater 3rd stand next to the key as it doth in the second instance, then the key is called sharp.

Simpson lists fourteen keys.

The passage in Playford on the Greek Moods is dropped from the editions from 1662 to 1670. It reappears in the 1672 edition, preceded by the following remarks:

> Of these Moods, though of little use among us, there is scarce any Author that has wrote of Musick but do give some account of them...therefore not intending to be singular, I shall give you this short Narrative.
> These Five Moods have no relation to those Moods mentioned in the former part of this Book [the earlier discussion refers to *Modus* in mensural notation]; those have reference to Notes and Time these only concern Tune. That which the Grecians called Mode or Mood, the Latins termed Tone or Tune: The design of either, was to shew in

---

[7]Pp. 28–29: "The lowest Note of this fift, beares the name of the Key...then divide that fift into his two thirds, and so you shall finde out all the Closes that belong to that Key."

[8]The first edition contains only part of the work. The second edition is reprinted, edited by Phillip J. Lord (Oxford: B. Blackwell, 1970). Later editions of Simpson's work appeared through 1775 or 1790.

what Key the Song was set, and how each Musical Key had relation one to another. These five appertained to the Grecians only, and had their several appellations from the Countries in which they were invented and practised. The Latins reduced theirs to Eight Tones or Tunes, and were by Church-men termed Plain-songs. These exceeded not the compass of six Notes, and was to direct how to begin and end in the proper Keys; which eight Tones or Tunes are printed in the Tenor Part of Mr. [Thomas] Morley's [1557-1602] [Plaine and Easie] Introduction [to Practicall Musicke],[9] p. 147.

It is hard to imagine a more confused presentation, especially in a work intended for beginners. But it certainly is refreshing to have Playford's opening admission of his reasons for including the passage at all.

Beginning with the 1683 edition, Playford dropped the entire section by Campion, and substituted a new discussion of composition and counterpoint derived from unnamed sources. There is no mention of modes or keys.

By 1694 a thorough overhaul was necessary. Henry Purcell (c.1659–1695) performed this task. After a fascinating demonstration of how to harmonize a melody, Purcell turns to keys:

There are but two Keys in Musick, *viz.* a Flat, and a Sharp; not in relation to the Place where the first or last Note in a Piece of Musick stands, but the Thirds above that Note. To distinguish your Key accordingly, you must examine whether the Third be sharp or flat, therefore the first Keys for a Learner to Compose in ought to be the two Natural Keys, which are A re and C fa ut, the first the lesser, the last the greater Third; from these all the other are formed, but adding either Flats or Sharps.[10]

Playford's 1697 edition is further modernized, and may have been prepared by Purcell before his death. Concerning the keys, there are

---

[9](London, 1597). Facsimile edition, ed. by E. H. Fellowes (London: Oxford University, 1937). Reprint ed. by R. A. Harman (New York: Norton, 1953). See Robert Stevenson, "Thomas Morley's 'Plaine and Easie' Introduction to the Modes," in *Musica Disciplina* 6 (1952):177–184 for a survey of Morley's theories, as well as a discussion of the apparent lack of understanding of Continental modal theory by English writers of the period.
[10]P. 105.

few changes. Sixteen keys are now cited. "These may be more thought of to puzzle Young Beginners, but not of any Use..."[11]

Another English, or to be precise, Scottish work of the early eighteenth century that is of interest in illustrating the state of modal theory in Britain is *A Treatise of Musick* (Edinburgh, 1721)[12] by Alexander Malcolm (1685-1763). Malcolm gives a full account of the major and minor keys, adopting the distinction between mode and key proposed by Saint Lambert about 1710.[13] The traditional modes arise in chapter 14: "Of the Ancient Musick." In his discussion of the modes, Malcolm seems to treating a phenomenon of the dim distant past. After noting the twelve modes, he writes "The material Point is, if we can find it, to know what they [the modal theorists] meant by these Distinctions, and what was the real use of them [the modes] in Musick; but even here where they [the theorists] ought to have agreed, we find they differed."[14] For Malcolm, only white-note scales on C and A are proper: "But we are to notice, that of all the 8ves, except c and a, none of them have all their essential Chords in just proportion."[15] There is a mention of the church keys, "but even here every Author speaks not the same way."[16] Malcolm's somewhat diffident attitude toward the modes alongside his thorough under-standing of major and minor keys stands in sharp contrast to some of his German and Italian- influenced contemporaries in works to be discussed in chapter 7.

German Works

The English works just discussed seem to have had virtually no effect on German musicians. Only the cosmopolitan Mattheson ap-pears to know any English writer, referring to Malcolm's 1721 *Treatise* within a year of its publication.[17] The developing French theories of major and minor seem to have had a similarly small influence prior to the 1710s. Only in authors such as Heinichen and

[11]P. 25.
[12]Facsimile edition (New York: Da Capo, 1970).
[13]Chapter 9.
[14]P. 564.
[15]P. 566.
[16]Pp. 567-568.
[17]Johann Mattheson, *Critica Musica*, I (Hamburg, 1722), p. 8. *Critica Musica* I and II appear in facsimile (Amsterdam: Knuf, 1964).

Mattheson, who decried the backward state of German musicians, is there a noticeable foreign influence in terms of major and minor. The only earlier reference to French influence of which I am aware is in a manuscript treatise, *Instructio Musicalis Domini Antonii Berthali* (1676) discussed by Helmut Federhofer.[18] Bertali writes "Finally, I am, along with many other virtuosi, of the French opinion that there are no more than two tones, one named by B moll, the other by B natural: e.g., D moll or D dur, or G moll or G dur."[19]

Between 1701 and 1713 three writers in Central Europe published presentations of the twenty-four keys: Thomas Balthasar Janowka, Johann David Heinichen, and Johann Mattheson. These presentations differ from one another in terminology, in the manner of presentation, in the ordering of the keys in relation to one another, and in the applicability of the keys to contemporary music as well as to older music.

Thomas Balthasar Janowka (1660?-1715?). Janowka's lexicon, *Clavis ad thesaurum magnae artis musicae* (Prague, 1701),[20] is perhaps most remarkable for its complete acceptance of the twenty-four keys for all music, past as well as present. Janowka appears to be in total ignorance of the traditional modes and defines both the modes and terms associated with them solely in relation to major-minor keys or contemporary usage. In his article on *cantus*, for instance, Janowka asserts that the eight church keys, divided into major and minor (based on *re-mi-fa* or on *ut-re-mi*), and listed with the traditional Greek names and affects, are the very church modes founded by Pope Gregory and St. Ambrose and used in the Catholic Church continually since then! Similarly, in the article *tonus* Janowka notes that earlier authors have established eight, twelve, or fourteen keys (*toni*). These figures are indeed the common numbers of modes claimed by various sources going back to the Middle Ages, but they do not refer to the

---

[18]Helmut Federhofer, "Zur handschriftlichen Überlieferung der Musiktheorie in Österreich in der zweiten Hälfte des 17. Jahrhunderts," in *Die Musikforschung* 11 (1958):274.

[19]Federhofer, *op. cit.*, p. 274: "Pro ultimo bin ich neben viellen anderen virtuosi der französischen Meinung, dass nit mehr als zwey Toni seindt, einer per B moll, der ander per quadro von ihnen genendt. V. g. aus den D moll oder D duro, aus den G moll oder G duro."

[20]The articles relevant to this study are translated into English in Appendix 1.

number of keys of the twenty-four major and minor, as Janowka intends them. Janowka defines *ambitus* not as a modal octave, but as the range of the human voice or of an instrument. And, finally, the article on *modus* returns to a medieval usage of the term, defining it only to mean interval.[21]

In his discussion of major and minor keys, Janowka presents a major and natural minor scale as a model, notes twelve pitches to the octave, and notates all twenty-four keys in ascending chromatic order, each with its proper key signature. In contrast to most earlier works, the complete scale is given for each key, not merely the tonic or tonic triad. He complains about incomplete key signatures in current use, particularly the Dorian signature for minor. Janowka also argues for another aspect of modern notation—correct spelling for all pitches, including even B-sharp instead of C in appropriate circumstances.[22] The only important aspect of keys not discussed concerns modulatory possibilities. Neither in the section on cadences (where previous theorists discussed this issue) nor elsewhere does the subject arise.

In its complete acceptance of the twenty-four keys, and its absolute silence concerning the old modes, Janowka's work surpasses even the works of Heinichen and Mattheson. But the *Clavis* went virtually unnoticed by Janowka's contemporaries. Mattheson, who often shows a remarkable knowledge of contemporary literature, did not know of the work in 1713. The use of Latin, quite unusual at this late date, and the apparently limited circulation of the work, were probably factors.

Johann David Heinichen (1683–1729). Unlike Janowka's *Clavis*, Heinichen's *Neu erfundene und gründliche Anweisung...des General-Basses* (Hamburg, 1711) is a practical work. In terms of its recognition of major-minor keys, Heinichen's treatise represents the culmination of the trend found in the practical works of Falck (1688), Speer (1687

---

[21]This usage of the term *modus* dates back to Boethius ("Modus est soni acuti gravisque distantia."), and was common among medieval and Renaissance theorists. In the MGG article on *Modus*, Heinrich Hüschen lists no works after the *Musices libri II*(Wittenberg, 1561) by Martin Agricola (1486-1556) which use this terminology. It appears, however, not only in Janowka, but also in Heinrich Buttstett's *Ut, mi, sol...*(c.1715; see chapter 7) and in Johann Gottfried Walther's *Lexicon* (1732) (p. 417).

[22]Both Heinichen and Mattheson use the older letter notation in 1711 and 1713, respectively.

and 1697), and Niedt (1700). There is virtually no mention of the modes, and major-minor keys are merely listed. But Heinichen progressed several steps beyond his predecessors and arrived close to the modern conception of the twenty-four keys. He did not present triads, but complete scales with their modern key signatures (like Janowka). He presented not just some keys, but all. The keys are not ordered arbitrarily, but divided into major and minor, paired according to relative majors and minors, listed according to their position on the circle of keys, and presented with a wide range of tonal modulatory possibilities. Perhaps what is most remarkable is that Heinichen presented this new development without fanfare. Unlike Werckmeister, who laboriously pondered each new point and continually questioned its value, and unlike Mattheson, for whom each new development, no matter how trivial, became the springboard for lengthy, self-righteous polemic, Heinichen presented the sum of his accomplishments as a *fait accompli*. Only in the preface does polemic intrude, when Heinichen complains about those supposedly learned theorists who often do not have any practical knowledge of music. In the body of the work, there are few such comments.

Major and minor are assumed, not argued. The Dorian form of minor is not accepted; Heinichen instructs the performer to use the minor sixth scale degree in all minor keys, even when it is not notated:

A minor has the same *ambitus* as C major; D minor the same as F major; E minor the same as G major, and so forth for all keys... In all minor keys one must ordinarily use the minor sixth of the key in which the piece is written, where it is not already indicated in the signature.[23]

The performer must be aware of changes of key:

When, in this manner, the signatures and the natural *ambitus* of each key have been firmly imprinted on paper as well as in hearing, nothing more is required than to keep attention fixed on where the beginning key, which often changes in a piece, modulates; and then one begins

---

[23]P. 104: "...a moll hat eben die Gräntzen/ welche c dur hat; d moll eben diese/ welche f dur hat; e moll, welche g dur hat/ und so fort durch alle Tone." P. 199: "In allen Tonen hat man ordinair mit der 6♭ des jenigen Tons, worinne das Stücke modulirt, zu schaffen/ wofern sie nicht allbereit mit vorgezeichnet."

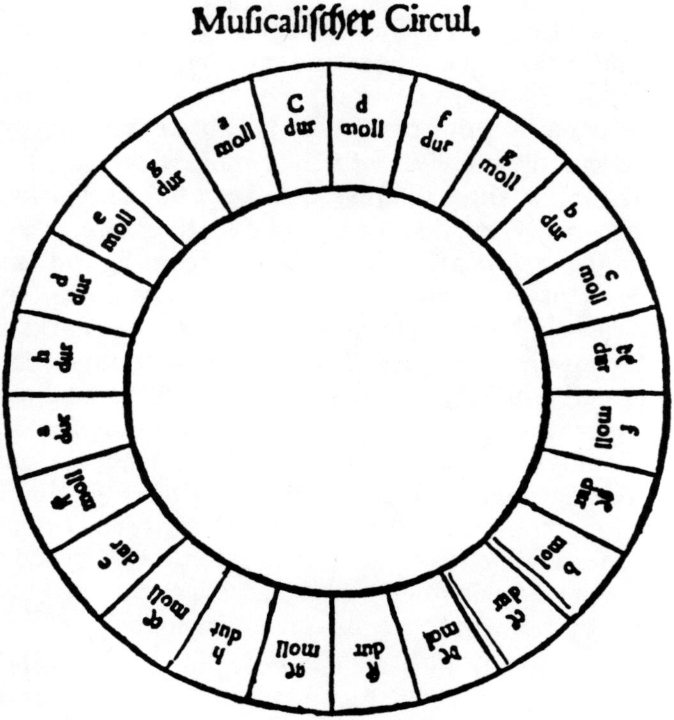

Muſicaliſcher Circul.

Fig. 6-1 Heinichen, *Anweisung*..., p. 261. [Courtesy of the New York Public Library Music Division.]

the signatures once again in this new key, just as they ordinarily appear according to the model.[24]

Finally, the musical circle (figure 6-1), for which Heinichen is perhaps most famous, is presented not as a revolutionary method of establishing a new tonal system, but as a practical convenience to aid in modulation from one key to another. Heinichen's circle offers not a simple circle of fifths, but an alternation of major and minor keys. It is intended as a practical guide to modulation. Heinichen allows

[24]P. 204: "Hat man sich solchergestalt die Signaturen und den natürlichen Ambitum jedes Tones, so wohl auf dem Pappiere/ als nach dem Gehöre recht feste inprimiret/ so mangelt nichts mehr/ als dass man wohl achtung gebe/ wohin der angefangene Ton, welcher in einen Stücke gar offt changiret/ ausweichet; und alsdenn fängt man in diesen neuen Tone die Signaturen wieder an/ wie sie nach dem Schemate gewöhnlich lauten."

modulations not only from one key to another in order in either direction, but also by using alternate keys (for instance, C major to F major). Skipping keys in this manner works for a single modulation, but, as Heinichen notes, is hardly possible for continued use.

Heinichen does not even take credit for the invention of the musical circle, only for its improvement. He relates that while he was studying with Johann Kuhnau (1660-1722),[25]

> my teacher told me something of the above-mentioned circle of [Athanasius] Kircher [1601–1680], but this gave me no satisfaction if I set out to go from a major key to a distantly- related minor key and vice versa... The well-known method of Kircher, to circulate through all the keys by fourths and fifths, is one of the most imperfect. For if one begins, e.g., from a major key, and continues by fourths or fifths until he returns to the first key, all twelve minor keys are left out.[26]

The reference to Kuhnau's teaching is at first puzzling. The only extant theoretical treatise of Kuhnau's, his manuscript *Fundamenta compositionis* (1703), written after Heinichen studied with him, presents only the traditional modes.[27] Another piece of evidence supports the assumption that Kuhnau recognized only the traditional modes. In a letter to Mattheson written in 1717, Kuhnau took exception to the major and minor keys, arguing for the retention of the Phrygian mode, and perhaps some others as well. (See p. 124.)

---

[25]Heinichen was a student at the Thomasschule in Leipzig from 1696 to 1702. Kuhnau was in Leipzig after 1682, and was Cantor at the Thomasschule from 1701 until his death in 1722, following which J. S. Bach assumed the post.

[26]Der General-Bass in der Composition(Dresden, 1728), pp. 840–841: "Mein Lehrmeister hatte mir zwar etwas von dem oben gemeldten Circul des Kircheri gesaget, allein dieser gab mir keine Satisfaction, so offt ich mir vorsetzte, aus einen Modo maj. in einen weit abgelegenen modum min. & vice versa zu gehen..." P. 837: "Die bekandte Arth des Kircheri, alle Modos per Quartas & Quintas zu circuliren, ist eine der unvollkommensten. Denn wenn man z. E. von einem Modo majori anfänget, und gehet so lange per 4tas oder per 5tas fort, biss man wieder in den ersten Modum gelanget, so sind alle 12 modi minores aussenblieben..."

[27]See Kurt Hahn, "J. Kuhnau's *Fundamenta compositionis*" in the *Kongressbericht Hamburg 1956* of the Gesellschaft für Musikforschung (Kassel: Bärenreiter, 1957), pp. 103–105. It is unclear from Hahn's account whether or not the section on modes is a copy of Christoph Bernhard's *Tractatus*. Johann Walther's *Lexicon* lists two other manuscript treatises by Kuhnau, but both are lost.

Two points are clear from this. First, discussions of circular harmonic progressions were not necessarily related to modal or major-minor theory. Second, circular harmonic progressions were handed down largely via an oral tradition, passed on by Kuhnau and others. Werckmeister stands alone among German writers in including "circles of the keyboard" in his published works (review chapter 5), although he does not actually write the progressions on a circle.

There does exist a graphic use of the circle to illustrate this type of progression a full generation before Heinichen. It occurs in manuscript treatises of Diletskii, written in Ukrainian and Russian around 1670. In discussing a number of techniques to extend a composition, Diletskii notes that one can go around the circle of fifths and return to the starting point. He offers two such circles, each with a brief cadential bass line transposed twelve times in order.[28] If Heinichen, his Central or Western European contemporaries, or for that matter any non- Slavic musician knew of Diletskii's circles prior to the late twentieth century, they never mentioned it. But the very fact that a circle and discussions of circular progressions appear over a wide geographic area, and that specific instances were unknown to contemporary theorists, reinforces the notion of an oral tradition.

According to Heinichen, Kuhnau thought that the origin of these circular progressions could be traced to Athanasius Kircher. The treatment of mode in Kircher's encyclopedic *Musurgia universalis* (*Tomus*, Rome, 1650; 650 pp. in 4°) is completely traditional, the only unusual feature being an extensive discussion of transposition.[29] The harmonic circle appears not in the discussion of mode, but as an abstract concept in the discussion of various types of keyboards and tuning systems. A particular keyboard with a sixteen-note octave is capable of such a *circulatio* but only after passing through three octaves.[30]

Although Heinichen had assumed that Kircher's circle used major and minor keys, Heinichen himself was actually the first

---

[28]I am indebted to Claudia Jensen for this information on Diletskii, presented as a paper to the AMS National Meeting in Vancouver in November, 1985. The works of Diletskii and Janowka, both of which offer modern notions ahead of their Western European contemporaries, suggest that a fuller investigation into Eastern European theory of this era may yield other dramatic findings.

[29]Mode is discussed in Book III, chapters 15–17, and Book IV, chapters 7–8.

[30]Pp. 457 and 462–463.

theorist to combine in print the concepts of circular harmonic progressions and key or mode theory.

In the *Neu erfundene Anweisung*, Heinichen shows little respect for the old modes, although he does note in the preface that one does not necessarily have to do away with them. After presenting the musical circle, however, he suggests that the old modes can now pass away.[31] But in the considerably enlarged 1728 edition of his treatise,[32] Heinichen provides a fuller explanation of his positions, both in the body of the text and in extensive footnotes. In the chapter on the musical circle, he gives four reasons for its utility.[33] He notes that even among musicians who accept the major and minor keys, there are many who insist that the old modes are necessary to learn the relationships between keys, and to learn which keys lie closer and which are more distant from one another. He cites Werckmeister's warning that he who does not know the modes will enter a labyrinth in his compositions and not know how to proceed.[34] Heinichen ridicules this position, asserting that the method of modulation formerly gained by understanding the modes is treated by him without reference to the modes. According to Werckmeister, one can modulate to those keys whose tonics are found in the tonic triad of the key or mode in which the modulation begins; for instance, if one begins in Ionian with the triad c-e-g, one can modulate to Phrygian with the triad e-g-b or to Mixolydian with the triad g-b-d. Heinichen notes that if this is true, then it is only the triad which is necessary. Second, the modulation by thirds and fifths is not the only possible one.

This is a crucial point. Earlier theorists, going back at least to Zarlino, had noted that the three principal cadences (whatever the terminology used) of a mode were to be made on the lower and upper notes of the species of fifth of the mode, and on the third which divides the fifth. This was maintained throughout the seventeenth century, with exceptions noted only where cadences on B would be necessary (Phrygian and Mixolydian). Heinichen is no longer willing to accept this. Not only does his circle pair each major key with its

---

[31]P. 267.

[32]Heinichen apparently began work on this version, titled *Der General-Bass in der Composition*(Dresden, 1728), not long after the 1711 manual. By 1722 the first part of the treatise was already set in type (see p. 938).

[33]Part II, chapter 5, pp. 837–916.

[34]Werckmeister, *Harmonologia musica*, p. 73.

relative minor (hitherto considered a distant relation in theory) but it also places the supertonic, the submediant, and the relative minor closer to the tonic of a major key than the mediant. Heinichen thus recognized that modulatory possibilities could be largely freed from the old modal bounds.

Heinichen also ridicules other aspects of modal theory. The assertion that the ambitus of a mode is an octave, give or take a few notes, is akin to saying that one should use only two or three fingers, or only twenty-four letters of the alphabet. Heinichen closes the discussion with the comment that such old stupidities (*Thorheiten*) should pass, since they are no longer applicable to our times.

Heinichen's more open antagonism toward the modes in the 1728 edition may have been inspired by Mattheson's polemic in the latter's *Das beschützte Orchestre* of 1717. Heinichen, one of the musicians to whom this work was dedicated, wrote to Mattheson on December 7, 1717:

> I am no special friend either of the old imprisoning musical modes, of the superfluous and decayed *ut, re, mi, fa,* or of other dusty musical fads. I admit readily that many times I have pondered deeply over the fact that, for whatever reason, there are still people in our time who seek to bring up and defend the long since decayed musical rubbish of antiquity...[35]

Johann Mattheson (1681–1764). Heinichen may have written the first work in the German language based on the twenty-four major and minor keys. But it was Mattheson who brought the battle between adherents of the major and minor keys and adherents of the church modes out into the open during the 1710s and 1720s. With a masterful understanding of the uses of publicity, Mattheson waged a relentless campaign against the use of the church modes and related antiquities to explain contemporary music. His wit, satire, irony, and sacrilegious attitude toward the idols of the past incited

[35]Published in *Criticae musicae*, II (Hamburg, 1725; facsimile edition, Amsterdam: Knuf, 1964), pp. 212–213: "...ich weder von den alten Kerkermässigen Modis musicis, noch von dem überflüssigen und Zeit-verderbenden ut, re, mi, fa, noch von andern bestaubten musicalischen Grillen, ein sonderbarer Freund bin. Ich gestehe gerne, dass ich vielmahls in tieffes Nachsinnen gerathen, woher es doch immer kommen müsse, dass es bey unsern Zeiten noch Leuthen gibt, welche die in der Music schon längst verfallenen rudera antiquitatis zu erheben, und zu defendiren, suchen?"

the upholders of the old order to respond with defenses of their opinions. On occasion this led to further rejoinders on both sides. As a result of his attacks, we have the comments of several musicians who might otherwise not have written at length on these subjects.

Mattheson was a prolific writer who published several thousand pages on music theory, criticism, aesthetics, performance practice, composition, and history. His writings consistently demonstrate familiarity with writings on music and other subjects by a wide range of authors, both contemporary and ancient, in German, English, French, Italian, Latin, and Greek. He is always out to show his superior knowledge of any topic. In volume 2 of his *Criticae musicae* (1725), for instance, he lists over 400 authors on music to be added to Brossard's list of 900 at the end of the latter's *Dictionaire*. That he kept abreast of contemporary developments is shown in his reference to Alexander Malcolm's *A Treatise of Musick* (Edinburgh, 1721) only a year after its publication. In addition to writing on music, Mattheson composed both vocal and instrumental music. As a true man of the Enlightenment, his life extended outside the world of music: he was secretary to the British Ambassador in Hamburg, and wrote and translated works on law, politics, diplomacy, and other subjects. Certainly he ranks as one of the most energetic persons ever associated with the history of music.[36]

It is ironic that Mattheson's first work, which began all the polemic, uses various aspects of traditional modal theory in the presentation of the major and minor keys, adopts as a whole a fairly tolerant attitude toward the church modes, and is not in general as radical as either Janowka's or Heinichen's works. *Das neu-eröffnete Orchestre* of 1713 (referred to hereafter as *Orchestre I*) contains a full exposition of the church modes, called the "Greek manners of singing," with the note that "church and chorale music sometimes use these modes even today, although with great freedom and changes."[37] In all his works, Mattheson was willing to allow the modes a place in church music. It is for contemporary music in the newer styles that he considered these modes to be inadequate.

---

[36]See Beekman Cannon, *Johann Mattheson, Spectator in Music* (New Haven: Yale, 1947), for a complete biography.

[37]P. 57: "...die zwölff Modi, oder Griechische Sing-Arten/ deren sich noch bissweilen heut zu Tage die Kirchen und Choral-Music, wiewol in grosser Freyheit und Veränderung bedienet."

The Italians and contemporary composers use another means to differentiate their modulations[38] and call

the first key	d f a	or d minor
the second key	g b-flat d	or g minor
the third key	a c e	or a minor
the fourth key	e g b	or e minor
the fifth key	c e g	or c major
the sixth key	f a c	or f major
the seventh key	d f-sharp a	or d major
the eighth key	g b d	or g major

...Although the above mentioned eight keys are easily the best known and most prominent [they are the church keys], yet the following are not less useful and acceptable:

9.	c d-sharp g	or c minor
10.	f g-sharp c	or f minor
11.	b-flat d f	or b-flat major
12.	d-sharp g b-flat	or d-sharp major
13.	a c-sharp e	or a major
14.	e g-sharp b	or e major
15.	b d f-sharp	or b minor
16.	f-sharp a c-sharp	or f-sharp minor

---

[38]The term *modulation* carried several meanings during this period. In this passage it connotes "types of compositions." See Alfred Mann, *The Study of Fugue*(New York: Norton, 1965), pp. 53–54, and William Mitchell, "Modulation in C. P. E. Bach's Versuch," in *Studies in 18th-Century Music, a Tribute to Karl Geiringer*(New York: Oxford, 1970), pp. 333–342.

...Whoever is eager to know all the keys must add the following:

17.	b e-flat f-sharp	or b major
18.	f-sharp b-flat c-sharp	or f-sharp major
19.	g-sharp b e-flat	or g-sharp minor
20.	b-flat c-sharp f	or b-flat minor
21.	g-sharp c e-flat	or g-sharp major
22.	c-sharp e g-sharp	or c-sharp minor
23.	c-sharp f g-sharp	or c-sharp major
24.	e-flat f-sharp b-flat	or e-flat minor

...According to the present division of the keyboard we have no more than twelve different tones, which are the twelve semitones of the chromatic octave, each of which can be changed once by the minor or major third; thus the twenty-four above-mentioned keys arise and remain just twenty-four.[39]

Mattheson goes on to note that no other author, with the sole exception of Heinichen, ever presented all these keys. Mattheson was apparently unaware of the listings of Ozanam, Frère, and Janowka.

Mattheson's presentation is in the tradition of Falck, Speer, and Niedt. Unlike Janowka, who paired parallel major and minor keys, or Heinichen, who paired relative majors and minors, Mattheson's ordering has no musical rationale. Not until 1717 did he pair parallel majors and minors, and not until 1735, in his *Kleine General-Bass-*

---

[39]Pp. 60–62: "Die Italiäner und heutigen Componisten gebrauchen sich einer noch andern Art ihre modulationes zu unterscheiden/ un nennen: Tonum primum d f a oder d moll... Obgleich obenstehende 8. Tone schier die bekanntesten und vornehmsten sind/ so sind doch folgende nicht weniger gebräuchlich und annehmlich... Wer alle Thone zu kennen begierig ist/ muss folgende darzu thun:...wir nach itziger Eintheilung des Claviers...nicht mehr als 12. differente Thone haben/ so eben die 12. Semitonia der chromatischen Octave sind/ deren jedes durch die tertia minores oder majores einmahl verändert werden kan/ also/ dass die vorgesetzte 24. herauskommen/ und dabey bleibet es." Two errors have been corrected here: no. 21 is g-sharp *minor* and no. 22 is c-sharp *major* in Mattheson.

Schule, did he present an "improved" musical circle, in which he claims it is "more comfortable" to modulate than in Heinichen's.[40]

When he comes to list the affects of each new key, Mattheson presents a mixture of old and new theory. He rejects the opinion that the entire affect of a mode resides in the major or minor third or in the key signature. For him each key has its own affect and is wholly independent of the others.[41] Indeed, throughout his life Mattheson insisted on the independence of each of the twenty-four keys. In *Orchestre I* he discusses first the affects that the ancients ascribed to the modes, then those of the moderns. Finally, he lists the affects for each key. Those keys which correspond by final and third to one of the old modes or to their common transpositions are referred to by name: D minor as Dorian, G minor as transposed Dorian, A minor as Aeolian, E minor as Phrygian, C major as Ionian, F major as transposed Ionian, G major as Hypoionian, and B-flat major as transposed Lydian. The inconsistencies can only be explained by Mattheson's desire to use old modal names in order to cite older theorists on the modal affects. F major is not Lydian, but B-flat major is transposed Lydian; G minor is transposed Dorian and D minor is Dorian, but the scale implied is Aeolian. How seriously Mattheson took the entire subject of affect is seen by the length of his discussion, encompassing over twenty pages.

Mattheson pokes fun at older authors for never referring to several keys in common use. He notes that D major is not listed by Kircher, nor is it found among the ancient modes: "From this, among other things, is seen the defect of ancient music."[42] About C minor, he remarks:

> It would be no idle curiosity to investigate whether it was by crass error or by a most profound ignorance that this most attractive key merited a place neither in the authentic, plagal, or transposed modes,

---

[40]In Mattheson's "improved" circle, pairs of major and minor keys alternate: C major, G major, E minor, B minor, D major, A major, F-sharp minor, C-sharp minor, and so on. See F. T. Arnold, *The Art of Accompaniment from a Thorough-Bass* (second edition, New York: Dover, 1965), p. 277, for an illustration of Mattheson's circle.

[41]P. 232.

[42]Pp. 242-243: "Daraus man defectum Musicae veteris unter andern zu ersehen hat."

nor even in the ecclesiastic or Gregorian tones. The stupidity of the ancients is hardly to be believed, much less excused.[43]

Like Heinichen and Janowka, Mattheson seems to project the twenty-four keys on the past and then wonders why no previous author took the trouble to mention them.

Thus, two conflicting attitudes toward modes and keys are present in *Orchestre I*. On the one hand, the twenty-four major and minor keys are presented as the basis of modern music, and although the old modes are mentioned, earlier authors are severely criticized wherever they failed to give the major and minor keys their due. Yet some aspects of the old modes are retained. Some of this ambivalent attitude toward the modes is explained by Mattheson's encyclopedic approach in *Orchestre I*. In his attempt to provide impressive data, Mattheson perhaps ultimately weakened the case for the twenty-four keys. But by introducing all this material, seemingly extraneous to the modern understanding of keys, Mattheson betrays the state of affairs in 1713 all the more clearly. Even a strong advocate of the new keys in German in 1713 felt it proper to try to relate the old modal names and affects to the new keys. It is significant that it was only in the 1728 edition, not that of 1711, that Heinichen protested so vigorously against using the names and attributes of the old modes. The two men's attitudes in 1711 and 1713 may not have been very different, if allowance is made for Mattheson's posturing.

[43]P. 245: "Es wäre keine schlecte Curiosite, zu erforschen/ ob crasso errore, oder profundissima ignorantia dieser so liebe Thon keine Stelle/ weder in Modis Authenticis, Plagalibus sive Transpositis, noch auch in Tonis Ecclesiasticis oder Gregorianis, meritiret habe? Die antique Dummheit ist fast nicht zu befreiffen/ vielweniger zu excusiren."

UT, MI, SOL,
RE, FA, LA,
TOTA MUSICA
ET
HARMONIA
ÆTERNA,
Neu=eröffnetes, altes, wahres, einsiges
und ewiges
FUNDAMENTUM MUSICES,
entgegen gesetzt
Dem neu=eröffneten Orcheſtre,

und in zwen Partes eingetheilet.

In welchen/ und zwar in dem erſten Theile/ des Herrn Authoris des Orcheſtre irrige Mennungen in ſpecie de Tonis ſeu Modis Muſicis,
wiederleget/

In andern Theile aber das rechte Fundamentum Muſices gezeiget/
Solmiſatio Guidonica nicht allem defendiret/ ſondern auch ſolcher
Nußen ben Einführung eines Canonis gewieſen/ dann auch behauptet
wird/ daß man vermeint im Himmel/ mit eben den Sonis, welche
hier in der Welt gebräuchlich/ muſiciren werde/
von
Johann Heinrich Buttſtett,
Des hl. Consiſtorii. Predigers Prediger, Kircke Organ.

Gedruckt ben Otto Friedr. Rechern/ Ac. Univerſit. Buchdr.
zu finden in Leipzig/ ben Johann Herbord Kloß.

Figure 7.1. Title page and Frontispiece to Buttstett's *Ut, Mi, Sol, Re, Fa, La* (1715?)

Chapter 7

Mattheson's Aftermath

Buttstett's Response

Johann Heinrich Buttstett (1666-1727), an organist at Erfurt, took sufficient offense at Mattheson's *Orchestre I* to publish an answer, thereby setting in motion a chain of reactions to Mattheson's works that dominated German theory of keys and modes for several decades. Buttstett's *Ut, mi, sol, re, fa, la, tota musica et harmonia aeterna* (Erfurt, 1715?)[1] is perhaps best described by its title page, reproduced in figure 7-1, opposite.

Ut, mi, sol, re, fa, la, the totality of music and eternal harmony, or newly published, old, true, sole, and eternal *Foundation of Music,* opposed to the *Neu-eröffnete Orchestre,* and divided into two parts, in which, and to be sure in the first part, the erroneous opinions of the author of the *Orchestre* with respect to tones or modes in music are refuted. In the second part, however, the true foundation of music is shown; Guidonian solmization is not only defended, but also shown to be of special use in the introduction of a fugal answer; lastly, it will also be maintained that someday everyone will make music in heaven with the same [solmization] syllables that are used here on earth.

Ut, mi, sol... is the first of a number of extremely conservative German works of the first half of the eighteenth century (others, to

---

[1]Published undated. Mattheson's *Orchestre I* had appeared in 1713. Buttstett notes in his preface to *Ut, mi, sol...* that he has promised the work already for a year (fol. 5r). Mattheson's *Das beschützte Orchestre* (referred to here as *Orchestre II*), written in answer to Ut, mi, sol..., was published by the middle of 1717 (letters to Mattheson in answer to *Orchestre II* were dated as early as December, 1717). This second *Orchestre* probably took a fair time in preparation; *Ut, mi, sol...,* therefore, was probably published in 1715 or early 1716. The date 1717, given by Walther Blankenburg and used in *RISM,* is almost certainly too late. See Blankenburg, "Der Titel und das Titelbild von Johann Heinrich Buttstedts Schrift 'Ut, mi, sol,...' (1717)," in *Die Musikforschung* 3 (1950):64–66.

be discussed later in this chapter, are by Murschhauser and Spiess). In his definition of the modes, Buttstett wanted to turn the clock back to the mid-sixteenth century, before Zarlino's differentiation of the affects of the modes according to the quality of certain important consonances. He defends the church modes, asserting that the placement of the semitone is the sole criterion for differentiating modes, so that all of Mattheson's keys are transpositions of only two modes. And, as he quotes Printz, transposition is "more a folly and a blunder which corrupts the harmony, than an art."[2]

In terms of solmization, Buttstett wanted to return to the status quo of the fifteenth century, before Ramos de Pareja advocated a seven-syllable solmization based on the octave.[3] Buttstett defends the medieval system of solmization with three hexachords and the technique of mutation. This is consistent with his acceptance of the modes as the sole basis of music. In major-minor tonality, there are only two basic scale constructions above the tonic that a beginning student has to learn. In the modes, however, there are six basic scale constructions. By learning a single hexachord construction, and using mutation where necessary, any modal melody can be easily learned. This very reason, given by Guido of Arezzo in his *Epistola de ignoto cantu* (c.1030) for the invention of this method, remains valid so long as such a large number of scales exist over the final.[4] Mattheson, in *Orchestre I*, advocated using letters of the alphabet (with suffixes to indicate accidentals) rather than solmization.

Yet despite his fervor, Buttstett, already in the title of his work, indicates the basic dichotomy between major and minor. The syllables are ordered ut-mi-sol, re-fa-la—the major and minor triads.[5] Walther Blankenburg has pointed out representations of the major and minor triads in the frontispiece.[6] Johann Lippius's *trias harmonica*,

---

[2]*Ut, mi, sol...*, p. 49; Printz's *Satyrischer Componist* (Dresden and Leipzig, 1696), Part I, chapter 2, par. 6: "...so ist Transponiren mehr eine Thorheit und Stümpelerey/ welche die Harmoniam verderbet/ als Kunst."

[3]*Musica practica* (Bologna, 1482).

[4]For Guido's writing, see Oliver Strunk, *Source Readings in Music History* (New York: Norton, 1950), pp. 121–125.

[5]The title is incorrectly listed as *Ut, re, mi, fa, sol, la* in Walther's *Lexicon* (1732), an inaccuracy continued in many later works, including even Ernst Ziller's monograph, "Der Erfurter Organist Johann Heinrich Buttstädt," (Halle/Salle: Waisenhauses, 1935), p. 81.

[6]Blankenburg, *op. cit.*

with its analogies to the Holy Trinity, so revolutionary a century earlier, had now become part of "ancient" tradition. In *Orchestre I*, Mattheson had derided such theological references to the triad, apparently unaware that it was precisely because of the analogy to the trinity that had Lippius coined the term in the first place.[7]

The *Orchestre* Defended

Mattheson answered Buttstett with *Das beschützte Orchestre (The Orchestre Defended)* (Hamburg, 1717; referred to hereafter as *Orchestre II*). It is a merciless satire of Buttstett's opus, beginning in the subtitle: "Ut, Mi, Sol, Re, Fa, La—Todte [Dead] (nicht Tota) Musica." The frontispiece, reproduced in figure 7-2 (next page), mocks Buttstett's admiration for solmization with a tombstone erected to Guido of Arezzo.

Mattheson derides Buttstett's scholarly pretensions, and ridicules the differentiation of modes based on the placement of semitones. Buttstett had asserted that there is only one natural semitone in music—mi, fa—and that it occurs twice in each diatonic octave, creating six primary modes. Mattheson's twenty- four keys are all transpositions of only two modes. Mattheson answers first by noting that Buttstett claims one semitone, two semitones per octave, and twelve semitones per octave. How can there be only one, yet also two and twelve of something? For Mattheson, all semitones are natural. If you ask a peasant to sing a song, says Mattheson, he will start on any comfortable pitch, and will sing D-sharp to E or D to E-flat just as easily as he will sing B to C or E to F. The keys in use in contemporary music are differentiated by the register of the final tone, the proportions of the tempered scale, and the triad, but in no way by the placement of semitones.[8] In later works, Mattheson extended his attack on octave species as a modal determinant by arguing that it was not until the end of the fifteenth century that modes were differentiated by octave species. The ancient Greeks differentiated modes by register, and octave species are not mentioned by Boethius.

---

[7]*Orchestre I*, pp. 109–110.
[8]P. 73.

Figure 7-2. The frontispiece to Mattheson's *Beschützte Orchestre* (Hamburg, 1717). The memorial is erected to commemorate the passing of Guido Aretino, six-syllable solmization, and the modes. Note the modal names on the twelve standing trees and two felled trees, the facetious acronymic "derivation" of the solmization syllables, and the several representations of Guido and the six syllables on the monument itself. (Courtesy of the Music Research Division, The New York Public Library.)

Mattheson argues that it was not until Gafurius and Glarean that the octave species were cited as the basis of the modes and that the problems of modal theory can be traced to those theorists.[9] This research is but one instance of Mattheson's familiarity with older as well as contemporary writings.

Mattheson accuses Buttstett of hiding the context of Printz's comment on transposition. According to Mattheson, Printz only complained about transpositions on untempered instruments, and did not intend to prohibit the use of keys such as C, F, B, and F-sharp minor and B, E, and A major.

The status of transpositions is an issue that differentiates German and French recognition of the twenty-four keys, and also shows a side of Mattheson's thinking that differs significantly from modern conceptions of the keys. For Janowka, Heinichen, and Mattheson, all the keys are equally original, in contrast to the French theorists

[9]See Mattheson's *Der vollkommene Capellmeister* (Hamburg, 1739; facsimile edition Kassel: Bärenreiter, 1954), chapter 9, pp. 60–68.

discussed in chapter 6 for whom most keys were transpositions of some more primary keys. But Mattheson stresses the individuality of each key to an extent unseen in Janowka's and Heinichen's works. In the meantone temperament advocated by Mattheson, the tuning of each key is indeed different from any other—each key is truly unique. (See Appendix 2 for Mattheson's tuning system.) That the C major scale is considered the diatonic genus is only an accident of notation, not a sign that it is more original than any other. He quotes from Werckmeister's *Hypomnemata musica* (1697):

> Why do upright musicians love transpositions so much? If they did not introduce pleasant variations, one would probably not think of them. The varied charm consists not only in the high or low register of the notes; rather, the difference and beat of the consonances and the dissimilarity of the tones and semitones impart an entirely different nature to the harmony.[10]

Similar sentiments concerning the uniqueness of each key are expressed by Mattheson in his letters to Johann Joseph Fux.[11]

Mattheson's concept of key is not entirely in agreement with modern conceptions in other aspects as well. He argues that semitone differences in a given scale are unimportant, so long as they do not alter the quality of the third:

> If I prelude for a peasant in the octave species d e f-sharp g a b c d (transposed Mixolydian), for instance, and then prelude in d e f-sharp g a b c-sharp d (transposed Ionian) and he notes the difference, I will reward him. But if I play C minor for him only a few times, and then play D minor, if he does not sense this difference, he has either no ears or no soul.[12]

---

[10]*Orchestre II*, p. 90: "Warum pflegen doch rechtschaffene Musici die Transpositiones also zu lieben? Wenn sie nicht angenehme Veränderungen brächten/ würde man wol an keine Transposition gedencken; Die veränderliche Angenehmligkeit bestehet nun nicht allein in der Höhe und Tieffe der Sonorum/ sondern die differenz/ und Schwebung der Consonantien/ und die Ungleichheit der Tonorum und Semitoniorum machen einer harmoniae eine gantz andere Natur."

[11]Published in Mattheson's *Criticae musicae II* (Hamburg, 1725; facsimile edition Amsterdam: Knuf, 1964), pp. 185-205. English translation by this author in "The Fux-Mattheson Correspondence: An Annotated Translation," in *Current Musicology* 24 (1977):37-62.

[12]P. 82: "Ich will einem Bauren/ e.g. aus der specie Octavae: d e fis g a h c d, Mixo-Lydii transpositi, und dann gleich darauf aus dem d e fis g a h cis d Jonici transpositi, (*cont.*)

A similar point arises in a letter from Johann Kuhnau to Mattheson, written, like Fux's letters, in answer to the *Orchestre II*.[13] Kuhnau, although praising Mattheson for his side of the argument, expresses doubts about dropping all of the old modes, particularly the Phrygian. Neither the major nor minor keys have a semitone above the final. How, Kuhnau asks, are Phrygian chorales to be elaborated in these new keys? Mattheson's answer is in two parts. First he notes that although all the keys begin with an ascent of a whole tone, is some keys there is a major tone (in the proportion 9:8), while in others the whole tone is a minor tone (in the proportion 10:9). Then he notes

> If, accidentally (outside of chorales), Phrygian and Hypophrygian phrases appear in a *galant* work, so long as it is required by the integrity of the song, this is not only possible, but must be considered as beautiful and moving.[14]

But, Mattheson argues, this is not the way to expand the number of modes or keys. Mattheson's insistence on the quality of the third as the sole criterion for differentiating the keys allows him virtually to ignore the remaining scale steps.

The same point is raised in the letter exchange with Fux. Fux notes that all of Mattheson's twenty-four keys are merely two modes, since they have the semitones in the same positions. Mattheson responds by listing twenty-four scales, each with the semitones in a different position, and each with the notation *dur* or *moll* based on the quality of the third, showing that "such changes of the semitones can contribute to the properties of today's modes little or not at all."[15] Some of these scales are rather bizarre, including, for example, f g-sharp a b-flat c d e-flat f, and d e-flat f g-sharp a b-flat c-sharp d, but

---

vorspielen/ und wann er den Unterscheid merckt/ will ich ihm einschencken. Ich will ihm aber ex. gr. das c. mol nur ein paar mahl/ und hernach das d mol anschlagen/ wann er diesen Unterscheid nicht empfindet/ so hat er entweder keine Ohren oder keine Seele."

[13]Printed in Mattheson's *Criticae musicae II*, pp. 229–239.

[14]*Criticae musicae II*, p. 242: "...wenn zufälliger Weise (ausser Chorälen) die phrygische und hypophrygische Clauseln, nachdem es die Anständigkeit des Gesanges erfordert, in einer galanten Arbeit vorkommen, so kan es nicht nur passiren, sondern muss für schön und beweglich gehalten werden..."

[15]See the author's English translation of the Fux-Mattheson letter exchange.

Mattheson notes that "none is so strange that I could not compose a true melody in it."[16]

Mattheson is not averse to arguing two sides of an issue. He states that there are only two types of modes or keys. But when he is charged with limiting compositional resources through this reduction in the number of modes from twelve to two, he retorts that each major and minor key is unique because of the differences in temperament—but there are still only two types of keys! If his hypothetical Thuringian peasant cannot differentiate Ionian from Mixolydian, how will he hear differences of a fraction of a tone? Each major or minor key is a transposition of the scale structure of all others; yet the scales can be changed without altering the key, so long as the major or minor third is maintained.

Finally, Mattheson still recognizes the use of the old modes for chorales:

> For, although one could get along according to today's style with two types of modes, yet the old modes, no less than the twenty-four contemporary species, should not therefore be wholly and completely discarded, because our beloved church songs, which in part are ordered according to the former, certainly merit much respect from everyone... I will present my opinion of their [the modes'] characteristics most briefly, in order to show that I am not one of those who despise the old modes or discard them entirely out of ignorance.[17]

Die Orchester-Kanzeley

Mattheson, always the public relations specialist, dedicated the *Orchestre II* to thirteen prominent contemporary musicians, to whom he appealed as to a jury for an "entirely impartial, free, and candid opinion" of his views. Of the musicians who wrote replies to Mattheson, a number commented specifically on modes and keys. All the letters, together with Mattheson's answers where questions were

---

[16]*Ibid.*

[17]*Orchestre II*, p. 382: "Denn/ ob man sich schon nach heutiger Art mit zwey generibus Modorum behelffen könte/ so dürffen doch die alten Modi, vielweniger die 24 Species hodiernae, darum nicht gantz und gar verworffen werden/ weil unsere lieben Kirchen- Gesänge/ die nach jenen theils eingerichtet sind/ leicht so viel Respect von jedermann verdienen... Ich will/ um zu beweisen/ dass ich nicht von denen sey/ die die alten Modos aus Unverstand verachten oder gäntzlich verwerffen/ meine Meynung von ihren Kennzeichen aufs kürtzeste hersetzen."

raised, were printed by Mattheson in *Criticae musicae II* (1725) under the heading: "The *Orchestre*-Chancellery, or testimonies, letters, findings, investigations, etc., by the former judges of the *Orchestre* trial."[18] Among the favorable comments specifically on the subject of the modes are those by Handel (with whom Mattheson had been close friends, and with whom Mattheson had fought a duel in 1704), Heinichen (excerpts of whose letter were presented on p. 112), and Johann Krieger (1651-1735).

Only Handel will allow the modes for those who practice old music:

> As concerns the Greek modes, I find that you have said everything that there is to say. Their knowledge is doubtless necessary to those who want to practice and perform ancient music, which formerly was composed according to such modes; however, since now we have been freed from the narrow bounds of ancient music, I cannot perceive what use the Greek modes have in today's music.[19]

Krieger's letter, which comments on each chapter of the *Orchestre II*, observes:

> I say this: the doctrine of solmization and modes belongs to ancient music... Concerning their use in today's music, I consider them unnecessary, troublesome, and inadequate things...[20]

Johann Kuhnau's doubts about giving up the Phrygian mode, included in his letter, have already been cited on p. 124.

Fux's Letters. By far the most important letter of this group, at least for the present study, is the one from Johann Joseph Fux, Capellmeister in Vienna, and later the author of the most important

---

[18]*Criticae musicae II*, pp. 179–288: "Die Orchester-Kanzeley, oder Gutachten, Briefe, Aussprüche, Untersuchungen, etc. der ehmaligen Scheides-Männer beym Orchester-Process."

[19]*Criticae musicae II*, pp. 210-211: "Quant aux Modes Grecs, je trouve, Monsieur, que vous avez dit tout ce qui peut dire la dessus. Leur connoissance est sans doute necessaire a ceux qui veulent pratiquer & executer la Musique ancienne, qui a ete composee suivant ces Modes; mais comme on s'est affranchi des bornes etroites de l'ancienne Musique, je ne vois pas de quelle utilite les Modes Grecs puissent etre pour la Musique moderne." Handel's letter, written in French, is printed along with Mattheson's German translation. The letter is dated February 24, 1719.

[20]*Ibid.*, pp. 216–219: "...Ich sage so: die Doctrin de Solmisatione & Modis gehöret ad Musicam antiquam...dem Nutzen bey der heutigen Musique nach, halte ich solche vor unnöthige, beschwerliche, und unzulängliche Dinge..."

counterpoint text since Zarlino, the *Gradus ad parnassum, sive manductio ad compositionem musicae regularem* (Vienna, 1725)[21]. He wrote on December 4, 1717, criticizing Mattheson's positions on modes and solmization. Mattheson replied on December 18. Fux and Mattheson each wrote one more letter, dated, respectively, January 12, 1718 and February 12, 1718.[22] The complete letter exchange is one of the most important documents we possess concerning developments of modes and keys in the 1710s and 1720s.

Fux appears here as a staunch defender of the traditional modes. For him, these are the basis of all music, ancient and modern, sacred and secular. Differentiations between modes are based solely on the position of the semitone in the diatonic octave. The twenty-four keys are, for him, only transpositions of Ionian and Aeolian odes. Fux also defends Guidonian solmization with six syllables, complete with the system of mutation, noting that he still uses it in Vienna.

Fux's position as expressed in these letters pertains directly to the interpretation of his *Gradus*, particularly with respect to the use of the modes. Mode is discussed in two passages in the *Gradus*, the first just before the study of fugue and the second, which presents much the same material but in more detail, later in the treatise. Fux notes that the subject of mode is highly complex, and announces his intention to mention only the most important points. Mode is defined by the placement of the semitones in a diatonic scale, and further by the placement of the fourth and fifth within the octave. There are six modes, and two forms of each. Josephus, the student in Fux's dialogue format, asks at one point whether all contemporary teachers have the same opinion of the twelve modes. Aloysius, representing Palestrina, the master, answers that there are differing opinions, but mentions only different countings of the modes.[23] There is no mention of major and minor keys eight years after the letter exchange with Mattheson.

---

[21]See Alfred Mann, *Steps to Parnassus* (New York: Norton, 1943) and *The Study of Fugue* (New York: Norton, 1965), pp. 78-138, for English translations of the passages on species counterpoint and fugue. The introduction and notes to *Steps to Parnassus* give complete bibliographical details and include a history of all previous translations. The 1725 edition appears in facsimile (New York: Broude, 1966). Several portions of the *Gradus*, some relating to the modes, that are not translated into English by Mann appear in translation in Appendix 3.

[22]See footnote 11 for publication and translation information.

[23]Latin edition of 1725, pp. 221–222.

Some modern commentators have argued that Fux used the modes in the *Gradus* merely for pedagogical purposes. Alfred Mann, for instance, writes in the introduction to *Steps to Parnassus*: "As a basis Fux chose the series of 'natural' tonalities, the old church modes which despite many attacks have, with the help of his teaching, proved their value throughout centuries of use."[24] In the *Study of Fugue*, Mann writes that Fux chose Palestrina as a model in order to use a style which emphasized equal treatment of all voices. This circumstance

> explains his retention of the modes, the theoretical basis of Palestrina's music. Indeed, in this presentation, Glarean's six authentic scales[25] offered Fux's student both a melodic-linear wealth which his own time had lost and the harmonic organization which it had conquered; studying the structure of the six basic modes and the essential intervals and cadences, he learned to understand the harmonic aspects of fugue while perceiving its melodic and linear aspects far more consciously than the limitation to two modes—major and minor—would allow.[26]

But Fux did not "choose" to use the modes; they were the only tonalities he recognized, as shown in this correspondence written eight years before the publication of the *Gradus*.

It should be emphasized here that Mattheson was not opposed to using the modes for teaching purposes or for church music. In 1731, his *Grosse General-Bass Schule* hailed an announced German translation of Fux's *Gradus*.[27] Mattheson himself may have planned a translation.[28] Fux and Mattheson were not arguing in 1717 over the best way to teach music or to teach some aspects of music; they were arguing about which tonal system was best for the understanding of their contemporary music.

---

[24]P. 12.

[25]Because of his peculiar nomenclature for the modes, Fux's usage follows Zarlino, not Glarean. See footnote 16 in chapter 1.

[26]Pp. 53–54.

[27]P. 181: "Ode on seeing a translation of Fux's *Gradus ad parnassum* announced in the catalog of the musical works of M. Telemann."

[28]Mann, *Steps to Parnassus*, p. 10.

Closely related to the question of Fux's purposes in using the modes is that of whether his work is to be understood as a general composition text, as a manual only intended for *a capella* style, or as a textbook in a purposely artificial style intended to make it timeless. This issue is of particular importance in our era because of the emphasis on strict counterpoint as an underpinning of tonal structure in a Schenkerian view of music. Fux's work has taken on an almost legendary status in part because the section on species counterpoint was used as a text by Haydn, Beethoven, and others.

Arnold Feil has argued that *Gradus* is a pedagogical work for beginners only, written in an artificial style, and that the modes are used to insure its isolation from contemporary practice.[29] Hugo Riemann asserted that the work was out of date before it was written.[30] Peter Benary expressed a similar sentiment, and summed up Fux's contribution to music theory in the *Gradus* as basically conservative.[31] Lorenz Mizler, in his 1742 German translation of the *Gradus*, notes after the second discussion of the modes that "what the capable Fux states here about the keys has all been set forth much more clearly in our time."[32] Certainly Mizler did not believe that a revolution in teaching had occurred in the seventeen years since the first publication of the *Gradus*.[33] In contrast to these positions, Helmut Federhofer argued that the work is a composition text. Counterpoint was a legitimate type of composition, and was a standard part of pedagogy, along with thorough-bass. The basic rules learned in the *Gradus* were applicable to all musical styles.[34]

The evidence of the entire *Gradus* argues that Fux did not choose an antique style of counterpoint for pedagogical purposes. Rather,

---

[29]"Zum *Gradus* ad Parnassum von J. J. Fux," in *Archiv für Musikwissenschaft*, 14 (1957):184–192.

[30]*Geschichte der Musiktheorie* (Leipzig, 1898), p. 415.

[31]*Die deutsche Kompositionslehre des 18. Jahrhunderts* (Leipzig, 1961), p. 80.

[32]Lorenz Mizler translation of Fux's *Gradus* (Leipzig, 1742).

[33]In fact, five years earlier, Mizler had criticized Johann Quirsfeld for including only a discussion of the twelve modes in the last edition of his *Lateinschul* manual *Breviarium musicum* (Dresden, 1717); see Table 4–1, item 14, for details on Quirsfeld's manual. Mizler notes "there are in fact twenty-four [modes], as should have been quite clear in his time." See Mizler's *Musikalischen Bibliothek*, II (Leipzig, 1737; facsimile edition Hilversum: Frits Knuf, 1966), p. 32.

[34]"Johann Joseph Fux als Musiktheoretiker," in *Hans Albrecht in Memoriam*, ed. Wilfried Brennecke und Hans Haase (Kassel: Bärenreiter, 1962), pp. 109–115.

all aspects of the *Gradus* present Fux's own views on the nature of contemporary music. After teaching counterpoint and fugue, Fux concludes his treatise with a study of the more complex dissonance usages in other styles in a manner not unrelated to that found in Christoph Bernhard's *Tractatus compositionis augmentatus*. The separate translations of Fux's sections on species counterpoint and on fugue (Alfred Mann's *Steps to Parnassus* and *The Study of Fugue*) can impart a misleading impression of the total scope of Fux's treatise to a reader familiar only with the English translations. The treatise as a whole amply demonstrates its similarity in overall design to Bernhard's work, even though the pedagogy of the two works is quite different. (See Appendix 3 for translations of some of the sections not covered in Mann's two translations.) Fux stands in the same Italian tradition that gave rise to Bernhard. In line with this tradition, Friedrich Wilhelm Riedel's hypothetical reconstruction of Fux's library rings true in that it contains not a single treatise presenting the major and minor keys.[35]

Gradus, then, is a composition text—an interpretation supported by the evidence of Fux's letter exchange with Mattheson. Fux as a composer wrote in both the old *a capella* style (*prima prattica*) and in more modern idioms. But the traditional modes were an intimate part of his thinking in all musical styles.

Later Works Concerning Mattheson. Although Mattheson wrote a number of works on composition after 1725, his opinions on the keys did not change substantially. In *Der vollkommene Capellmeister* (Hamburg, 1739,[36] he adopts the distinction between key (*Ton* or *Ton-Art* [that is, type of tone, the modern German term]), which gives the location of the final pitch, and mode (*modus*), which gives the scalar structure of the octave.

Buttstett's *Ut, mi, sol...* was not the only work written in answer to Mattheson's *Orchestre I* of 1713. Franz Xaver Anton Murschhauser (1663-1738) published in 1721 the first volume of a projected two-volume treatise, *Academia musico- poetica* (Nuremberg, 186 pp. in folio). The section on modes includes three separate parts: the eight

---

[35]"Johann Joseph Fux und die römische Palestrina-Tradition," in *Die Musikforschung*, 14 (1961):14–22.

[36]Facsimile edition (Kassel: B+renreiter, 1954). English translation by Ernest Harriss (Ann Arbor: UMI, 1981). See Part I, Chapter 9.

psalm tones, the eight Gregorian modes, and the twelve church modes used for "figural" music.[37] The work was severely criticized by Mattheson in *Critica musica I* (1722) in a section entitled "The compositional light-snuffers" ("Die melopoetische Licht-Scheere"). This subtitle is in answer to the inscription found on some copies of Murschhauser's work: "in order to bring a little more light to the excellent Herr Mattheson."[38] Possibly as a result of this criticism, or for other reasons, the second volume never appeared.

In 1745, Meinrad Spiess (1683-1761) published a lavish work, *Tractatus musicus compositorio-practicus* (Augsburg, 220 pp. in folio + a lexicon), in which, once again, the twenty-four keys are rejected as transpositions of only two modes.[39] The work was reprinted in a second edition only a year later. Spiess was a member of Lorenz Mizler's *Korrespondierenden Sozietät der musikalischen Wissenschaft* (of which J. S. Bach was a member), and was highly regarded in many circles as a theorist and a teacher. The *Tractatus* was listed along with Mattheson's *Der vollkommener Capellmeister*, Marpurg's treatise on fugue, Heinichen's thorough-bass treatise, and other works on composition, as recommended acquisitions for a mid-eighteenth- century music library by J. A. Hiller.[40]

Among other comments, Spiess notes that modern composers have limited themselves to only two modes. The Phrygian mode is used in church but not in the opera house; this is because God has blinded opera composers to the beautiful melodies possible in this mode to prevent them from profaning the mode. The old modes are superior to the new keys since there are more compositional possibilities and affects in them, and it is easier to compose a fugue. Although the motivation for Spiess's conservative position may be similar to that of Fux and Buttstett, Spiess's recognition of mid-eighteenth-century reality concerning use of major and minor keys

---

[37]"Von denen Tonis Choralibus, und Figuratis," pp. 106–186.

[38]"Um dem vortrefflichen Herrn Mattheson ein mehres licht zu geben..."

[39]Pp. 34–36.

[40]See Vincent Duckles, "Johann Adam Hiller's 'Critical Prospectus for a Music Library,' " in *Studies in 18th-Century Music, a Tribute to Karl Geiringer* (New York: Oxford University, 1970), pp. 177–185.

sets him apart from his predecessors. In any event, Mattheson, then 64 years old, did not lift his pen, and Spiess was spared a fresh onslaught of polemic. By 1745 the arguments of the 1710s and 1720s had begun to fade into the past.

Chapter 8

The Persistence of Modal Theory

Traditions of modal and major-minor thinking had persisted in German theory from the early seventeenth century through the early eighteenth century. But to an observer in the 1720s, it might easily have seemed that the modal tradition had come to an end. Works of Janowka (1701),[1] Heinichen (1711 and 1728), and Mattheson (several works beginning in 1713) are firmly grounded in the twenty-four keys. And after all the dust had settled from Mattheson's debates of the 1710s with various upholders of the modal tradition, there seemed little doubt as to the victor. Buttstett's *Ut, mi, sol...* (c.1715), attacking Mattheson's work of 1713 and defending traditional modal theory, had been derided by Mattheson's *Orchestre II* (1717). And the judgment of contemporaries was clear: of the "jury" of thirteen musicians to whom *Orchestre II* was dedicated to decide the merits of the issues, only Fux had fully defended Buttstett's position. Murschhauser's attempt "to bring a little more light to the excellent Herr Mattheson" (*Academia musico-poetica*, 1721) backfired to such an extent that after a stinging review by Mattheson, its second volume was never published.

Among major works of the period, only Fux's *Gradus ad parnassum* (1725) used the modes as its sole basis. And whatever Fux's intentions, his German contemporaries clearly viewed use of the modes in *Gradus* as part of Fux's instruction in the *prima prattica*, not in any way as a commentary on their contemporary music. This is clear from Mattheson's praise of the work as well as from comments in Mizler's 1742 German translation.

---

[1] See chapters 6 and 7 for complete references to the works cited in these opening paragraphs.

German works of the 1720s and early 1730s uniformly back up this assessment of the recognition of major and minor keys. All use only the twenty-four keys. These works include several by Mattheson and Heinichen: by Mattheson, *Das forschende Orchestre* (Hamburg, 1721), *Critica musica* I and II (Hamburg, 1722 and 1725),[2] *Grosse General-Bass-Schule* (Hamburg, 1731),[3] and the *Kleine General-Bass Schule* (Hamburg, 1735); by Heinichen: *Der General-Bass in der Composition* (Dresden, 1728). Other works of the period using the twenty-four keys are the *Treulicher Unterricht im General-Bass* (Hamburg, 1732) by David Kellner (c.1670–1748),[4] an early manuscript treatise (c.1730) by Johann Adolph Scheibe (1708–1776),[5] and the *Museum musicum* (Schwäbische Hall, 1732) by Joseph Majer (1689–1768).

Majer's *Museum* was a popular work, appearing in a second edition in 1741. It contains elaborate illustrated discussions of musical instruments along with basic information on a variety of subjects. Majer modeled his treatment of tonal materials on the "world-famous Mattheson," and printed an ode by Mattheson praising his work. The twenty-four keys appear in a table divided into four groups of six each: those whose major third is a natural pitch, those whose major third is a sharp, those whose minor third is natural, and those whose minor third is flat.[6] (Compare this to the groupings in the works of Speer, discussed on p. 84.) Only brief mention is made of the old modes "of the ancients;" they are not enumerated, nor are any details of their structure given, save to note that Ionian and Aeolian, the only two named, are the same as major and minor scales.[7]

But despite these appearances, the modal tradition was alive during this period, and was reasserted in the 1730s. Indeed, the modal tradition persisted in some form until the very end of the eighteenth

---

[2] Facsimile edition (Amsterdam: Knuf, 1964).

[3] Facsimile edition (Hildesheim: Olms, 1968).

[4] Elwyn Weinandt, in "David Kellner's Lautenstücke," in *Journal of the American Musicological Society* (1957):29–38, makes the rather astounding assertion that Kellner's work was the "first theory book to be based on major and minor keys."

[5] The *Compendium musices theoretico-practicum* is published as an appendix to Peter Benary's *Die deutsche Kompositionslehre des 18. Jahrhunderts* (Leipzig: Breitkopf & Härtel, 1961). Benary dates the manuscript between 1728 and 1736, giving 1730 as an approximate date. The keys are discussed on pp. 16–18.

[6] Pp. 50–51. Majer is not fully consistent in his groupings: e.g., G-sharp major (*Gis dur*) has a natural third (C), but C-sharp major (*Cis dur*) has an accidental third (F).

[7] Pp. 60–61.

century, recurring in a variety of works directed at different segments of the musical community.

Walther's *Lexicon* and its Influence

Modal theory was once again interjected into current discourse in what is probably the most impressive work of music scholarship produced by the eighteenth century: the *Musicalisches Lexicon* (Leipzig, 1732)[8] of Johann Gottfried Walther (1684–1748), a work that includes extensive biographical, bibliographical, and historical information as well as definitions of terms. The principal discussion of mode appears under the heading *modus*, covering nine pages, one of the lengthiest discussions in the work. A translation of the entry *modus musicus* appears in Appendix 6. Only the salient points are surveyed here.

The first and longest portion of the article treats the traditional theory of twelve modes. Mode is "the way to begin a song, to continue it properly within certain bounds, and to end it appropriately." The diatonic scale with its two semitones is the basis of the twelve authentic and plagal modes. The discussion of each mode individually is extensive, including the derivation of its name from the Greek, its ambitus in several registers, alterations of the ambitus, and a list of church songs composed in that mode. Walther defends the integrity of each mode by correcting various chorale melodies that have been "corrupted" over time. He notates each mode in scalar form in all its transpositions, with the semitones isolated. All the modes except Lydian appear in more than twelve transpositions: Phrygian and Ionian in thirteen (Phrygian with scales on both E-flat and D-sharp; Ionian with scales on both G-sharp and A-flat), and Dorian, Mixolydian, and Aeolian in fourteen (with scales on both E-flat/D-sharp and A-flat/G-sharp). Thus, key signatures with double sharps (for example, F-double sharp in Ionian on G-sharp) are necessary.

Walther then turns to a brief consideration of the modern teaching of the modes. Most of this passage is a paraphrase of Mattheson. There are twelve notes to an octave, each of which can have a major or minor third above it, which gives rise to the twenty-four major and minor keys.

---

[8] Facsimile edition (Kassel: Bärenreiter, 1953).

In the concluding paragraphs of the article, Walther avoids taking sides between the new and old systems. Instead, Walther presents the assets of each system. But the result is confused and in part contradictory. The older teaching is recommended in that the key signature is more easily discovered, and thus one knows better which notes belong to which mode. (Walther seems to have taken Mattheson literally when Mattheson argued that all sorts of scales were possible in each key.) But the newer teaching shows how to use the notes of the key in cadences and other passages, and what notes must be used if the signature agrees neither with the new or the old modes. Following Mattheson's reasoning, Walther notes that the whole tones on the keyboard are not all of the same size, so that each of the twenty-four keys has a different arrangement of major and minor tones, although the semitones appear in either the major or minor pattern in all.[9] This is contrasted with the older type of teaching, in which all transpositions are the same. But surely on any given keyboard, transpositions of either type of mode will give the same result. Walther himself is unsure of the thrust of this argument, and notes that there is not universal agreement whether the difference between a major tone and a minor tone is in fact audible.

The article closes with a statement of neutrality, "in no way taking sides in the heated disputes, both past and present; leaving it to each reader to decide which type [of modal theory] he prefers, and [believing] that either will lead to success in both figured music and chorales." But despite this disclaimer, Walther does in effect take a position on the modes. The old modes are discussed fully, with musical examples of each. Their integrity is assumed, and there is a repertoire of music—chorales—that mandates knowledge of them. Walther offers no similarly strong case for the major-minor keys. He presents no specific repertoire that requires knowledge of major and minor. Indeed, he implies in the final discussion that the old modes can deal adequately with major-minor music. Nowhere does he mention that the quality of the third over the final is or should be a crucial differentiating factor. Lurking throughout the discussion is this question: if the old modes can cope with all music, and there is no clinching improvement in the new modes, why should the old modes be abandoned?

[9] See Appendix 2 for Mattheson's recommended tuning system, and review chapter 7 for Mattheson's arguments.

It might be argued that in a book concerned in large part with a historical perspective, the system of modes would be presented more fully than a relatively new system of keys. The *Lexicon* is, after all, not a composition text. As the title indicates, Walther wanted to cover "not only those musicians, in old as well as in recent times, likewise in different nations, who distinguished themselves in theory and practice, and what is known of each, or what he left in writings; but also the technical terms or other words used in music in the Greek, Latin, Italian, and French languages." It is, therefore, instructive to turn to Walther's earlier manuscript treatise on composition, the *Praecepta der musicalischen Composition* (1708),[10] to see how much the discussion of mode in the *Lexicon* reflects Walther's thinking as a practicing musician.

In fact, the sections on the traditional modes in the *Lexicon* agree extensively with the corresponding passages in the *Praecepta*. Among the changes in the discussion of mode that Walther made in preparing the *Lexicon* are the following:

1. The ordering of the modes follows Zarlino in the *Praecepta*, and Glarean in the *Lexicon*.

2. Walther discusses many aspects of mode in more detail in the *Lexicon*: ambitus, authentic and plagal, cadences, the combining of modes, and repercussio.

3. Walther offers fewer chorale melodies for each mode in the *Lexicon*, but discusses deviations from the modal ambitus in greater detail, including reasons why such deviations are to be understood as corruptions.

4. In the *Praecepta* there is no mention of the major and minor keys. Even when Walther notes that Dorian, Aeolian, and Ionian

---

[10] The *Praecepta* was published, edited by Peter Benary (Leipzig: Breitkopf & Härtel, 1955). Walther may not have held the highest opinion of his *Praecepta*; in the autobiographical sketch he submitted for inclusion in Mattheson's *Ehrenpforte* (Hamburg, 1740), he did not mention this manuscript treatise. There is a comparison of the treatment of mode in the *Praecepta* and the *Lexicon* in Hermann Gehrmann's monograph, "Johann Gottfried Walther als Theoretiker," in *Vierteljahrsschrift für Musikwissenschaft* 7 (1891):574–575. Gehrmann reports that Walther's treatment of modes in the *Praecepta* is close in content to that found in the 1703 manuscript treatise of Johann Kuhnau. Kuhnau's *Fundamenta compositionis* is discussed by Kurt Hahn in the *Bericht über den internationalen Musikwissenschaftlich Kongress* (Hamburg: Bärenreiter, 1956), pp. 103–105. It appears that Walther did not know of Kuhnau's treatise, since it is not mentioned in the article on Kuhnau in the *Lexicon*.

are the only modes still in common use, there is no implication that the major-minor differentiation is any more essential than any other scalar variation. Compare this to works of Werckmeister, discussed in chapter 5, in which the limitation to two or three modes is accompanied by the explanation that these represent a major-minor differentiation.

Therefore, the content of much of the discussion on modes in the 1732 *Lexicon* was actually written some twenty-four years earlier, in 1708, before Heinichen's musical circle was published, and before Mattheson's defenses of the twenty-four major and minor keys first appeared. Indeed, Walther may have begun the work on the *Lexicon* as early as 1710, before these Heinichen and Mattheson works.[11] If it is remarkable that a thoroughly conservative treatment of mode should appear at all in 1732, it is all the more surprising that it should be even more conservative than the treatment by the same author in 1708. Not all the changes in 1732 can be explained as giving a fuller picture of mode in the past. The discussion of the integrity of each modal ambitus, for example, is clearly addressed to the contemporary composer and performer.

Walther as an organist and composer was intimately involved with chorales. The vast majority of his compositional output is based on chorales: including trio sonatas and fugues on chorale tunes. A lifetime spent working with these melodies must have convinced him that the modes were indeed an important part of contemporary music.

The conclusion is inescapable that the treatment of mode in the *Lexicon* must be taken as Walther's view of the situation in 1732. Peter Benary argues that in the *Praecepta* Walther introduced the modes only for the purposes of church musicians, and that he realized that such a thorough presentation was anachronistic.[12] This point of view is contradicted by the evidence of the *Lexicon*. But even in 1708, Walther could have used the works of Werckmeister, Falck, Speer, Niedt, or those of any number of foreign writers (Janowka, Brossard, or other French writers) as models to present a closer approximation

---

[11] See Hans Eggebrecht, "Walthers Musicalisches Lexikon in seinen terminologischen Partien," in *Acta musicologica* 29 (1957):10–27. The first part of the *Lexicon*, containing only the entries beginning with A, was published in 1728. By July, 1729 the entire work was completed except for minor emendations.

[12] Benary, *Die deutsche...*, p.35.

of the major and minor keys, had he wished to. Werckmeister, whose works include a well-reasoned advocacy of the major-minor differentiation of the modes, was, like Walther, deeply involved in sacred music. In any event, the *Praecepta* contains a more conservative view of mode than most other contemporary works, and certainly more conservative than any other work by such a young musician—Walther was only 24 at the time. Perhaps the most remarkable aspect of Walther's view of the modes is that Walther thought very highly of Mattheson, and praised him in a two-and-a-half page article in the *Lexicon*, one of the longest devoted to a single person.

The Influence of Walther's *Lexicon*. Immediately on its appearance and for some years thereafter, Walther's *Lexicon* was the foundation of musical knowledge in Germany. As such, it exercised a powerful influence on all later writings. It was not until rather late in the eighteenth century that writers complained about the relevance of the *Lexicon* to contemporary practice.[13] Discussions of the modes in several publications can be traced in part to Walther's influence.

A particularly clear instance of such influence is afforded by Joseph Majer's *Museum musicum*. The first edition of this work (1732), discussed on p. 134, is based solely on the twenty-four keys. Majer refers in the preface to this edition to Walther's just-published *Lexicon*, but does not seem to have been influenced by the work. But when Majer prepared the second edition of his work for publication in 1741, he added a long appendix to the discussion of the twenty-four keys, stressing the importance of knowing the old modes in addition to the keys. This is especially true for church organists who deal with chorale melodies. Each mode is discussed, with the ambitus, affect, final, and so forth, listed.[14] Although this section was almost certainly added under the influence of Walther, Majer's exposition of the modes contains information not found in Walther's *Lexicon*. There are references to authors not mentioned by Walther, and the listing of affects is more complete. That Majer considered these changes important is demonstrated by other portions of his

---

[13] See Hans Eggebrecht, *op. cit.*, pp. 21–24.
[14] The 1741 edition appeared under the title *Neu-eröffneter Theoretischer & Praktischer Music-Saal*. The chart of the twenty-four keys appears on pages 64–65; the interpolated section on the modes covers pages 75–77.

work that remain untouched in the 1741 edition, including even the preface, which still refers to Walther's *Lexicon* has having been published "this year"[!]

Another work influenced by Walther is the *Kurtzgefasstes musicalisches Lexicon* (Chemnitz, 1737).[15] The work was prepared by the publishers Johann Christoph and Johann David Stössel, who recognized the market for a work that was cheaper and more compact than Walther's. Although their preface lists eighteen different authors as sources, most of the work is derived from Walther. The Stössel *Lexicon* came under attack from many quarters for the quality of the articles and revisions of other authors' works. Mattheson, in his *Ehrenpforte* (Hamburg, 1740), asks, for example, "What kind of man is it who always writes *Semitonium* instead of *Semiditoni*? He can hardly know his business."[16] Jacob Adlung, in his *Anleitung zu der musikalischen Gelahrtheit* (Erfurt, 1758),[17] warns his readers not to try to save money by buying the Stössel work instead of Walther's: "leichte Geld, leichte Waare" ("You get what you pay for"). Adlung notes later that the Stössels are probably not the authors, but the publishers.[18] The question of who actually wrote and/or compiled the material was apparently unknown even to contemporaries.

The discussion of the traditional modes, including their history, theory, and practice, appears under several headings: *Modi Cantus Ecclesiastici Octo* (p. 232), *Modi Musici* (pp. 232–234), *Modus in Genere* (p. 235), and *Modus in Specie* (pp. 235–237). The presentation of the twenty-four keys derives from Mattheson's discussion of 1713 (*Toni*, pp. 397–398). What is significant for the present study is not the quality of the Stössel *Lexicon*, but that a work aiming for the popular audience in 1737–1749 devoted so much space to the modes.

The Mid and Late Eighteenth Century

Works that Continue to Discuss the Modes. Numerous German works continue to present the traditional modes in some form right through the end of the eighteenth century. Although these

---

[15] Later editions in 1743 and 1749.

[16] P. 128.

[17] Facsimile edition (Kassel: Bärenreiter, 1953).

[18] P. 130.

works use the twenty-four keys as the basis of contemporary music, all the authors felt it important to include the discussion of the modes. The variety of reasons is not without interest, for it demonstrates the prevalence of continued interest in the modes. In some works, the discussion is present for the sake of a particular pedagogic approach. In others, the presentation is addressed to organists or others who deal with older music. And in some, aesthetic issues are primary. But for all, some knowledge of the modes is considered to be an essential for the well-educated musician. This is in sharp contrast to French and English attitudes of the late seventeenth and eighteenth centuries already cited in earlier chapters.

The following works that fall into this category are listed chronologically:

1. Lorenz Mizler (1711–1778), who was a pupil of J. S. Bach, and a translator of Fux's *Gradus*, included both modes and keys in his *Anfangsgründen des Generalbasses* (Leipzig, 1739). The same passage recurs as a footnote running from page 165 to page 172 in his translation of Fux's *Gradus* (1742).

2. Georg Andreas Sorge (1703–1778) also discusses modes and keys in chapter 11 of Part I (pp. 22–33) of his *Vorgemach der Musicalischen Composition* (Lobenstein, 1745).

3. The most extensive discussion of the modes in the works of Friedrich Wilhelm Marpurg (1718–1795) appears in his *Abhandlung von der Fuge* (Berlin, 1753). He discusses modes and modal fugal answers on pp. 56–73. In his other works, Marpurg mentions the modes only to show that they have become the major-minor keys. In his *Handbuch bey dem Generalbasse* (Berlin, 1762), for instance, he notes that it was only after centuries of working with octave species that musicians realized that the principal differentiation of keys should be the quality of the third, and not the placement of the semitones (p. 17). His *Anleitung zum Clavierspielen* "according to the more beautiful practice of the present time" (Berlin, 1755)[19] does not mention the modes.

4. Jacob Adlung (1699–1762) discusses the modes fully in his encyclopedic *Anleitung zu der Musikalischen Gelahrtheit* (Erfurt, 1758).[20] His discussion reveals the persistence of various attitudes. In general, Adlung held liberal views on the propriety of various

---

[19] Facsimile of the 1765 edition (Hildesheim: Olms, 1970).
[20] Part I, chapter 2 (pp. 153–156) and chapter 3 (p. 170).

styles of playing or composition. In a discussion of whether or not to use Picardy-third cadences in minor chorales, Adlung appends the following recommendation: "Do in Rome as the Romans do. When a player is to be heard in a foreign place, he will do well to inquire about the practices there so that he will not be held ignorant by the pedants... Yet I also see no reason why one cannot occasionally, for variety's sake, make use of those types of playing which are called old."[21] Adlung was Buttstett's successor as organist and teacher in Erfurt upon the latter's death in 1727. Buttstett's conservative biases clearly did not influence the choice of his successor.

5. Johann Lorenz Albrecht (1732–1773) discussed both tonal systems in his *Gründliche Einleitung in die Anfangslehre der Tonkunst* (Langensalza, 1761). Albrecht may have been a protégé of Jacob Adlung. Among other similarities between his work and Adlung's, he copies Adlung's peculiar notation of * and ♭ for major and minor (C* means C major; C♭ means C minor; and so forth).

6. Johann Philipp Kirnberger (1721–1783), a pupil of J. S. Bach, is one of the major theorists of the late eighteenth century. He accepts only the major and minor keys for most contemporary music, but presents a very strong case for the maintenance of the modes in sacred music in his *Kunst des Reinen Satzes* (Berlin and Königsberg, 1776).[22] Not without significance is that he begins the discussion of keys and modes with the traditional modes, not with the major and minor keys. A similar defense of the modes appears in the article *Kirchentöne*, probably by Kirnberger, in the *Allgemeine Theorie der Schönen Künste*, an encyclopedic work on all the arts, published in several editions from 1771–1799. Among the points made in this article is a comment that the concepts authentic and plagal are also applicable to major-minor music. The openings of two arias by [Karl Heinrich?] Graun (1704–1759) are cited, one being labeled authentic, the other plagal:

---

[21] P. 677: "Ländlich, sittlich. Wenn ein Spieler sich an einem fremden Orte hören lässet, thut er wohl, wenn er sich nach der dasigen Gewohnheit erkundiget, damit er nicht von den Pedanten vor unwissend gehalten werde... Doch sehe ich auch keine Ursache, warum zur Veränderung man nicht bisweilen solcher Spielarten sich bedienen könne, welche man alt nennet."

[22] Facsimile edition (Hildesheim: Olms, 1968). See Part II, pp. 41–67. English translation by David Beach and Jurgen Thym (New Haven: Yale, 1982), pp. 314–335.

Example 8–1.

Of- fe- sa ad im-   pla- ca- bi- le, cru- de-   le   *etc.*

Ah!   pur trop- po, io l'a-   mo an-co- ra

7. Johann Joseph Klein (1740–1823) presents a full exposition of the modes in his *Versuch eines Lehrbuches der Praktischen Musik* (Gera, 1783).

8. Daniel Gottlob Türk (1756–1813) includes a full discussion of the modes in his *Klavierschule* (Leipzig and Halle, 1789).[23]

Several of these writers introduce the modes largely for the sake of church music—mostly, but not necessarily exclusively, for chorales. But this does not exclude a strong defense of their use. The most impassioned appeal on behalf of the modes occurs in Kirnberger's treatise. At several points, Kirnberger notes that the modes are capable of greater expressivity than the modern keys:

> We have various old church songs which are so full of feeling and expression that they cannot be transformed to the new manner without a marked diminution of their worth. The old keys, moreover, have greater variety of harmony and modulation than the newer type allows in such simple songs, where one makes do with the tonic chord, and with its upper and lower dominant [that is, with the I, IV, and V chords]. As an example, I will accompany the song *Ach Gott, von Himmel sieh darein* with the harmony which its key suggests, and set above it the same song as it is set or performed by some recent

---

[23] Facsimile edition (Kassel: Bärenreiter, 1962).

143

composers or organists. One cannot have the slightest sensitivity if he does not find this song expressive and admirable in the second harmonization, and, on the other hand, very trite and offensive in the first. [See example 8-2.][24]

Example 8-2. Kirnberger, *Kunst des Reinen Satzes,* **II, p. 48**

[The lower line is incorrectly labeled Aeolisch; corrected to Phrygisch in the errata list at the end of Kirnberger's treatise.]

[24] Kirnberger, *Kunst des Reinen Satzes,* p. 47: "Wir haben verschiedene alte Kirchenlieder, die so voll Empfindung und Ausdruk sind, dass sie ohne merkliche Verminderung ihres Werthes nicht können nach der neuen Art umgesetzet werden. Die alten Tonarten haben überdem mehr Mannigfaltigkeit der Harmonie und der Modulation, als die neuere Art in so einfachen Gesängen zulässt, wo man sich insgemein mit dem Accord der Tonica, und ihrer Ober- und Unterdominante behilft. Ich will zum Beyspiel das Lied: Ach Gott, vom Himmel sieh darein, mit der Harmonie, die seine Tonart an die Hand giebt, begleiten, und dasselbe Lied, wie es von einigen neuen Tonsetzern oder Organisten gesetzt oder vorgetragen wird, hersetzen. Man müste nicht das geringste Gefühl haben, wenn man das nemliche Lied bey der ersten Harmonie nicht ausdruksvoll und vortreflich, bey der zweyten hingegen nicht äussertst schaal und ekelhaft finden sollte."

...Nowadays the old keys are too much ignored, especially in Protestant countries, where almost without exception sacred music is executed very poorly; this is one of the reasons that today's music has sunk so low, even in Catholic countries, that it can hardly be differentiated from theatrical music... On the other hand, one should listen to a composition by good masters worked out in the true church keys, a mass by Prenestini [Palestrina], Leonardo Leo [1694–1744], [Antonio] Lotti [1667–1740], Franc[esco] Gasparini [1668–1727], Frescobaldi [1583–1643], [Luigi] Battiferri [early seventeenth century],[25] Fux, Handel, J. S. Bach, Froberger [1616–1667], [Johann] Zelenka [1679–1745] and others. One should hear even a single song! What power! What dignity becoming the church and religion! What grandeur of expression! Clearly it is not the keys alone that make this effect, but no one could deny that they contribute most strongly to it.[26]

In his suggestions for setting chorales in an appropriate manner, Kirnberger does not recommend that a composer use only the pure diatonic mode for the entire composition. He suggests instead that the best way to use the modes is to keep the melody and bass within the modal scale, and use leading tones or b-flat in the inner voices. But he does recommend using cadences proper to each mode.

If Kirnberger's is the most impassioned appeal on behalf of the modes, similar sentiments are expressed by Sorge (who, for example, complains about the blindness of those who prelude to Phrygian

---

[25] Nearly a half-century earlier, Walther in his *Lexicon* could not specify birth or death dates for Battiferri, nor could he cite more than a handful of publications. It is possible that Kirnberger included Battiferri's name based on the fugue discussed at some length in Marpurg's treatise on fugue of 1753. See Alfred Mann, *The Study of Fugue* (New York: Norton, 1965), pp. 181–184, for the composition and Marpurg's analysis translated into English. If this was indeed Kirnberger's only acquaintance with Battiferri, it casts some doubt on Kirnberger's knowledge of the music on which he expends so much energy in praise.

[26] Kirnberger, *Kunst des Reinen Satzes*, p. 66: "Heut zu Tage werden die alten Tonarten, zumal in protestantischen Ländern, wo die Kirchenmusik fast durchgangig sehr schlecht bestelte ist, zu sehr vernachlässiget; dies ist eine mit von den Ursachen, warum die heutige Kirchenmusik, selbst in katholischen Ländern, so tief gesunken ist, dass man sie fast nicht mehr von theatralischen unterscheiden kann... Man höre dagegen eine von guten Meistern in den wahren Kirchentonarten ausgearbeitete Musik, eine Messe von Prenestini, Leonardo Leo, Lotti, Franc. Gasparini, Frescobaldi, Battiferri, Fux, Hendel, J. S. Bach, Froberger, Zelenka, u.a. Ja man höre dagegen blos einen simpeln Choral! welche Kraft! welche der Kirche und der Religion anständige Wurde! welche Hoheit des Ausdrucks! Freylich sind es die Tonarten nicht allein, die das bewürcken, aber niemand wird läugnen können, dass sie aufs kräfftigste dazu beytragen."

chorales in E major or E minor or even C major), Adlung, Albrecht, Klein, and Türk. Klein notes that the modes have contemporary usages (p. 68), while Türk comments that they are still in use mostly, not *only*, because of chorales.

A sense of historical distance from the modes pervades the later works in the preceding list. Mizler, in the footnote to his 1742 translation of the *Gradus*, notes that the modes that Fux describes are no longer the basis of contemporary music. And already in 1758, Adlung prefaces his explanation of modal terminology by noting that the jargon "may not be entirely foreign to readers of books."[27] Marpurg includes a discussion of modal fugue answers with this explanation:

> We could be spared this section were it not that there are still certain songs in the church, Protestant as well as Catholic, which are set in these old keys, and which consequently must be practiced according to them... However, since these old keys may not be known to everyone, before we show how the answer must be arranged in them, we will first explain them.[28]

Yet Klein introduces the modes after complaining in the foreword about introductory texts that are full of unnecessary material.

Works that Omit the Modes. Many writings of the mid and late eighteenth century, particularly those whose scope is confined to secular music, avoid any mention of the modes at all. Into this category fall not only other works by some of the authors discussed in the preceding section, such as Kirnberger's *Grundsätze des Generalbasses* (Berlin, [1781]), but also the three great instrumental treatises of the 1750s: the *Versuch über die wahre Art das Clavier zu spielen* (Berlin, 1753)[29] by C. P. E. Bach (1714–1788), the *Versuch einer gründlichen Violinschule* (Augsburg, 1756)[30] of Leopold Mozart (1719–1787), and

---

[27] Adlung, *Anleitung zu der musikalischen Gelahrtheit*, p. 170: "...welche den Bücherlesern nicht gantz unbekannt seyn dörfen."

[28] Marpurg, *Abhandlung von der Fuge*, p. 56: "Wir könnten dieses Absatzes überhoben seyn, woferne nicht in der Kirche, sowohl bey den Protestanten als Catholischen, annoch gewisse Lieder und Gesänge vorhanden wären, die aus diesen alten Tonarten gesetzet sind, und die folglich darnach ausgeübet werden müssen... Da diese alte Tonarten aber vielleicht nicht jedermann bekannt seyn mögten, so wollen wir selbige zuförderst erklären, bevor wir zeigen, wie der Gefährte darinnen eingerichtet werden müsse."

[29] English translation by William Mitchell (New York: Norton, 1949).

[30] English translation by Editha Knocker (London: Oxford University, 1951).

the *Versuch einer Anweisung die Flöte Traversiere zu spielen* (Berlin, 1752)[31] of Johann Joachim Quantz (1697–1773).

Quantz's only reference to the modes occurs during his explanation of the incomplete key signatures still in use. After noting the origin of incomplete signatures in the days of the modes, Quantz recommends that composers avoid these, since such signatures only necessitate adding sharps and flats in the course of a piece that should be in the key signature[32]–echoing an argument found already in Janowka's *Clavis* of 1701.[33] Only Leopold Mozart felt a need to explain the absence of a discussion of the old modes. In a footnote to the passage on keys, Mozart writes: "To a violinist my explanation of the keys will of a surety be more useful than if I prattle to him of the Dorian, Phrygian, Lydian, Mixolydian, Aeolian, Ionian, and by adding the Hypo, yet six more keys of the Ancients. In the Church they enjoy the right of liberty; but at Court this is not suffered."[34]

The final demise of the modes as an aspect of contemporary practice is found in the works of Heinrich Christoph Koch (1749–1816). Both his *Versuch einer Anleitung zur Composition* (Leipzig and Rudolstadt, 1787)[35] and *Lexikon* (Frankfurt, 1802)[36] show little sympathy for the modes, even though the latter is in some sense a scholarly work. The second volume of the *Versuch* dismisses the modes as no longer in use except for a few old church songs–a sentiment reflected in the *Lexikon*.[37] The latter work reveals its lack of sympathy both through its attitude and the level of accuracy. In the article on key (*Tonart*) the discussion of mode is historical, whereas the major and minor keys refer to contemporary music. According

[31] English translation by Edward Reilly (New York: Free Press, 1966).

[32] Pp. 60–62 of the English translation.

[33] See the article *Tonus* in Appendix 1.

[34] P. 64 of the English translation.

[35] Facsimile edition (Hildesheim: Olms, 1969).

[36] Facsimile edition (Hildesheim: Olms, 1964)

[37] Column 1542: "Most of our chorale melodies are actually set in the old keys. But many of them have gradually been modified in various places according to our modern keys, so that now only a few are still extant which fully correspond to the usage of the old keys." "Die mehresten unserer Choralmelodien sind eigentlich in den alten Tonarten gesetzt; aber viele derselben sind nach und nach in verschiedenen Stellen nach unsern modernen Tonarten modifieirt worden, so, dass anjetzt nur noch wenige vorhanden sind, die dem Gebrauche der alten Tonarten völlig entsprechen."

to Koch, the old modes were "commonly practiced until about the end of the seventeenth century."[38] Of these modes, only the Ionian and Aeolian scales remained. These two are superior to the remaining modes for the purposes of harmony, because each has the same quality of third over the tonic, fourth, and fifth. It is the imperfection of the remaining scales that led to their demise. The article on the *Kirchentöne* presents only the church keys. Any reader desiring more information is referred to Forkel's history of music, or to the works of Fux, Murschhauser, Printz, or Vogler.

What is clear from works by Koch, by some of his predecessors, and by most of his colleagues whose eye was primarily on contemporary secular styles, is that by the end of the eighteenth century the modes and music that required the modes were no longer a necessary concern for many musicians. But whether from the appeals of a Kirnberger to retain a glorious past that he himself experienced, or from a new generation of historicizing writers, the subject of the church modes remained in the public eye in German-speaking areas of Europe. The later works cited earlier in this chapter appeared during the era of Beethoven's education. His explorations of modal turns of phrase in some later works, whether in the *Heiliger Dankgesang* of the A-minor String Quartet, op. 132, or portions of the *Missa Solemnis*, op. 123, did not arise in a vacuum, but at the end of a continuous tradition of modal thinking that had nourished German styles of composition throughout two centuries.[39]

---

[38] Column 1542: "und bis gegen das Ende des 17ten Jahrhunderts allgemein ausgeübt worden sind."

[39] Sieghard Brandenburg surveys some of the literature discussed here as well as later sources in his fascinating study of "The Historical Background to the 'Heiliger Dankgesang' in Beethoven's A-minor Quartet Op. 132," in *Beethoven Studies 3*, ed. Alan Tyson (Cambridge: Cambridge University Press, 1982), pp. 161–191.

Chapter 9

Epilogue

German theory over a period of nearly two centuries maintained two parallel traditions: one insisting on the continued relevance of the traditional modes, the other emphasizing the essential differentiation into major and minor. Only after 1750 did a sense of historical distance begin to permeate the modal tradition.

To be sure, there are numerous changes in details from generation to generation, but the overall outline remains the same. Just as Lippius had proclaimed two types of modes in 1610, each with three possible finals, so Janowka, Heinichen, and Mattheson between 1701 and 1713 presented two types of modes, each with twelve possible finals. The increasing number of keys with accidentals in the signature found in treatises of the late seventeenth century are anticipated by the free attitude toward transposition found as early as Zarlino. Already in 1605, Johann Kretzschmar, in a singing manual, had discussed transpositions by moving ut to the notes D, E, F, G, A, and B-flat, generating seven of the twelve possible transpositions of each mode, with key signatures up to two flats and four sharps. And in 1606, Giovanni Paolo Cima, outside Germany to be sure, had published a short piece written out to begin on all twelve notes in the chromatic octave.[1] So it is possible to trace back at least to the early years of the seventeenth century the two primary aspects of the twenty-four keys: the differentiation of modes based on the quality of the tonic triad, and the use of numerous transpositions. Indeed, from a long-range perspective, Mattheson's view of twenty-four keys is similar to Lippius's view of the modes. Both accepted the major-minor triad as the differentiating factor, but allowed scalar

[1]. Giovanni Paolo Cima (c.1570–c.1622), *Partito de ricercari & canzoni alla francese* (Milan, 1606), reprinted, edited by Clare G. Raynor (N.p.: American Institute of Musicology, 1969). See pp. 62–71 and 89 of the reprint.

alterations between different transpositions, either in the tuning differences or in actual scale content.

During this whole period, one can point also to numerous authors maintaining the essence of the modal system: the works of Magirus and Burmeister, which expand the function of the semitone in modal differentiation, the elementary manuals, and the composition treatises by Herbst, Bernhard, and Printz, among others. Even those seventeenth-century writers who did present a major-minor differentiation often tried to do so within the framework of the modal system: review Crüger's introduction of a thirteenth and fourteenth mode, and Werckmeister's insistence that knowledge of the modes is necessary even for those who only write and play in major and minor keys. The absence of newly published works based solely on the modes from the late 1680s through the early eighteenth century might be interpreted as a sign of their diminishing influence. But the virulence of the attacks engendered by Mattheson's *Orchestre* series—attacks by Buttstett, Fux, and Murschhauser, and even the questions raised by Kuhnau—indicates the persistence of the modal tradition. These musicians may not have published on the modes in the preceding two decades for much the same reason that Fux did not write about solmization: "I have never had any reason to doubt the usefulness of this invention, and have never thought to write about it."[2] And if the manuscript treatises of Kuhnau (1703) and Walther (1708) are taken into account, the apparent gap in the modal tradition between the works of Printz and Buttstett is illusory.

Although Mattheson's polemic may have helped to drive some defenders of the modes out of the public eye, Fux's counterpoint treatise and Walther's *Lexicon* appeared in 1725 and 1732, both emphasizing the traditional modes, and each deriving its modal viewpoint from a different tradition. Fux's *Gradus* stands in a line of Italian and Italian-influenced treatises going back through Bononcini and Bernhard—a tradition whose origins lie in Monteverdi's argument that the new monodic style is based on the structures of the *prima prattica*. Walther's *Lexicon* is yet another German work testifying to the importance of chorales and the modal theory that dealt with them. Walther's *Lexicon*, coupled with the continued use of the modes in church music, influenced many later eighteenth- century

---

[2] In Fux's letter of January 12, 1718 to Mattheson. See "The Fux-Mattheson Correspondence: An Annotated Translation," by this author in *Current Musicology* 24 (1977):51.

German writers to include some comments on the modes. It is not until the closing years of the eighteenth century that Türk, in 1789, felt compelled to explain the modes in terms of the major and minor keys, noting for instance that the chorale melody *Ein' feste Burg ist unser Gott* is in Ionian mode which is the same as a major scale. In addition to Türk, Adlung, Marpurg, and Kirnberger advocate continued knowledge of the modes as absolutely essential to church music.

The present study chronicles these two traditions of modes and major-minor keys during the seventeenth and eighteenth centuries. Two basic questions were asked of each treatise and theorist. What tenets were held by a given theorist? And what role to do those tenets play in the conceptual universe of that theorist and his times? Presenting such a chronicle has the obvious result of allowing future scholars of this period—whether of the music or of the theory—to place their subject of study within the historical frame of its generation.

In addition, by chronicling the attitudes of each generation of theorists, this study calls attention to the inadequacy of views, many of them commonly held, that arise from a progressive view of the history of theory. The progressive fallacy can lead to paradoxically contradictory results. It can lead historians both to isolate a tenet from a theorist's framework because that tenet seems to foreshadow future developments, while at the same time misinterpreting the implications of that very tenet because that tenet connotes different things to the generation under study and to the future generations that motivated the historian's interest in the first place. Consider recognition of Ionian and Aeolian modes by Glarean and Zarlino in the sixteenth century. Assuming that recognition of these modes is in some sense recognition of major and minor succumbs to the obvious error of ignoring the many arguments presented by these theorists for adding these modes and their plagals to the traditional eight. This assumption then compounds the error by considering Aeolian the model for the minor mode; throughout the seventeenth century, and well into the eighteenth century for some theorists, it was Dorian, not Aeolian that was the model for minor. To believe that Glarean added "major and minor" modes to the traditional eight requires a belief in an astounding prescience on Glarean's part—a prescience that leaps two centuries into the future, bypassing the consensus of generations of musicians, to a music and a theory Glarean could hardly have imagined.

A no less serious byproduct of the progressive fallacy is the desire of many historians to protect the theorists that they study from the charge that they are "behind their times." In order to demonstrate that a theorist is progressive, and, perhaps, even "ahead of his times," historians easily misinterpret the importance of that theorist as a reflection of important aspects of his own era. The larger trends of historical evolution, such as the eventual dominance of major and minor keys, arise in history only as abstractions of the contributions of individuals. In order to make such abstractions, we must decide that the mainstream is more important than any of the offshoots occurring along the way. There is nothing amiss with this assumption if we are only interested in the largest picture. But when we get down to the individual theorists and the concerns of an individual era, such large-scale perspectives do us little good. A supposedly conservative trait can be rationalized so as to protect the theorist from having been behind the times. But it can also be incorporated into the conceptual universe of that theorist or era, giving rise to new perspectives.

Consider the persistence of modal thinking in Germany well into the eighteenth century, alongside of major-minor thinking. Clearly, the duality of these traditions is one of the salient features of the musical-intellectual scene. One of the most impressive aspects of German music of the high Baroque is the wide range of harmonic resources and idioms—many of which arose from modal mannerisms. A J. S. Bach was equally at home in the world of modal chorales as he was in major and minor music. And voice leadings in many of his tonal pieces derive from a wider range of resources than those suggested merely by major and minor. The first half of the *Fugue in C minor* (*Well- Tempered Clavier*, I) offers several exemplary passages. See example 9-1.

Example 9-1. J. S. Bach, *Fugue in C minor (Well-Tempered Clavier,* **I)**

Think first of the brief episode that precedes the entry of the third voice. In a fugue in minor the fugal answer in the dominant is in minor. In measures 5–7 of this fugue, this minor dominant is transformed into a major dominant to prepare for the third subject entry in the tonic. Of the many possible ways of performing this task, this piece opts for a rising chromatic scale from G to B-natural as the structural basis of the episode in measures 5–6. See example 9-2. The rapid root progressions by fifth that support this rising line seem to be suggested more by various modal possibilities than by a direct dominant-to-tonic model. That is, the progression uses neither a single diatonic scale nor secondary dominants as its basis. Rather, Aeolian and Dorian forms of a C minor scale are suggested as A-flat and A- natural occur in sequence. Viewed from the perspective of each chord that is preceded by a chord built on its upper fifth, the sequence from C^{min} to F^{min} with D-natural in the scale suggests perhaps a Dorian F minor, the sequence from D^{min} to G^{min} suggests an Aeolian G minor, E-flat^{maj} to A-flat^{maj} with D natural in the scale suggests even a Lydian scale on A-flat. Only after this sequence does the more tonal II^7 to VII^6 to I lead into the tonic on measure 7.

Example 9-2

The next episode, measures 9–10, changes the local key from C minor to E-flat major, preparing for the subject entry in that key in measures 11–12. The progression that accomplishes the change of key is a series of descending root progressions by fifth: C^{min} to F^{min} to B-flat^{maj} to E-flat^{maj} to A- flat^{maj}. A-flat^{maj} then becomes IV in the key of E- flat. The progression is distinctly tonal in character. With typically Bachian ingenuity, the progression, along with the texture and motives, is simply reversed or inverted to return from E-flat major to C minor in measures 13–14. The descending scales in the bass in measures 9–10 become rising scales in the soprano in 13–14. The roots of the chords appear in reverse order: E-flat to B-flat to F to C. But the B-flat triad in measure 14 changes from major to minor, imparting a modal flavor caused by two factors. First, the change from major to minor makes the D-natural on the downbeat of measure 14 sound in retrospect like a Picardy-third at a minor cadence reverting to its natural form in the next phrase. Second, the B-flat major triad as subdominant leading to F minor imparts a Dorian flavor to the measure.

Such richness of harmonic resources persisted in German and Austrian music into the later eighteenth century as well. For one of the striking differences between the music that has continued to survive in concert repertoire from the eighteenth century to the present and that music that has not survived in the active repertoire is in fact the richness of the harmonic vocabulary and voice-leadings in the music we traditionally think of as the great works of that era. Might the persistence of a modal tradition in church music and in pedagogy have been a factor in stimulating the richness and variety of harmony in composers of the Viennese school? If this is indeed the case, then the persistence of modal thinking in German music should be regarded as one of the features leading toward the Viennese Classical style, not an archaism and a liability.

This very aspect of modal influence is addressed by Kirnberger's harmonization of the same chorale melody in major-minor keys and using the modes. Review example 8-2, on p.144. There is a striking contrast between his bland tonic-dominant-and-subdominant harmonization in the major-minor system and the richly varied harmonic language in his modal rendering. Kirnberger and many of his contemporaries often regarded the use of major-minor keys as implying simple tonic and dominant harmonizations.[3]

---

[3] There were also theorists and composers who were unsympathetic to such modal harmonic resources. One of the most curious documents reflecting this attitude is the *Zwölf Choräle von Sebastian Bach, umgearbeitet von [Abbé] Vogler, zergliedert von Carl Maria von Weber* (Leipzig: C. F. Peters, [c. 1810]). Vogler prints a dozen J. S. Bach chorales and his own reharmonizations side by side, with annotations by the young Carl Maria von Weber explaining why each of Vogler's versions is better than Bach's. Although many of Vogler's emendations simply eliminate groups of dissonant nonharmonic tones, in quite a few passages Vogler made changes in order to produce simple tonal harmonies where Bach had used complex voice-leadings with modal implications.

With such a perspective, the entire focus of many concerns changes. As a single example, consider Walther's discussion of tonal resources. One might view Walther's retention of modal theory in 1732 as an anachronism. But from the perspective being argued here, there is no need to protect Walther from the charge of being behind his times. It may well be that his presentation of the modes, as a reflection of his understanding of the music of his time, was more important to the evolution of the Classical style than the remarks of those theorists who only saw in modal theory a useless remnant of the ancient past.

Indeed, given Walther's personal commitment to modal theory, and the fact that such interest in the modes was not at all anomalous in the 1730s in Germany, what is perhaps most significant is not the presence of modality, but rather that Walther thought it necessary to include a summary of major-minor key theory—a theory which he did not fully understand, and certainly did not fully support. Was it only out of fear that Mattheson might lay down the gauntlet for him too that his *Lexicon* included the twenty-four keys at all?

If the *C-minor Fugue*, usually considered a piece entirely within the major and minor keys, includes a range of harmonic resources that might be profitably thought of as enriched by modal voice-leading habits, many other J. S. Bach compositions contain music whose modality raises entirely separate theoretical issues. Perhaps the most important among these issues concerns the basis of our assumptions about harmonic directionality in this music. Whether they analyze Bach compositions according to a traditional-harmony approach, or according to Schenkerian ideas, I believe that virtually all analysts assume that certain harmonies inherently represent goals and that other harmonies inherently represent varying states of motion leading toward those goals. A dominant-tonic succession, for instance, is a motion from a relatively mobile chord to a resolution of that mobility (however temporary or incomplete the individual circumstances may make that resolution).

But on what grounds can we consider these harmonic-directional norms to be universal in Bach's music when he also writes various modal voice-leadings and harmonic successions that seem to deny this directionality. I refer not only to those obviously modal chorale harmonizations whose harmonic successions stubbornly resist major-minor interpretations, such as one of Bach's settings of *Herr Gott, dich loben wir* (example 9-3). For these harmonizations are difficult not because they use fifth-progressions in problematic ways, but because they lack root-progressions by descending fifths and because they contain many successive step-related root-position triads.

Example 9–3. J. S. Bach *Herr Gott, dich loben wir (Gesamtausgabe, vol. 39, no. 75)*

Even more problematic are those Phrygian chorale harmonizations that seem to be in minor keys, but whose structure seems to be framed not by the minor tonic triad but by the dominant. Example 9-4 offers the opening two phrases and the conclusion of two Bach harmonizations of *Ach Gott vom Himmel sieh' darein.*

Example 9–4. J. S. Bach *Ach Gott, vom Himmel sieh' darein (Cantata 153).*

Example 9-4 (cont.)

(*Cantata 2*)

In this chorale, whose melody is Phrygian (a view supported by Walther; see p. 216), Bach's harmonizations seem at first to begin on the dominant chord of a minor key. The first two phrases appear to rhyme harmonically, with open and closed cadences. But Bach concludes the final cadence of the melody on the apparent dominant of the key. Perhaps instead of thinking of the opening harmony as a dominant, he conceived of the opening and concluding harmonies as being the conclusive chords in the Phrygian mode. After all, many theorists had regarded the cadence on the fourth degree of the Phrygian scale as a final cadence (see pp. 64-65). Are the norms of harmonic directionality leading from dominant to tonic reversed here? That is, does the "minor tonic" chord drive toward the "major dominant" rather than the other way around? The question is inescapable here, for these chorales are the presumably conclusive finales of multi-movement cantatas, not internal movements followed by other music. Hence an explanation of the concluding Phrygian cadences as internal cadences (such as the Phrygian cadence that ends the middle movement of the *Brandenburg Concerto No. 3*) is not operable here. After all, Johann Gottfried Walther, following many other authors, explicitly differentiates the half cadence (which he calls *Clausula dissecta*) from the final cadences in Phrygian mode (see footnote on p. 219 in Appendix 4).[4]

Interpreting the issue of harmonic directionality pertains not only to the final cadence, but to the first two phrases as well. For if the "dominant" is the conclusive chord, are we to understand the very opening succession as the reverse of what we normally mean by dominant-to-tonic? In other words, are the two opening phrases best analyzed as open-ended to close-ended or the reverse?

I am aware of only a single eighteenth-century discussion of these issues of harmonic directionality in modal music. It occurs in a survey of the modes by the harmonically-oriented theorist Georg Andreas Sorge (1703 -1778) in his *Anleitung zur Fantasie* (Lobenstein, [1767][5]). Sorge, like most of his contemporaries, begins his brief discussion of modes by articulating a sense of historical distance from a living tradition:

> The modes are for the most part quite unnatural and affected. Yet it is good if an organist knows them.[6]

Similarly, he closes his discussion with the following, after expressing surprise that anyone could have ever thought of writing a piece in the A-mode without using g-sharp.

> The old teaching of the modes only concerns the melody and not the harmony necessary to it. Our good ancestors composed melodies without questioning the harmony from which the melody must arise. That is correctly called missing the point.[7] If it happened that those tones [accidentals] which the key required according to the law of nature could be introduced in the middle voices, it was good, and they [the composers] were satisfied if only the melody could remain within their paltry limits [set for the modal scale]. In addition, they often took the freedom to sing, for example, f-sharp, g-sharp, or c-sharp instead

[4] Note that from a Phrygian perspective the key signatures of both chorales are correct. (Phrygian transposed up and down by a fifth).

[5] The date appears only in the dedication.

[6] P. 42. "Sie sind meistentheils sehr unnäturlich und gezwungen. Jedoch ist gut, wenn sie ein Organist kennet."

[7] Sorge probably intends here not to join the common eighteenth-century debate over whether harmony or melody has priority, but rather to note that a melody note must be thought of along with its harmony. The melody g-a for him simply makes no sense at a cadence in the key of A minor because a dominant-to-tonic cadence requires g-sharp.

of f, g, and c, without having the sharps attached to the notes. Nature was so strong that it made them follow its law without having specified it.[8]

Between these passages, Sorge does not offer the usual explanation of octave species, ambitus and the like. Instead he explains how several modes relate to modern practices:

> Phrygian is no other key than our A minor, only with this difference, that the dominant chord e g-sharp h begins and ends, as the chorale *Ach GOtt vom Himmel sieh darein* illustrates. Nowadays we can still use this mannerism of beginning and ending with the dominant chord, especially in those pieces in which a concerto, symphony, or sonata does not fully conclude, as happens with the Andante. This type of ending awakens a desire to hear something additional.[9]

It would quite be helpful to us if such a discussion concerning harmonic directionality in modal music could be located in the works of earlier theorists closer to composers who were actually continuing to write music that retains significant modal aspects. But we should not expect to find such an explicit discussion much earlier than this. An adequate vocabulary for discussing this issue does not appear outside the works of Rameau and those influenced by him (either directly or indirectly; Sorge is clearly one of the latter). Earlier theorists who discussed various aspects of modality were largely silent on the issue of harmonic directionality (Werckmeister, Fux, Buttstett, etc.) and never applied this issue to harmony in modal

---

[8] P. 43. "Die alte Moden-Lehre gehet also nur auf die Melodie, nicht aber auf die darzu nöthige Harmonie. Die guten Alten machten Melodien, ohne die Harmonie, aus welcher die Melodie entspringen muss, darum zu fragen. Das hiess recht: Rechnung machen ohne Wirth. Traf es nun so zu, dass diejenigen Töne, welche die Tonart nach dem Gesetz der Natur erforderte, in denen Mittelstimmen konnten angebracht werden, so war es gut, und sie waren zufrieden, wenn nur die Melodie in ihren armseligen Schranken bleiben konnte. Dabey aber nahmen sie sich oft die Freyheit, z.B. fs gs cs an statt f g c zu singen, ohne dass sie Creuze oder Erhöhungs-Zeichen vor die Noten fassten. So stark war die Natur, dass sie nach ihrem Gesetze thaten, ohne es vorgeschrieben zu haben."

[9] P. 42. "Der Phrygius ist keine andere Tonart als unser A moll, nur mit dem Unterschied, dass der herrschende Accord e gs h anfänget und endiget, wie der Choral: Ach GOtt vom Himmel sieh darein, herzeuget. Wir können diese Art, mit dem herrschenden Accorde anzufangen und zu endigen, noch heutiges Tages gebrauchen, sonderlich in denen Stücken, mit welchen ein Concert, Sinfonie oder Sonate nicht völlig geendiget wird, wie mit dem Andante geschiehet. Diese Art zu schliessen erwecket ein Verlangen ein mehrers zu hören."

pieces or passages. And those theorists who were interested in these harmonic questions did not apply this perspective to any discussions of the modes. Rameau and the French and English contemporaries who soon adopted his ideas were not interested in modality. And German theorists did not begin to fully adopt his perspective until after the mid-century. As a result, our attitudes toward these issues cannot rely on contemporaneous perspectives.

To be sure, a full exploration of these issues far exceeds the scope of the present study. Having established the existence of a modal tradition, what is needed now is a complementary study of seventeenth and early eighteenth-century theories of harmonic progression—not as imperfect anticipations of Rameau's theories or any other eighteenth-century approaches, but as complete perspectives in their own right. Armed with modal and harmonic approaches in agreement with contemporaneous thought, we will then be able to explore the musical repertoires of that era not only as steps on the way to tonality, but also as unified creations in their own right.

Translations of Articles from *Clavis ad thesaurum magnae artis* (Prague, 1701) by Thomas Balthasar Janowka

The following selections contain all the material on modes and keys relevant to the present study. These include the articles on Song (*Cantus,* pp. 7–10), discussing mode in sacred music, and Tone (*Tonus,* pp. 287–304), discussing key in secular music. Two additional articles follow on subjects formerly associated closely with modal theory, but here treated independently: *Ambitus* (p. 3) and Cadence (*Cadentia,* pp. 5–6). Finally, portions of the articles on Notes (*Claves,* pp. 17–20) and Accidentals (*Chromatica signa,* or *Diaeses chromaticae,* pp. 12–15) appear, indicating Janowka's relatively modern attitude toward several aspects of notation. Parts of these articles restate material already in the article on Tone. Various other passages are treated in footnotes to explain the particular meaning of a given term.

Musical examples are transcribed according to the original with all substantive additions (mostly corrective accidentals) in brackets. Minor changes, such as the addition of a missing bar line, or the correction of an obviously incorrect pitch, have been made without comment. All footnotes are by the translator.

Song (*Cantus*)

Song is used in a two-fold manner in the Catholic Church. There is, first, ecclesiastical song, otherwise known as plain chant; secondly, figured song. The first kind is not improperly called monophonic for the reason that all singers sing the same song together in unison at the same intervals. The second kind is called polyphonic for the reason that it is sung by more than one voice. Those who established monophonic music were St. Ambrose and Pope Gregory the Great, after whom it has been called Gregorian continuously up to today. The first kind of song is also called monastic from the fact that it was sung by monks, and *chorale* from the fact that it was sung by a chorus. And it is two-fold, namely *dur* and *moll*. They call it *dur* when the voice has to sing on the note B natural, which is called *dur* among them. They call it *moll* if B flat is to be sung on the note *fa moll*.

According to this division of this song, they also establish a two-fold scale, namely *dur* and *moll*. Moreover in this plain-song there are held to be primarily eight tones or modes, by which all songs are governed. They call the first Dorian, the second Hypodorian, the third Phrygian, the fourth Hypophrygian, the fifth Lydian, the sixth Hypolydian, the seventh Mixolydian, and the eighth Hypomixolydian. And these modes are defined as different dispositions in all manners of voices, whether in their seriousness or in their brightness. These names are obtained from the nations which were attracted to different modes. The notes of these modes, from which they begin and in which they end everywhere nowadays, are the following: No. 1, D; No. 2, G; No. 3, A; No. 4, E; No. 5, C; No. 6, F; No. 7, D; No. 8, G. See the *Ars magna consoni & dissoni* by Johann Speth,[1] and others; with whom Franciscus Murschhauser does not agree with regard to the eighth, he putting it with a minor third in his *Octitonis organico*.[2] The first four modes are in *re mi fa*, or with a minor third (a semiditone). The latter four are in *ut re mi*, or with a major third (a ditone). And according to this variety, the first tone differs from the seventh, and the second from the eighth.

The characteristics of these modes have been attributed to them from antiquity; the first wanders morosely and worriedly. The second proceeds by a harsh seriousness. The third proceeds by a strong protest of indignation. The fourth would have the form of

---

[1]Johann Speth (1664–after 1719), *Ars magna consoni et dissoni...auf die acht Chor-oder Choral-Thon eingericht...* (Augsburg, 1693). Ten toccatas from this organ collection (which, according to Walther's *Lexicon*, is a compilation of compositions by several composers) are reprinted as volume 9 of *Liber organi: Suddeutsche Orgelmeister Johann Speth*, edited Gregor Klaus (Mainz: B. Schotts Söhne, 1954).

[2]In fact, the *Oct-tonium novum organicum, octo tonis ecclesiasticis, ad psalmos & magnificat* (Augsburg, 1696) by Franz Xaver Anton Murschhauser (1663–1738) agrees with Janowka with regard to the eighth mode. It is the seventh mode that differs, Murschhauser setting it with a flat in the signature and a final on D, following the older ordering of the church keys. See *Gesammelte Werke für Klavier & Orgel: Krieger und Murschhauser*, edited Max Seiffert (Leipzig, 1917), pp. 75–118.

adulation. The fifth would contain moderate wantonness. The sixth would sound a mournful elegance. The seventh would proceed by almost hostile leaps. The eighth would have a proper and almost matronly tone.

Song of figural or polyphonic music is defined as the art of singing and playing of musical degrees and proportions according to specific measurements; thus the types of song are named from the variety of musical figures or notes and the variety of musical characters.

Moreover, song of figural music is three-fold, namely: natural, *moll*, and *dur*. Natural or diatonic occurs when the music proceeds through the seven diatonic notes *a b c d e f g*, which is inferred if neither flats nor sharps are placed at the opening of any song at the beginning of the staff after the clef. The song is said to be *moll* when the five chromatic notes, or only some of them, are to be taken as flatted; and this is observed from one or several flats placed at the opening of the song, always after the clef on the staff. The song is named *dur* when the five chromatic notes (*b-flat c-sharp d-sharp f-sharp* and *g-sharp*), or only some of them, are to be taken as sharped while singing, which is indicated by one or more sharps placed at the opening of the song after the clef. This matter can be better understood in the article on notes [*claves*]. Let the student of music observe the following examples of this doctrine. See example A1-1.

Example A1-1

Natural Song

Moll Song

Dur Song

Tone (*Tonus*)

Tone generically means any sound; in particular it is sometimes taken for a musical interval, and sometimes for a specific rule of composition...

Tone as a rule of song is defined and differentiated one way in chant, and another way in our figural music. The manner in which it is differentiated in chant is examined under the term song [*cantus*]. Tone of figural music (which is the subject matter of this section) also ought to be defined and differentiated. As observed today, it is defined as the agreement of the sixths and sevenths from any note contained in the octave with the quality of the semiditone [minor third] or the ditone [major third] from that same note. From this definition it is evident that tone is of two types, no matter whether some speak of eight, twelve, or fourteen tones in chant or than in figural music, or whether some speak about them according to the progression of diatonic fifths and fourths as in the case of twelve or fourteen modes. Thus, these two types are truly referred to as the minor tone (or of the minor third), and the major tone (or of the major third). For all compositions should have either a minor or a major third above any chosen base or final note (whether this final is chosen as a natural or chromatic note, and whether it is called *a* or *b-flat*, etc.), and according to this choice, the major or minor sixths and sevenths *generally* enter into this song. I say *generally*, and not *absolutely*, for it occasionally happens that the selection of the third and of the sixth and seventh does not agree regarding their being major or minor.

Hence, in the first place, in cadences, even though the song is of the minor tone, and the third is the same, at the end of the song it is most frequent that the third be major, as seen in example A1-2. Secondly, in response to the needs of the text or another valid reason, the tone was often mixed; consequently the sixths or sevenths change from major to minor, or vice versa, as in example A1-3, in which the major seventh to *g*, which is *f-sharp*, changes to the minor seventh, *f*, at the sign NB.

Example A1-2

166

Example A1-3

Both the minor and major tone, according to its base (*basis*), or the note from which it begins and in which it ends, are twelve-fold; for that is how many notes are found in the octave taken in its entirety—which is clearly demonstrated in the twenty-four examples placed below.

Objections which could be raised against this I remove to another time.

Thus observe FIRST, that having chosen the minor third, the sixths and sevenths should regularly or preferably be minor, just as to the contrary having chosen the major third, the sixths and sevenths should be major, always keeping in both tones, whether major or minor, the major second, the minor [perfect] fourth, and the consonant [perfect] fifth. E.g., the base or final note *a* with the minor third *c* is selected in order to arrange a song; then regularly and preferably you should add or play in thorough-bass the minor sixth and seventh, namely *f* and *g*, with the major second, namely *b*, the minor fourth, namely *d*, and the consonant fifth, namely *e*, added. See number 1 among the twenty-four examples set down below. And if you wish to compose this song with the major third, namely *c-sharp*, the major sixth and seventh, namely *f-sharp* and *g-sharp*, also ought to be chiefly used; the second is once again major, namely *b*, the fourth minor, namely *d*, with the consonant fifth, which is *e*. And this is shown as number 2 among the examples.

You will find this observation already in compositions of the most recent composers; unless it is observed that the work is deficiently notated, as happens in songs which begin from the note *d* of the minor tone, and end in the same, if they do not have the minor sixth, namely *b-flat*, placed at the beginning of the staff. The same should be understood for the same reason of a song in *g* of the minor tone, if in the position of the note *e* the flat sign is not affixed. For this minor tone, in both types of song presented, essentially requires the minor sixth and seventh. One can sometimes take a specific note of a tone other than that in which you begin—and during a song in these two examples it may be necessary to place the major sixth *b-natural* in the first, or *e-natural* in the second by reason of mixing. Yet it is preferable that this *b-natural*, used less often and less commonly, be indicated by the natural sign placed before the similar note (*b-flat*), rather than not placing the flat sign at the beginning of the staff at the sixth, in which case you must write the flat everywhere during the song. For if you make an exception to the rule, or if you do that which should be in the place of the rule as an exception contrary to the principles of all art, you will express by many symbols that which can be expressed by few. For the sake of brevity, let there be only a few examples to show this; in longer examples, however, this would be clearer. See example A1-4.

Example A1-4

In this example the flat signs are placed here and there throughout the song, which is poor:

In this example the flat is placed at the beginning of the staff for the sixth [of the key], which is best:

The same, but in the opposite sense, or vice versa, ought to be understood of the major sixth and seventh.

Observe SECOND that what is said here in the definition of the sixth and seventh within the octave should also be understood in the double or higher octave, and so on successively. For all octaves have the same arrangement—so that what is asserted concerning one should consequently be understood concerning the second, the third, etc. For that reason it was decided only to give examples below which are within one octave, whether for all twelve tones, both natural and chromatic, or for joined notes[3] in both genera of music (namely the pure diatonic and the shared diatonic). Review here what is said in the article on the pure and shared diatonic genera of music,[4] and then proceed to the following observation.

Observe THIRD that tone thus considered differs from the genera of music in four ways: Firstly, as the director from the directed. For in order that genus be correctly established by the octave (the same of the higher octave, etc.) a work has a rule of tone. Secondly, whereas genus primarily concerns whether the notes are diatonic or chromatic, tone is considered primarily by whether the notes are major or minor. Thirdly, that the genus of music can vary while the tone remains the same, namely major or minor. This is seen here in the appended examples in *g- sharp* and *d-sharp*. And that this distinction be more clearly elucidated, it has produced here the third observation. Fourthly, that genus concerns immediately the orthographical position, while tone can be recognized in the abstract. Whence in a musical work of more than one voice a musical virtuoso recognizes from the first chord whether it is a major or minor tone, even if he is ignorant of the base note, that it, whether it is *e* or *d*.

Observe FOURTH that often care should be taken in the positioning of a song or prelude or any other musical work as to whether it should be composed with flat notes or with sharp notes (that is, in the joining of these chromatic notes to diatonic ones). For

---

[3]Concerning *joined notes*, see the article on notes (*claves*), pp. 174-75 below.

[4]The relevant portions of the article *Genus musicae* are: "Today's genus can be shown to be duple according to the duple consideration of notes in use: either pure diatonic or mixed and shared diatonic. It is said to be pure diatonic when it proceeds *chiefly* by diatonic notes, and this happens twice in music, namely if the composition is composed in *a* minor or *c* major... Genus is said to be mixed or shared which is composed from diatonic as well as chromatic notes, and according to the plurality of the former or the latter it can be properly called diatonic-chromatic or chromatic-diatonic. It is the first if diatonic notes prevail, the second if chromatic notes prevail in any song."

if by the placement of these chromatic notes natural and diatonic notes can be left in their places, the song ought to be fashioned with these diatonic notes. Whence of the following two examples the second is most rarely in use. Granted it is permitted so long as the sound is considered in the abstract, or even so long as the keys on the keyboard, accepted by their common names, are deemed of equal status. Nevertheless, as far as the position of the chromatic keys is concerned, the flats ought to be selected and preferred to the sharps. Consequently the flat-diatonic- chromatic genus ought to be used, as you see in the example A1-5.

Example A1-5

g♯ b♭ c c♯ d♯ f g g♯

g♯ b♭ c c♯ d♯ f g g♯

There you see the note names in both examples written in the same manner, according to the common acceptance of the keys on the keyboard. For if the tones are considered with the genera of music, and if the nature of the keys on the keyboard and of the song ought to be expressed by *dur* and *moll*, thus the note names of both these examples should be criticized. However, the main reason why the first example is preferred to the second is that in the first, three natural notes, namely *c*, *f*, and *g*, are found, while in the second there is found no note which keeps its own natural name taken from the property of its position on the staff. To be sure, it is admitted that on the keyboard the notes *c* and *f* appear in the second example, yet here they are not in the position of *c* and *f* (called natural), but are placed in the position of lower keys, namely *b-sharp* and *e-sharp*, not *c* and *f*. For the first (*c*) is joined to the note *b*, and the second (*f*) is joined to the note *e*. The reader should take note of this.

Similarly, care should be taken that where you have used notes with flats you do not presume to use sharps in one and the same song by changing their positions. Certain composers are in the habit of doing this in order to annoy others, contrary to the primary and in every way naturally clear principles of art, more in violation of skillful composition than in its achievement. See example A1-6.

Example A1-6

I said in observation four that if several accidentals happen together, those are to be chosen by which the largest number of natural keys can remain in their place. If the arrangement were equal by the placing of either type of accidental when you added sharps or flats, and an equal number of fundamental or natural notes remained, what is the reason for placing the composition in sharps or flats? In this case you have a choice, and this happens in two tones, namely in *d-sharp* with the minor third and *f-sharp* with the major third. The former, as a rule, is preferably placed in flats, the latter in sharps. See example A1- 7.

Example A1-7

[Only the example of D♯-minor vs. E♭-minor is shown.]

Observe FIFTH that the organization [of the notes in each key] is the same whether the voice [or melody] proceeds by tone or semitone, as I have done in the twenty-four examples, or if the voice proceeds by skips, for example, by thirds, fourths, fifths, etc. Any organization by single steps is the same as organization by thirds, etc., unless a tritone or some other faulty progression prohibits it.[5] Whence in the following examples I placed the progression only of tones and semitones. And for the ease of every reader I have indicated in the examples by white noteheads those notes which move from one to another by whole steps, and by black noteheads those which move by semitone.

Observe SIXTH that in the following examples I did not duplicate the sharps and flats at the beginning of the staff in octaves. They are sufficient in one place in order that the gaze of the eyes may not be uselessly frightened by their number and by the multiplied necessity of seeing them—for all octaves have the same arrangement.[6] And thus let these be examples of both types of tone, namely minor and minor, for all twelve notes contained within the octave. See example A1-8.

Example A1-8

The minor tone from A of the pure diatonic genus:

The major tone from A of the sharp-diatonic-chromatic genus:

[And so forth through all keys in ascending chromatic order.]

And if you ask which of these tones, considered with their lowest notes, are most usable in music, the answer is those tones which are of the pure diatonic genus, or the diatonic-chromatic. And according to this, twelve or fourteen tones are usually chosen. The remaining chromatic-diatonic are rare, and usually have their place only among organists in preludes, or if in responding to a priest who is singing in chromatic notes they are compelled to play in the same. This would happen before the Agnus dei in the mass, and after the Magnificat between Commemorations in Vespers.

---

[5]That is, instead of conjunct scales, Janowka could have written out the notes of each key in sequences of thirds, fourths, and so forth.
[6]Note that Janowka does not always follow his own advice in this matter. See the G major example in example A1-1.

With respect to these examples, I ask most politely those devoted to the syllables *Ut Re Mi*, etc., and consequently the defenders of the ancient French scale, whether that scale is sufficient for distinguishing all these tones? It will be if in *A la mi re* (for example) it will keep all the syllables (that is, *la mi re*) and if it will not take notes from other scales, not to mention chromatic notes, of which their scale makes no mention. My scale will certainly always render to each key its own in whatever tone. Cadences in these tones are made on the consonances considered and then used from the first or final note of the song. Thus in the first, it cadences on *d, a, f* and *b-flat*, and the fourth, namely *g*.

Ambitus

Ambitus in music is said to be the compass or circumference and the limit of any human voice or of instrumental sound. It is assigned to the former by nature, and to the latter by the agreement of musicians.

Cadence (*Cadentia*)

Cadence is an ending of one or more voices, which happens in three ways according to the bass or lowest note. Either firstly, the bass proceeds to the lower second, either to the whole tone or to the semitone. The antepenultimate note of the close [*clausula*] commonly used in this cadence is the seventh; the penultimate, the major sixth; and the last the octave–see example A1-9.

Example A1-9

To the tone.   To the semitone.

Or secondly, the bass proceeds to the lower fourth. The antepenultimate notes of the close commonly used in this cadence are, in different voices, the fifth and third; the penultimates, the major sixth and major [augmented] fourth; and the last the tenth and octave—see example A1-10.

Example A1-10

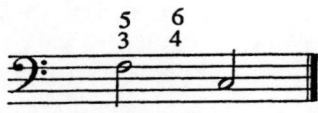

To the lower fourth.

Or thirdly, the bass proceeds to the lower fifth or hypodiapente, in which closes the antepenultimate notes commonly used in different voices are the minor [perfect] fifth and fourth, or the major or minor sixth and the minor [perfect] fourth, the penultimates are the fifth and major third, and last the octaves—see example A1-11.

Example A1-11

To the fifth:

major   minor
sixth   sixth

Notes (*Claves*)

Musical notes are letters from the alphabet, or constructions from them, and thus are defined: they are letters of the alphabet and constructions from them, belonging to an interval or space of a line or lines, indicating the height or depth of the human voice or of instrumental sounds...

Moreover these notes are of two kinds: some of them are called diatonic, others chromatic. The diatonic are those which are called natural, fundamental, and essential. They are seven, namely *a b c d e f g,* and they have their own position on the line or in the spaces as the example demonstrates. See example A1-12.

Example A1-12

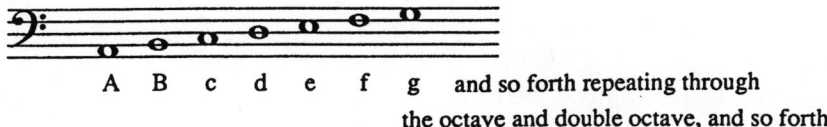

A B c d e f g and so forth repeating through
the octave and double octave, and so forth

The five remaining notes are said to be chromatic, namely *b- flat c-sharp d-sharp f-sharp* and *g-sharp,* and agree with the latter part of the definition: NB, "or constructions from them (that is, from the letters)." These five chromatic notes are sometimes called *moll,* and sometimes *dur,* according to the diversity of the chromatic signs ♭ and ♯ .

These five notes are also called joined, since they do not have their own place and location on the staff, but are joined to the first seven with regard to their positions; as will be evident to one considering them from which position they derive their different names. For example, if the ♯ is placed in the second space in the bass clef, then that note will be called *a- sharp.* If on the second line of the same bass clef a flat is placed before the note, then the same key sounds on the keyboard on the organ, yet it is called *b-flat* and not *a- sharp* from the other representation of the note, in order to explain the flat note according to the place it has on the staff. The same is to be understood of *c-sharp, d-sharp,* etc. See example A1-13.

Example A1-13

b♭ d♭ e♭ g♭ a♭

a♯ c♯ d♯ f♯ g♯

Accidentals (*Chromatica signa*)

Accidentals are those signs by which chromatic notes are indicated; and they are two: the flat and the sharp... Yet sometimes these two chromatic signs, ♭ and ♯, also denote the diatonic notes; but then those notes are placed under another name and in a position other than that which they have elsewhere as diatonic notes. Thus if a sharp is placed before the note *e,* or before a number or in place of the number itself, connoting the same, then indeed *f* should be struck on the keyboard; yet it will not be called *f,* but *e-sharp.* (All this is to be seen in the example below.) The same is properly understood of *b-sharp,* which sounds the same as *c,* and is to be seen in the example. The same also holds when other diatonic keys are struck in the place of chromatic ones: as when *g* should be touched in place of *f-doublesharp* (as you see in the third example). This happens in a song with sharps already notated at the beginning of the staff for specific notes: let a sharp be placed before the same notes right next to the note or number itself, and thus it is not called *g,* but *f-doublesharp* in order to make a better distinction and explanation of the song. The same is said of flats. It has been decided to add examples.

Example A1-14

The greatest attention should be given to this or similar matters in playing: namely whether such a sharp or flat is placed superfluously, as copyists occasionally do, or whether such a sharp or flat is necessary and of substance. This ought to be inferred from the passage or from the composition. Certain people place sharps before the note or number in order to remove all doubt from the mind of the player. Whether or not this is necessary, let the excellent reader judge.[7]

---

[7]Janowka does not use the double sharp, either in pitch names or pitch notation. On the staff, he assumes that a sharp added to a note already sharped in the signature raises the note another half step. Thus the use of a sharp before F in the third part of example A1-14. In the text, this pitch is referred to as *fis* (*f-sharp*), not *fisis* (*f-doublesharp*), the latter notation being alien to him.

Mattheson's Tuning System

Mattheson, in his *Exemplarischen Organisten-Probe im Artikel vom General-Bass* (Hamburg, 1719), discusses the various tunings of intervals on pages 52-112. He recommends a tuning of the chromatic octave in which the tonic, subdominant, and dominant chords in C, E, and G majors are tuned to pure thirds and pure fifths. The sole remaining pitch in the chromatic octave is B-flat, tuned to a major third below D. This system gives rise to four sizes of semitones:

15:16—the major semitone

24:25—the minor semitone

Together, the major semitone and minor semitone add up to a minor tone (9:10)

25:27—the major limma, the difference between the minor semitone and the major tone

128:135—the minor limma, the difference between the major semitone and the major tone

and to four sizes of whole tones:

8:9—the major tone

9:10—the minor tone

Together, the major tone and minor tone equal the major third (4:5)

225:226—the major tone plus the diaschismate (2025:2048), which arises from the addition of two major semitones

125:144—the major tone plus the diesis (1125:1152), which arises from the addition of the major semitone and the major limma.

Table A2-1 (opposite) presents a chromatic octave, with the pitches represented by string lengths. The placement of the different sizes of half tones and whole tones are noted. In table A2-2, the step progressions in each major key are presented, as shown by Mattheson on pages 57-59. Table A2-3 shows the tunings of all diatonic intervals over the tonic in all the major keys, as shown by Mattheson on page 60.

Table A2-1. Mattheson's Tuning of the Chromatic Scale

String length:	3600	3456	3200	3072	2880	2700	2560	2400	2304	2160	2000	1920	1800	1728
Pitch:	C	C#	D	D#	E	F	F#	G	G#	A	A#	B	c	c#

Semitone relationship:

C–C#	C#–D	D–D#	D#–E	E–F	F–F#	F#–G	G–G#	G#–A	A–A#	A#–B	B–c	c–c#
$\frac{24}{25}$	$\frac{25}{27}$	$\frac{24}{25}$	$\frac{15}{16}$	$\frac{15}{16}$	$\frac{128}{135}$	$\frac{15}{16}$	$\frac{24}{25}$	$\frac{15}{16}$	$\frac{25}{27}$	$\frac{24}{25}$	$\frac{15}{16}$	$\frac{15}{16}$

Whole-tone relationship:

$\frac{8}{9}$, $\frac{9}{10}$, $\frac{9}{10}$, $\frac{8}{9}$, $\frac{8}{9}$, $\frac{9}{10}$, $\frac{125}{144}$, $\frac{9}{10}$, $\frac{9}{10}$

$\frac{8}{9}$, $\frac{225}{256}$, $\frac{8}{9}$, $\frac{9}{10}$, $\frac{8}{9}$, $\frac{9}{10}$

According to tables A2-2 and A2-3, the structures of C and E majors, and of F and A majors, are identical. Mattheson then presents examples of all the major keys with various chromatic pitches added in order to show that even these keys have different structures.

Table A2-2. Tunings of Each Major Scale in Mattheson's System

Scale degrees:	1-2	2-3	3-4	4-5	5-6	6-7	7-8
Key:							
C major	8:9	9:10	15:16	8:9	9:10	8:9	15:16
C# major	8:9	225:256	128:135	9:10	125:144	9:10	24:25
D major	9:10	8:9	15:16	9:10	8:9	9:10	25:27
Eb major	225:256	8:9	24:25	125:144	9:10	8:9	24:25
E major	8:9	9:10	15:16	8:9	9:10	8:9	15:16
F major	8:9	9:10	25:27	9:10	8:9	9:10	15:16
F# major	9:10	125:144	24:25	9:10	8:9	225:256	128:135
G major	9:10	8:9	15:16	8:9	9:10	8:9	15:16
Ab major	9:10	125:144	24:25	8:9	225:256	8:9	24:25
A major	8:9	9:10	25:27	9:10	8:9	9:10	15:16
Bb major	9:10	8:9	24:25	225:256	8:9	9:10	25:27
B major	9:10	8:9	15:16	8:9	9:10	125:144	24:25

Table A2-3. Tunings of Intervals Over the Tonic in Each Major Scale in Mattheson's System

Scale degrees	1-2	1-3	1-4	1-5	1-6	1-7	1-8
Key							
C major	8:9	4:5	3:4	2:3	3:5	8:15	1:2
C# major	8:9	25:32	20:27	2:3	125:216	25:48	1:2
D major	9:10	4:5	3:4	27:40	3:5	27:50	1:2
Eb major	225:256	25:32	3:4	125:192	75:128	25:48	1:2
E major	8:9	4:5	3:4	2:3	3:5	8:15	1:2
F major	8:9	4:5	20:27	2:3	16:27	8:15	1:2
F# major	9:10	25:32	3:4	27:40	3:5	135:256	1:2
G major	9:10	4:5	3:4	2:3	3:5	8:15	1:2
Ab major	125:144	25:32	3:4	2:3	75:128	25:48	1:2
A major	8:9	4:5	20:27	2:3	16:27	8:15	1:2
Bb major	9:10	4:5	96:125	27:40	3:5	27:50	1:2
B major	9:10	4:5	3:4	2:3	3:5	25:48	1:2

Translations from Johann Joseph Fux's
Gradus ad parnassum

Fux's *Gradus ad parnassum* (Vienna, 1725; 279 pages in folio)[1] has been used as a counterpoint treatise by numerous musicians since its appearance. Large portions of *Gradus* appear in English translation by Alfred Mann in two works: *Steps to Parnassus; The Study of Counterpoint* (New York: Norton, 1943) and *The Study of Fugue* (New York: Norton, 1965). But the treatise contains sections other than counterpoint instruction. The entire work is organized as follows. Asterisks indicate portions translated here.

Book I (pp. 1–42) contains twenty-three chapters on music, notes, the mathematical operations involved in generating intervals, the generation of intervals, and tuning. The last chapter, "Concerning the System of Today's Music" (pp. 36– 42), includes a discussion of consonances and dissonances, types of voice leading, and the rules of interval progression. Alfred Mann translates a portion of this final chapter in *Steps to Parnassus*, pp. 20–22. The remainder of Book I is not translated into English.

Book II (pp. 43–279) is entitled The Dialogue.

The preparatory discussion covers pp. 43–45 (*Steps to Parnassus*, pp. 19–20, 22–23).

Species counterpoint with a cantus firmus covers pp. 45–139 (*Steps to Parnassus*, pp. 25–139).

*A brief discussion covers resolutions of suspensions in the absence of a cantus firmus (pp. 139–140).

---

[1]Facsimile edition (New York: Broude, 1966).

Imitation and fugue covers pp. 140–217 (*Study of Fugue*, pp. 78–138). This includes the first discussion of mode on pp. 143–146 (*Study of Fugue*, pp. 80–83). Fux takes note of the different placement of semitones in the six octave species: d, e, f, g, a, c. A brief discussion follows concerning tonal answer in fugues and the need for maintaining diatonic subjects and answers, "for otherwise we would never fully understand the true nature of the modes."

*Various ornamental figures are discussed on pp. 217–220.

*Mode is discussed on pp. 221–231.

*Various types of fugal answers are discussed on pp. 231–239. The conclusion of this section surveys meter signatures and tempo.

Taste (pp. 239–242).

Church Style (pp. 242–243).

A Capella Style (pp. 243–273)

Mixed Style (with independent concerted instrumental parts; p. 273).

*Recitative Style (pp. 274–279).

The dialogue portion of *Gradus* features two characters: Josephus the student and Aloysius the teacher. Aloysius presumably represents Palestrina. But when Aloysius refers to Palestrina in one passage, he does so in the third person. In the following translation, all footnotes are by the translator. Musical examples are rendered in treble and bass clefs, notes tied across barlines are rendered in the modern manner, and some examples written on multiple staffs are rendered on a single staff.

Passage 1: pp. 139–140. This brief explanation concludes the study of species counterpoint and precedes the study of imitation and fugue.

Aloys.: I will now introduce you to imitation and fugue which occur without a cantus firmus. But first I must show you another manner of resolving some dissonances without the restriction of a cantus firmus—for example, how a ninth can resolve into a sixth or a tenth, how a seventh can resolve into a tenth, and how a fourth can resolve into a sixth or a third in the manner shown in example A3-1.[2]

Example A3-1

Jos.: Why are these resolutions used in the absence of a cantus firmus, yet not when there is one?

Aloys.: Do you not see that both voices move at the resolution, and that that cannot be done with a cantus firmus which does not move? The difference therefore is that these resolutions do not occur where oblique motion is necessary. Now let us return to composition for two voices without the restraining bonds of a cantus firmus.

Passage 2: pp. 217–239. This passage follows the study of fugue.

Concerning the figures *variation* and *anticipation* [pp. 217-220]

Aloys.: Variation is nothing other than irregular diminution. It is differentiated from regular diminution in that regular diminution may take place only when notes progress by skips of a third, as in example A3-2.

Example A3-2

[2]The end of this sentence appears to be garbled in Fux: "for example, a ninth into a sixth and a tenth into a third; a fourth into a sixth and a third" ("V. G. Nonam in Sextam, & Decimam in Tertiam; Quartam in Sextam, & Tertiam..."). The sentence has been translated to agree with example A3-1. Haydn noted this garbled sentence and emended it in his copy of the *Gradus*; see Alfred Mann.

185

Variation occurs when notes proceed by step, as in example A3-3.

Example A3-3

This example demonstrates clearly that variation departs from the common rules of counterpoint in that it proceeds by skips from a consonance into a dissonance, and then from a dissonance into another dissonance—this is certainly not allowed in counterpoint, but is commonly admitted in composition. Example A3-4 illustrates several types of variation.

Example A3-4

Such variations, as well as others not much different, which alter little the essence [of the counterpoint], can be validly employed in ordinary composition. They are shown in example A3- 5.

Example A3-5

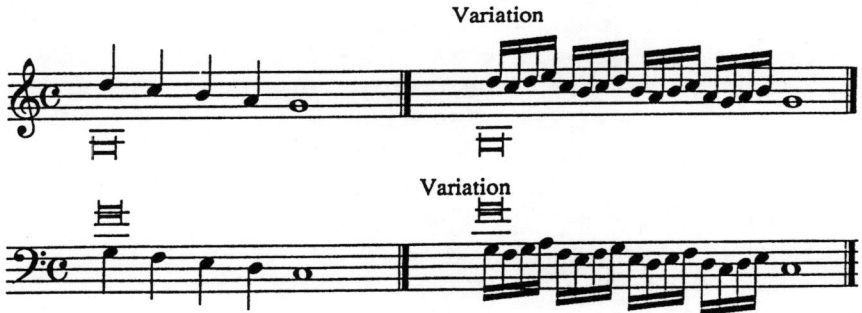

Anticipation occurs when half the duration of a preceding note is taken away and added to the following note.

Example A3-6

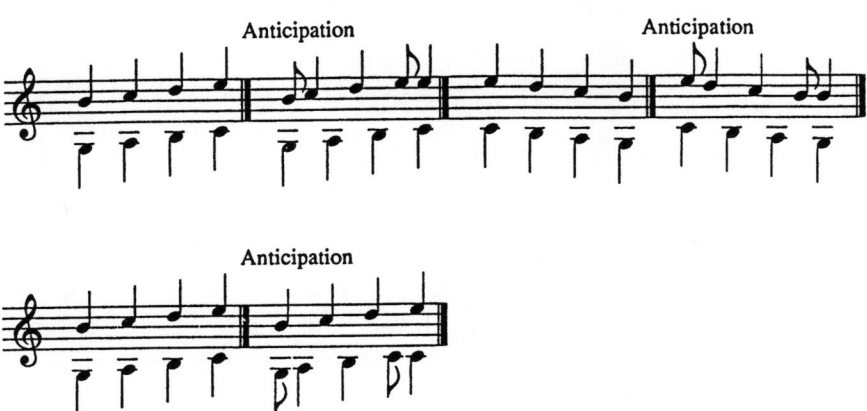

Let these few examples suffice. For a composer today need not introduce variations, since more of them than are sufficient are added *ad nauseum* by singers to such a degree that they appear to be gurgling more than singing.

Jos.: From what cause do these variations and departures from the rules of counterpoint have their origin?

Aloys.: From what was just said it is clear that singers were the originators; they were so little content with regular diminutions, and so fond of showing off the flexibility of their voice, that they devised such variations. Would that this longing for variation had remained within the limits of modesty, so that the musicians who varied did not change the essence [of the counterpoint]. How fortunate would composers have thus been! But oh, what a disappointment! This insatiable appetite and audacity for variation proceeded so far that not only the essence of the harmony (the basis of which was created so carefully and painstakingly) has been perverted with indifference, but also the composer himself can hardly recognize his own creation on which he has toiled. Even greater censure and derision are due to those musicians who, even though they are endowed with no talent, succumb to the same extravagance of the impulse for variation and twist their face into a thousand forms, so that not even a harlequin's masks are so varied, and in place of one note they produce nearly five sounds at once. Indeed, this folly goes so far that some engage in a rivalry for their own glory, in which the victory is granted to the swirling notes and neither the music nor the text is perceived. Yet who can stand against this torrent? It is the fault of the times and of the customs that all undertakings good in their beginning fall in time into evil.

Jos.: Although as a student it is not my place to judge this matter, yet I dare to affirm that such destruction of the harmony never pleased me. Meanwhile, as to how variations are made, I am satisfied. Now it remains to treat transposed modes and then irregular fugues.

Aloys.: A full understanding of the natural modes should precede a discussion of the transposed modes. Since I only touched upon this material earlier in the discussion of simple fugue,[3] I take it upon myself here to treat it more extensively and in as much detail as is necessary.

---

[3]*Gradus*, pp. 143–146 (*Study of Fugue*, pp. 80–83). See the summary of this discussion at the beginning of this appendix.

Concerning the Modes [pp. 221–231]

Treating the subject matter of the modes is just like imposing order on the primeval chaos of antiquity. Indeed, there is so much diversity of opinion among writers, older ones as well as more recent ones, that there seem to be almost as many authors as there are opinions. I do not have much admiration for the Greek authors, for it is beyond dispute that at its beginning their music was quite poor in intervals, as Plato shows in *The Timaeus*.[4] Whence it is not surprising that as they added more species of tetrachords and octaves as time went on, the number of modes grew too. The modes of the Greeks received their names and number not so much from species of octaves as from the diversity, talents, and manner of expression of the peoples: hence the Dorian, Hypodorian, Phrygian, Lydian modes, and so forth, which names indicated the diverse talent or manner of expression used by any one of these peoples according to the established custom, just as today we call an aria Italian, French, or English, and so forth. Since no more than a shadow of Greek music remains for us, I am amazed that there still exist some who use these foreign terms for the modes of our contemporary music, and dare to obfuscate this subject matter, intricate enough as it is, by empty names. We would rather pass over those things that cannot be used and leave them to music history, and proceed with the more recent meaning of those who teach twelve modes: six authentics or principal modes and six plagal or collateral modes.

Jos.: Do not all modern teachers hold this opinion of the twelve modes?

Aloys.: Not at all. Some, proceeding perhaps from chant, believe that there are eight, others, that there are more or fewer. I will explain how these opinions are to be assessed, and then add my own opinion.

Here you must recall those things that we declared above concerning simple fugue: namely that there are six different species of octave according to the varied position of the semitone, and

---

[4]See Plato, *The Timaeus and the Critias*, transl. by Thomas Taylor, foreword by R. Catesby Taliaferro (Princeton: Princeton University Press, 1944), pp. 69–74 and 122–125. Plato describes the creation of harmony in the world soul in terms of the Pythagorean scale and its intervals. Thus, many intervals of later music are not present.

consequently there are just that number of principal modes, namely d, e, f, g, a, c, whose scales were already presented in the cited passage, yet which I regard in no way superfluous to repeat anew.

Example A3-7

There are just so many different species of octave because there are just so many semitones in different positions in relation to the first note. Therefore, just so many principal modes and not any more necessarily have been established. For all other possible octave scales must be reduced to one of those species as transposed modes.

Example A3-8

These then are the transposed modes of the first mode d, for their semitones coincide with that mode in the same positions; likewise, as they maintain the same solmization, their species differ in no way.

[There follow similar examples of transpositions of the remaining modes: the E-mode transposed to a and b, followed by the comment "and some others of no great use;" the F-mode to g and c, followed by the comment "although others are made by the aid of flats or sharps, they are little used;" the G-mode to a, b-flat, c d, e, f; the A-mode to b, c, d, e, f-sharp, f, g; and the C-mode to d, e-flat, e, f, g, a, and b-flat.]

Jos.: And thus I conclude from what was said and demonstrated that there are exactly six natural modes.

Aloys.: Withhold your judgment for a brief while, Joseph, and remember what was said in Book I concerning the division of the octave: namely that it can be divided in two manners, harmonically and arithmetically. By harmonic division, the fifth is placed below and the fourth above. By arithmetic division, the fourth is below and the fifth above. The reason why this duple division is instituted was explained in Book I, and to repeat it here would be superfluous.[5]

From that double division of the octave arise two different species of the octaves. Thus there are two modes, differing by their species, of which harmonic division produces one, named authentic, and arithmetic division produces the other, named plagal. It thus follows that because there are twelve species of octave, there are that number of modes.

Example A3-9

Octaves divided harmonically, and the modes thereby arising

That these systems are produced from the harmonic division, there is no doubt. But there is great controversy whether the sequence shown by Gioseffo Zarlino and many others regarding the formation of the plagal modes is born of arithmetic division.

[5]Chapter 15, pp. 21–24.

Example A3-10

And Zarlino himself in Part 4, chapter 9[6] on modes, places the following system from the octave c:

Example A3-11

Here the lowest note remains and is a true product of arithmetic division. Therefore, if plagal modes arise from arithmetic division, which is the case, their form must be expressed by the following systems:

Example A3-12

Jos.: By this manner, there would exist only five plagal modes.

Aloys.: Precisely, because the octave F to f, on account of the tritone which thereby arises, cannot be divided arithmetically, as I have said elsewhere.

Jos.: What, therefore, is to be believed in such a perplexing matter?

Aloys.: I will tell you, after we have considered the use of the difference between the authentic and plagal modes. It must be assumed from Zarlino's opinion that the beginning, the end, and the cadences in modes of both type are in common. Thus there is no difference between them except that the authentic mode should have its melody [*modulatio*] in high notes, and the plagal mode should have its melody in low notes. This author [Zarlino], however, does not

---

[6]*Istitutioni harmoniche.* See p. 382 of the 1573 edition for example A3-11.

demand that subjects in authentic modes always ascend, while those in plagal modes to the contrary descend, as his examples demonstrate:

Example A3-13

From these examples it is clear that there is no difference between those two modes other than that the melody of the plagal is lower and that its subject ends in collateral intervals, namely e and b.[7] Giovanni Maria Bononcini [1642–78], in addition to low modulation, and on account of this, wishes subjects in the plagal mode to descend to the fourth [below the final].[8]

Angelo Berardi [c.1636–94], hardly a contemptible writer, appears to distinguish authentic mode from plagal by name only, without regard either to ascending or descending subjects or to high or low melodies. To the contrary, he introduced a lower melody in the authentic mode than in the plagal, as his examples reveal.[9]

---

[7]That is, notes borrowed from another mode in which they are the principal notes.

[8]*Musico prattico* (Bologna, 1673); facsimile edition (New York: Broude, 1969), p. 123. Bononcini notes that the only difference between authentic and plagal modes is that the authentic mode ascends a fourth above the plagal, and the plagal descends below the authentic. The same passage recurs in the second edition of 1688.

[9]Angelo Berardi, *Miscellanea musicale* (Bologna, 1689). The examples here illustrate compositions in the various modes. Example A3-14 shows the tenor-bass opening of a four-part composition in the Dorian mode (p. 180) and the soprano-alto opening of a four-part composition in the Hypodorian mode (p. 181). Thus Fux's comment below about the piece in the plagal mode beginning higher than that in the authentic mode refers to the choice of voices, not to the range of the melody in relation to the modal final, as was traditionally meant by the terms authentic and plagal. Example A3-15 is Berardi's composition illustrating the third mode (p. 183). As proved by numerous seventeenth-century theorists, and as Berardi himself notes, "composers commonly begin and end their songs composed in the third tone on A." ("Communemente li Compositori nelle loro cantilene fatte sopra il terzo tuono, cominciano e finiscono in A la, mi, re" p. 183.) See, for instance, Johann Andreas Herbst's cadences for the E-mode illustrated in example 4-4, p.65.

Example A3-14

Authentic

Plagal

Who is there, well-versed in music and knowing the opinion of other authors, who will attribute this last example to the plagal mode, since the nature and melody of the subject are seen to resemble more closely the form of the authentic mode? We must also wonder greatly about the following example introduced by the same author [Berardi] in his example of the third or E-mode, which, so that you may better ponder it, I place here in its entirety.

Example A3-15

Do you see that neither the entry of the tenor nor the final cadence corresponds to this mode, so much so that there is no reason why this composition should not be assigned to A or Hyperphrygian[10] as the proper mode? I could introduce not a few examples by Palestrina and thereby show that this aspect of the modes [namely, the difference between authentic and plagal] was not of great concern to that most illustrious man. In pondering this, I believe that unless an authority contradicts this, even those same distinguished authors did not know what others had established concerning the modes; or else the distinction between authentic and plagal was deemed of so little importance that it was not worth their effort to take note of it. In earlier times, when our sense of hearing was more delicate and could be aware of such subtlety, this distinction might have had value. But in this age of ours, in which the insatiable desire of our ears scarcely allows itself to be circumscribed by reasonable limits, it is easy to judge what is to be made of that opinion [concerning authentic and plagal] that restricts the breadth of music.

Jos.: What, then, is to be advised in such great disagreements among authors on such an ambiguous matter?

Aloys.: I will tell you, Joseph, but as advice rather than as a rule. Set aside the plagal modes and attend to the six modes d, e, f, g, a, c with their transpositions, in the manner that was taught above and should still be followed concerning simple fugue, and proceed in your melody [*modulatio*] as far as you wish through the proper intervals of the mode in which you are working. You can then be sure that the composition, if worked out according to the rules of harmony, modulating through various intervals, and adorned with

---

[10]It is unclear from whom Fux, who otherwise identifies modes by final pitch or by Zarlino's nomenclature, derived this name for the A-mode. Zarlino had called it Aeolian. Review pp.10-11 of the present study.

grace, is sufficiently authentic to be free from those things being plagal.[11]

Jos.: Perhaps the plagal modes are necessary in chant?

Aloys.: Not at all. It suffices to understand the intonations and the ecclesiastical modes, knowledge of which is necessary for choir singers. Follow the advice given just above without the restriction of the plagal mode, and you will achieve good work.

Jos.: Now that I have understood from you that there are no more than six modes of figured music, I would also like to know the order of them that you hold, which you believe to be the first, second, third, and so forth.

Aloys.: Gioseffo Zarlino and many others in that generation held c or Dorian as the first mode. Since then, almost all more recent performers assign the first place to d, then called Phrygian. For us, it suffices to show that there are no more than six modes different in species, and it matters little what the order is. Moreover, I am not opposed to you following the custom of using the common names.[12]

Concerning the Various Subjects of Fugues [pp. 231–237]

Aloys.: Mention was made not long ago of irregular fugues or subjects. By irregularity I mean the treatment of subjects of which the answering part responds properly to the first part without the help of sharps or flats, just as with subjects within the diatonic genus. For even if one departs from the rigor of the diatonic genus in other matters, yet such subjects that are arranged according to the manner which we will discuss here can nevertheless have their own regularity. Now you, Joseph, must propose your own subjects, different from those which we have already used.

---

[11]The Greek root *plagios* denotes slanted or oblique, connoting something borrowed, whence the term plagal arises. In its other sense, *plagios* conveys the sense of something devious or treacherous, whence the word plagiarize is derived. Fux's pun here combines both meanings.

[12]By the "common names," Fux means the traditional nomenclature, extended by Glarean to include A- and C-modes. Lorenz Mizler, in his German translation of *Gradus* (1742), places a footnote here: "Our author has without doubt erred when he calls C the Dorian mode, and D the Phrygian. It is well known that C is Ionian and D Dorian." (P. 165: "Unser Verfasser hat sich ohnfehlbar nur verstossen, wenn er hier C. die dorische Tonart und D. die phrygische nennet. Es ist bekandt dass C die jonische, und D die dorische sey.") See footnote 16 on p. 11 of this study for other writers who have used Zarlino's nomenclature.

Jos.: I will do so indiscriminately, as they come into my mind.

Aloys.: In what way will you make the answer to the subject in example A3-16?

Example A3-16

Jos.: In my unfounded opinion, I believe that it can be done in two ways. In one manner, in which the last note of the answer ends suitably in the mode. In the other manner, by following solmization.[13]

Example A3-17

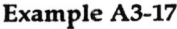

Aloys.: Each of the two manners is legitimate, but for a different reason. The first is legitimate because its last note lands properly on the final of the mode. The second is legitimate because it has the support of solmization on its last note. [See footnote 13.]

Jos.: Which, however, do you deem the better?

Aloys.: The second manner of answering is better for two reasons. Firstly, because in this manner the doctrine of singing is better taken into account. Secondly, because the answer does not depart so far from the course of the subject. And I strongly recommend to you that you abstain, wherever possible, from changing the subject without a good reason. More attention should be paid to the melody than to the mode, because a defect of the mode can easily be compensated for by the voice leading [*modulatio*] of the other part, namely by suspending the modally pertinent note above that note standing outside of the mode, as in example A3-18.[14]

---

[13]By solmization, Fux means that the second answer in example A3-17 ends with semitone fa mi, just as the subject did.

[14]In example A3-18, the modal final of the answer should be D. Instead, to reflect the *fa mi* semitone of the subject, the answer ends on E. Fux argues that the D suspended above this E supplies the modal final missing in the answer.

Example A3-18

The same reasoning pertains to the following subject.

Example A3-19

The two subjects in examples A3-16 and A3-19 can be called regular or irregular in different respects. They are irregular because they are not disposed in their own proper mode, and therefore require the assistance of a flat to produce that semitone appearing in the upper part in both examples. They can be called regular according to the mixed genus so much in use today.

Jos.: What do you mean that the subjects are not disposed in a proper mode?

Aloys.: If I show you a mode in which that semitone can exist without a flat, will it not be clear that the subject belongs to that mode?

Jos.: Yes. It seems so to me. But which mode is it?

Aloys.: Mode A. As in example A3-20.

Example A3-20

etc.

Jos.: This matter is clearly worthy of observation.

Aloys.: Putting a flat at the beginning, before a piece, indicates a mode transposed a fourth higher, in which case the subjects are called regular and are in agreement with their mode. See example A3-21.

Example A3-21

In our times, when the mixed genus has advanced so far, not much attention is paid to such subtleties, even though they are, nevertheless, necessary to a true understanding of the modes. Proceed now to other subjects.

Example A3-22

Jos.: I see that the sharp before the third note is in error, yet without it I find myself at a loss to answer the subject properly. What is the cause of the error?

Aloys.: It is the interval of a seventh between the first and third notes of the subject, for the note between them is not of sufficient strength to compensate for the impropriety of that skip. Therefore, in those subjects in which a skip of a fourth occurs between the first and second notes, attention should be directed mostly to the third note, so that the interval by which it is distant from the first note in the subject will be the same in the answer. Since the skip of a sixth occurs between the said notes in the first part, the same interval

199

therefore must be offered by the answering part, as in Example A3-23.

Example A3-23

etc.

  Jos.: The subject and answer [*modulatio*] in this manner appear to go outside the limits of the mode.[15]

  Aloys.: Not at all. Since in the first part the subject does not end on the octave of the mode [that is, on the final of the mode], how can the answering part end on the fifth of the mode? Furthermore, are not all intervals of the subject and answer contained within the octave of the mode naturally? If, however, by placing a sharp at the beginning of the piece a transposed mode arises, then the answer must be made somewhat differently, as in example A3-24.

Example A3-24

etc

As a result, because of the nature and difference of the mode, the answering part to one and the same subject must sometimes be made in different manners. Now turn your attention to another subject.

Example A3-25

  Jos.: Although I have spent much time searching for the answer to this subject, I have not been able to find it.

---

[15]That is, the answer ends on E, with C against it in the first part, implying a cadence on C. A C-cadence would be a foreign cadence in the G mode.

Aloys.: To this subject there can be two manners of answering. The first is made according to the mode, the second according to solmization. If you wish to relate the answer to the mode, the subject must be transferred from the chromatic genus to the diatonic in the following manner:

Example A3-26

In this case, the answer presents itself of its own accord, as in example A3-27.

Example A3-27

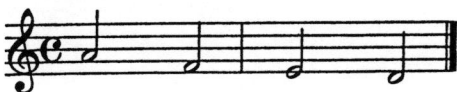

Returning to the chromatic genus, it will have this answer:

Example A3-28

Jos.: Could not the entire subject be maintained in the answer, retaining all its semitones as in example A3-29?

Example A3-29

Aloys.: No, because E-flat is much too foreign and not at all suitable in the D-mode. It would be otherwise if the subject were constructed thus:

Example A3-30

Here E-flat is introduced into the subject as an essential note.

The second manner of answering the subject, one reflecting solmization, is that in example A3-31.

Example A3-31

This manner, in that it is less disruptive to the subject, should in my opinion be preferred over the first answer, namely that in example A3-28.

Almost the same subject, if it is taken ascending, agrees properly with both the mode and the half steps in its answer:

Example A3-32

Jos.: With your leave, Master, let me propose one or two subjects for violins which are more spread out, and I will try to answer them as well as I can.

Example A3-33

[The next excerpt carries the erroneous
meter signature of 6/4 in the original.]

Aloys.: These subjects are adapted to today's excesses. But take
care, Joseph, of using subjects of such immense length and breadth
in four-part composition—for it can hardly be done with such extravagant and diffuse subjects without one part hindering the others.
Meanwhile, the answer, insofar as the subject allows one, was made
properly in that where in the first part there is a skip of a fifth, you
used a skip of a fourth in the answer, and where the first part skips
a third, you used a second in the answer, according to the nature of
the mode. Indeed, you made the answer so well that I have con-
fidence that you have paid close attention to what was said above
and will have no problem finding answers to any sort of subjects.

The selection of subjects matters a great deal. For truly not all
subjects indiscriminately can be used equally well. Thus the choice
of a subject must be judiciously considered.

[There follows on pp. 237-239 a brief discussion of tempo and meter markings, and the types of notated values to be used as suspensions in different tempos.

Pages 239-242 are a discussion of taste, or aesthetic judgment, in which Fux argues against taste being merely a matter of one saying, "I like this." Rather, only those things that are proper deserve our attention. This discussion leads into a survey of various compositional genres. Under the heading of the Sacred Style (*Stylus Ecclesiasticus*, pp. 242-243), Fux treats the *A Capella* style (pp. 243-273) (which for him means choral writing unaccompanied or with doubling instrumental parts) and the mixed style (p. 273) (with concertato instrumental parts). Under a capella style, Fux discusses first vocal compositions written in the diatonic genus in the style of Palestrina. The *Kyrie* from Fux's *Missa vicissitudinis* appears in its entirety. Following a discussion of this and other compositions, Fux turns to choral compositions with organ, quoting the *Kyrie I* and *Christe* from his *Missa in fletu solatium*, as well as other compositions. Concerning the mixed style (*Stylus Mixtus*), Fux quotes no examples, noting that it is the commonly used style of sacred music, and warning that the proper end of sacred music should be to arouse a spirit of devotion.]

Concerning Recitative Style [pp. 274–279]

Aloys.: Recitative style is nothing other than speech expressed by means of music, or, in other words, oratorical speech. Just as a speaker modulates his voice in various ways for different types of speech, now making it loud, now soft, now raising it, now lowering it, striving to represent the character of the feeling which he has conceived in his mind to express, the composer of music likewise must make his music according to the variety of the text. In setting recitative texts resembling ordinary speech, the music must make the voice somewhat relaxed. When expressing strife, a passionate voice can be used, even crying out, with frequent changes in the bass. The dignity of inspired text is portrayed by music full of seriousness, with few changes of the bass, which is well suited to the sacred style, where the recitative is frequently accompanied by instruments, as in example A3-34.

Example A3-34

Jos.: What do I behold? It seems that the instrumental chords, which consist mostly of dissonances, depart from the rules of counterpoint altogether.

Aloys.: This departure is considered good according to the nature of recitative, in which the treatment cannot be handled in the usual manner because the bass does not move in a way that allows the dissonances to be resolved as usual. Thus, in this style one should pay attention less to the harmonies than to the expression of the meaning of the words.[16] Recitative can be made in this manner or otherwise according to the character of the text where we express our feeling in a devout prayer to God.

Concerning secular music, namely of the court and theater, common sense teaches that since it has a different purpose, it should be made differently. For secular music has the goal of entertaining the spirits of the listeners and arousing various emotions. The emotions usually expressed in recitative are the following: anger, pity, fear, power, vexation, delight, and love, etc.

Anger can be expressed by a rapid melody, mostly in high notes. And it if is more vehement, it is expressed in such a cry that the voice is broken off. And this is always effected by figures of shorter notes ascending to the high register along with numerous bass changes. It is of the utmost importance to be attentive to the station of the angry person. If he is a king, in no way should he carry on in unmanly crying, but preserving his royal dignity he should show his indignation by a majestic seriousness. This should also be observed with all the other affects.

Pity demands a tearful, but in no way interrupted voice, which is expressed in longer notes and numerous dissonances with the bass remaining for longer durations in the same place.

Fear demands a lower, hesitating voice.

Strength is depicted by a vehement voice and by intense and secure seriousness.

Delight employs an effusive, yet soft and gentle type of voice.

The affect of love is expressed in the voice by caressing, tenderness, and affection. Since certain other affects are commonly joined with love, they too must be expressed to a greater or lesser degree.

In addition, the following punctuations of rhetoric[17] should be observed, too: the comma, colon, semicolon, period, question mark,

---

[16]Note the difference in attitude between Fux, who throws up his hands in despair at understanding the basis of such progressions, and Christoph Bernhard, who in his treatises of the mid-seventeenth century related even the most extravagant types of dissonances to the basis of *prima prattica*. Review the discussion of Bernhard on pp. 66-68.

[17]As Fux uses the term *punctuation* and the various types of punctuation marks here, he refers to the divisions of speech indicated by these punctuation marks more than to the marks themselves.

exclamation point, and parentheses; for everything should be in one of these divisions.

If you wish the meaning of a comma, it is done in the following manner:

Example A3-35

The semicolon in music is made in almost the same way. The comma very often is continued without a break, such as when the meaning of the text demands such continuity.

The colon usually ends in the following way:

Example A3-36

The period [*punctum*] is made in the same way if the sentence [*periodus*] and the thought are finished but the speech continues with the same subject. If another sentence is introduced immediately, a formal cadence is commonly employed, making the separation.

Example A3-37

If, however, the thought is completed, then the period should be made in the following manner:

Example A3-38

The question mark is also expressed in various ways according to the meaning of the speech:

Example A3-39

The exclamation point is indicated in the following way:

Example A3-40

A sentence enclosed in parentheses should be produced by a softer voice, as when an aside is directed to the audience so that it is not understood by the other actors. Knowing how to use all these punctuations is learned more by use and by observing the works of good composers than by rules.

Jos.: This, then, is the teaching of recitatives. What sort of teaching do you give concerning the composition of arias?

Aloys.: What shall I teach definitively concerning an arbitrary music which is subject to frequent changes? I do not censure the attempt to find out about new things; rather, I praise it greatly. For indeed, if a man of middle age were to appear today dressed in the style of fifty or sixty years ago, certainly he would expose himself to ridicule. Music, too, must be suited to the times. But never have I found a tailor familiar with the new fashions, nor have I heard tell of one, who attached shirt sleeves to the thigh or to the knee; nor of any architect who was so foolish as to put the foundation of a building on top of the roof. Yet we see and hear such things everywhere in music, not without bringing disappointment to those of taste, and shame to art when the fundamental precepts of nature and art are deliberately inverted from their proper place by rules turned upside down, and the foundation is put above while the other parts are put below without regard for the proper foundation. Indeed, Joseph, no matter how much you strive for novelty and invention by exerting all the powers of your times, nothing can overturn, much less destroy, the rules of art which imitate nature and which achieve the ends of nature. If you now work on music with continual practice, and attain thereby a facility in it, I do not doubt that you will achieve the fame of an eminent composer.

[The concluding sentences, which form the peroration of the *Gradus*, appear at the end of both segments translated by Alfred Mann.]

Translation of Article *Modus musicus* from Johann Gottfried Walther's *Lexicon*

The entire article (pp. 409-415) appears here in English. Of the examples that merely illustrate the transpositions of each mode, only the example that illustrates transpositions of the first mode (Dorian) has been retained; this results in some minor rephrasings in later passages, indicated in square brackets. All footnotes and all bracketed examples are by the translator.

In seeking examples of certain chorales cited by Walther, I have first attempted to locate a chorale prelude setting of that chorale by Walther himself. Failing that I have turned to the works of his contemporary and relative, J. S. Bach.[1]

Where no instance of the melody could be found there, I consulted the chorale collection by Johannes Zahn, *Die Melodien der deutschen evangelischen Kirchenlieder*.[2]

Musical mode is the way to begin a song, to continue it properly within certain bounds, and to end it appropriately. Among the Greeks twelve of these were recognized, namely six principal modes and the same number of subsidiary ones (or, as they themselves called them, *nomoi* or *tropoi*). These were named according to the sequence of letters to which they subsequently were accommodated: Dorian, Hypodorian, Phrygian, Hypophrygian, Lydian, Hypolydian, Mixolydian, Hypomixolydian, Aeolian, Hypoaeolian, Ionian, and Hypoionian. What the actual relationship among these twelve types of song was has not yet been settled, and most probably

---

[1]Concerning the relationship between Walther and J. S. Bach, see *The Bach Reader*, ed. Hans T. David and Arthur Mendel (New York: Norton, 1966), p. 26, *passim*.
[2](Gütersloh, 1889). Facsimile edition (Hildesheim: Olms, 1963).

will not be settled very easily. In any case, what happened to them is what has happened in various towns to some streets which still carry the names of certain professions (for example, locksmiths, furriers, blacksmiths, etc.) whose members used to live there in earlier times although not one of those artisans is now found there. Accordingly it may well be said that nothing remains but the name. Just this, it seems to me, has also happened to the just-mentioned modes. Only the Greek names are left, and these names have been attached to diatonic melodies set on the following six notes: D, E, F, G, A, and C. As for the origin of these modes, without doubt it follows from the fact that it is not possible for a singer always to proceed by whole tones [in a scale or melody], for such a progression (consisting of nothing but whole tones) would be a modulation without modulation,[3] and a pure mishmash in which nothing at all could be accomplished. See example A4-1.

Example A4-1

[sic]

    etc.

   Thus, nature has placed the interval of a semitone twice, and ordered the semitones in unequal positions in the octave of each of the above-mentioned six notes. This unequal position plays the greatest role in the proper transposition of the said diatonic modes to the modes called chromatic, in which the semitone must appear again in the same place that it had in the diatonic mode. (The position of the semitone is most important only so long as the difference between the major and minor tone, observed in the *Istitutioni harmoniche*, Part III, chapter 13 of Zarlino[4] and the *Harmonicorum libri 6*,

---

[3]*Modulation* does not carry its modern meaning here. The phrase appears to mean "a melodic structure without structure."

[4](Venice, 1558). Facsimile edition (New York: Broude, 1965); second edition (Venice, 1573), facsimile edition (Ridgewood, N.J.: Gregg Press, 1966).

Proposition 25 of Mersenne,[5] is not brought into this calculation[6]). Yet the sequence of the whole tones also must not be neglected, but must be followed along with that of the semitones; and the whole tones must again be placed in just the same positions which they had in the diatonic mode. Thus, the manner by which the transposition of each diatonic mode should appear according to the signatures, if each should be taken through all the twelve notes found in an octave, shall be shown in the following presentation; for knowledge of this teaching is absolutely essential, especially to organists who have the most to do with chorales, of which many were composed and handed down in these old modes. Now follows the first mode, according to the above-noted order of the letters, according to the sense of the ancients, and as well according to today's usage in monasteries and nunneries:

1. *Dorius modus* (Latin), *Mode Dorien* (French), *Modo Dorio* (Italian) or the Dorian manner of singing (which probably was used by the Dorians, a Greek nation) means: when a melody is contained between the notes *d* and *d'* (to calculate according to the tenor) or between *d'* and *d''* (according to the discant), when it touches on the notes written down in example A4-2 within that ambitus, and makes the ordinary bass cadence on *D*.[7]

Example A4-2

Since in this species of octave the semitone appears after the second and sixth degrees, the complete transpositions of this mode are seen as in example A4-3, according to the signatures.

[5](Paris, 1635-1636).
[6]Mattheson had insisted on differentiating all transpositions from one another according the varying placements of major and minor tones and several sizes of semitones. Review pp. 123 and 125 and Mattheson's tuning system presented in appendix 2.
[7]Walther defines the ordinary bass cadence in the article *Cadence parfaite* on p. 125 of the *Lexicon* as a cadence in which the bass descends a fifth (that is, a dominant-to-tonic cadence).

Example A4-3

Here follows the listing of some well-known chorales set in this mode:

1. JEsus Christus unser Heyland, der von uns den GOttes Zorn wand.

2. Christ lag in Todes-Banden.

3. Christ ist erstanden von der Marter alle.

4. Mit Fried und Freud ich fahr dahin.

5. Auf meinen lieben GOtt trau ich in Angst und Noth.

6. Wir gläuben all' an einen GOtt &c according to the long melody.

7. Jesulein, du bist mein, weil ich lebe.

214

8. Ach GOtt thu' dich erbarmen.

9. Vater unser im Himmelreich.

10. Als Christus gebohren war &c. The same: Singen wir aus Hertzens-Grund.

Although there is sometimes one note more or less in the ambitus of some of the songs listed (for example, the ambitus of the song *Vater unser im Himmelreich* [see example A4-4]

Example A4-4 [Melody from *Cantata No. 101* by J. S. Bach]

even exceeds it by a minor third above the octave, which is said to have happened to express the glory of the soul at the words *ruffen an* found in the first verse; this song also uses *b-flat* instead of *b* in the last phrase), and furthermore, although in some songs *c-sharp* and *g-sharp* appear instead of *c* and *g*, which are required in a rigorous interpretation of the mode–yet even here the exception proves the rule, because the notes of the mode dominate these alterations in most melodies (as examination of the appended songs will show), and it is to be presumed that the *c-sharp* in particular was brought into Dorian in imitation of Ionian, chiefly on account of the cadence. This usage is also to be understood in the same way in the following mode, which is named

2. *Hypodorius* (Latin), *Hypo-Dorien* (French), *Hypodorio* (Italian) or Subdorian (from *hypo* and *dorios*), because it touches on the same diatonic pitches as the previous mode, and forms its final cadence on D. But whereas the ambitus of the former is contained between *d'* and *d''*, the ambitus of the latter is contained between *a* and *a'*, and

proceeds, accordingly, a fourth below the former—example A4-5—as the following church songs prove by their low ambitus if they are played from the note *D*:

Example A4-5

1. Hilff GOtt, dass mirs gelinge &c. or: Wenn meine Sünd mich kräncken.

2. Von GOtt will ich nicht lassen &c. or: Helfft mir, GOttes Güte preisen.

3. JEsus Christus unser Heyland, der den Tod überwand.

4. GOtt Vater der du deine Sohn.

5. Was mein GOtt will das gescheh allzeit.

NB. The final note of the melody is the black note *d'* in example A4-5. The transposed systems of this mode are the same as with the previous mode.

3. *Phrygius modus* (Latin), *Mode Phrygien* (French), *Modo Frigio* (Italian) or the Phrygian manner of singing (which is said to have been used especially by the Phrygians, a Greek nation) means: when a melody is contained between the notes *e* and *e'* (to calculate according to the tenor) or between *e'* and *e"* (according to the discant), and touches upon the notes written down in example A4-6 within that ambitus.

Example A4-6

Since in this disposition and species of octave the semitone appears after the first and fifth degrees, the complete transpositions of this mode, according to the signatures, [can thereby be calculated]. Here follow a few church songs set in this mode:

1. Es woll uns GOtt genädig seyn.

2. Ach GOtt vom Himmel sieh' darein.

216

3. Christus, der uns selig macht.

4. Aus tieffer Noth lasst uns zu GOtt.

5. Da JEsus an dem Creutze stund.

6. Ach HErr mich armen Sünder.

7. Christum wir sollen loben schon.

8. HErr JEsus Christ wah'r Mensch und GOtt.

Although already in the first two melodies *f-sharp* appears once in each instead of the *f* required according to the system of this mode, the rule cited above in the discussion of the first mode is also valid here: in that in the first example *f* occurs three times opposing one *f-sharp*—example A4-7:

Example A4-7

Also, in the second example *f-sharp* falls aside if the first four notes are sung a tone higher as is directed in some song books, namely in the manner found in example A4-9 instead of that found in example A4-8.

ExamplesA4-8

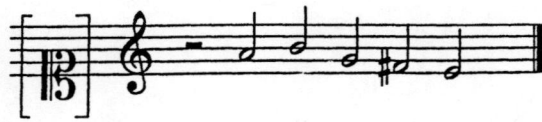

Example A4-9

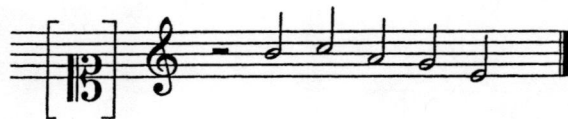

Since *f* is entirely characteristic in this mode, it follows from this that the principal cadence cannot progress from *B* to *E*, but must be executed in the bass from *A* to *E* (*la mi*, according to solmization) in the manner found in example A4-7. Also, since the offensive phrase marked with the + in example A4-7, no doubt corrupted by time, can be rectified by a more convenient bass motion, and the *f-sharp* can be removed, it seems to me that it would be quite good to do so, perhaps in the manner noted in example A4-10.

Example A4-10

218

A similar correction could also be undertaken of the *f- sharp* immediately following in the middle voice, which can just as easily be done away with. As for the song: *Christum wir sollen loben schon &c.,*

Example A4-11 [Melody from *Cantata No. 121* by J. S. Bach]

which is a translation of the hymn: *A solis ortus cardine*, which Coelius Sedulius prepared in the first half of the fifth century (if the melody was also composed at that time, it would certainly be old enough!)—it should be, according to the opinion of some, in the Dorian mode, especially on account of the beginning, and the end should be a *Clausula dissecta;*[8] others, however, think it is Phrygian, among whom is Glarean, who calls it a most elegant example of Phrygian in Book II, chapter 36, p. 164.[9] In the first case, if an organist plays a prelude to this chorale on *D*, it is very easy for a singer to begin properly. In the second case, however, if he places his prelude in *E* and the singer is supposed to begin on *D*, they both must understand each other well. But should this chorale have suffered the same fate as *Der du*

---

[8]*Lexicon*, p. 170: *"Clausula dissecta* means: when the bass voice descends a fourth or ascends a fifth, and one note appears, as it were, to be cut off from the cadence. Printz counts this species among the *Clausulas perfectas* on p. 27 of Part I of his *Satyrischer Componisten* [Dresden and Leipzig, 1676 and 1696]; Conrad Matthaei, however, places them among the *imperfectas* on page 8 of his *Bericht [von den Modis Musicis* (Königsberg, 1652)]. The proper final bass cadences of the so-called Phrygian and Mixolydian modes and their plagals do not belong here."

[9]*Dodecachordon* (Basel, 1547); facsimile edition (New York: Broude, 1967). English translation by Clement A. Miller (N.p.: American Institute of Musicology, 1965).

bist drey in Einigkeit &c. (which will be discussed in its place[10]), the latter opinion is probably the safest.

4. *Hypophrygius modus* (Latin), *Mode Hypo-Phrygien* (French), *Modo Hypofrigio* (Italian) or Subphrygian (from *hypo* and *phrygios*) is the name of the mode which consists of the same diatonic pitches as the previous one, and forms its final cadence on E in the same manner. But whereas the ambitus of the former is contained between *e'* and *e''*, the ambitus of the latter is contained between *b* and *b'*, and thus proceeds a fourth below the former—see example A4-12.

Example A4-12

By the letter of the law, this mode should maintain this ambitus: [Cyriacus] Snegassius [1546-1597], in his *Isagoge musica[e libri duo]* (chapter 8, *notione 2, de ambitu*),[11] noted that this mode rarely descends to the lowest note *b*; rather, this semitone, with which it should reach the *c* from below, is taken above, and the ambitus even ascends to *d'* on occasion. Thus it happens that there is only a small difference between this and the preceding mode. And the following church songs confirm this:

    1. Mitten wir in Leben sind mit dem Tod umfangen.

    2. Erbarm dich mein o HErre GOtt.

    3. HErr GOtt dich loben wir.

    4. Mensch, wilt du leben seeliglich.

    5. O grosser GOtt von Macht.

This last chorale, to be sure, reaches the lowest *b*, but not the upper *b'* [example A4-13], and is commonly performed transposed.

---

[10] See below under the Hypomixolydian mode.
[11] (Erfurt, 1591).

Example A4-13 [The melody is taken from the chorale prelude by Walther, number 77 in his *Gesammelte Werke für Orgel*, ed. Max Seifert, revised by Hans Joachim Moser (Wiesbaden: Breitkopf & Härtel, 1958.)]

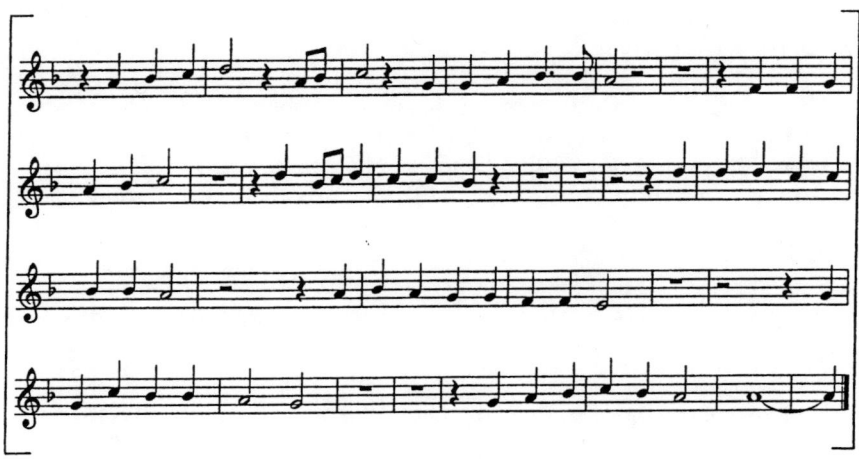

The transpositions of this mode are the same as those of the foregoing.

5. *Lydius modus* (Latin), *Mode Lydien* (French), *Modo Lidio* (Italian), or the Lydian manner of singing (which was supposedly used by the Lydians, a Greek nation in Asia Minor descended from Lud, son of Sems), means: when a melody is contained between *f* and *f′* (to calculate according to the tenor) or between *f′* and *f″* (according to the discant), and touches upon the notes written down in example A4-14 within this ambitus, and cadences on F.

Example A4-14

Since in this disposition the semitone appears after the fourth and seventh degrees, the complete transpositions of this mode, according to the signature, [can thereby be calculated]. No church songs are found set in this and the following mode, because as already cited from Glarean above in the article *Modi Cantus Ecclesiastici Octo*, even at that time, now 183 years ago,[12] the hymns and other pieces set in this mode had degenerated and had been changed into the transposed Ionian mode by means of the *b-flat* which crept into this mode. Concerning this, I will insert only a few passages from the aforementioned author: in the eleventh chapter of the second book, p. 93, he writes the following:

> However, early ecclesiastical musicians were pleased with the Lydian and HypoLydian because of the harshness of the [species of] fifth, especially in the songs called Graduals, also in the Passion of the Lord, sung during Holy Week, in which the Evangelist, as the grave narrator, has this [species of] fifth suitable for narration. But our time makes changes mostly at random, or rather it corrupts while it seeks softness more than it cares to esteem dignity.[13]

And in the nineteenth chapter, on p. 115, he puts it in the following form:

> I am also of the opinion that some have conspired to make Ionian and Hypolonian modes out of all Lydian and HypoLydian modes, but this has had little success. And therefore songs, especially Graduals, are not distorted very much.

And in yet another passage on page 130 he says:

> We have said previously that this mode is not used in our time by singers, who turn all its songs into the Ionian by substituting *fa* for *mi* on the *b* key. This custom has prevailed so much that now one rarely finds a pure Lydian in which *fa* has not been introduced somewhere, in a conspiracy as it were, formed against it and with its banishment decided on openly.

6. *Hypolydius modus* (Latin), *Mode Hypo-Lydien* (French), *Modo Hypolidio* (Italian), or called Sublydian (from *hypo* and *lydios*), which proceeds in the diatonic pitches of the previous mode, and also makes its final cadence on *F*, but departs from the former in that its ambitus is contained between *c* and *c′* (to calculate according to the tenor) or between *c′* and *c″* (according to the discant), and accordingly maintains its ambitus a fourth lower than its authentic mode.

---

[12]1547+183=1730. Apparently this section of the article was not proofread after 1730. See also footnote 11 in chapter 8.

[13]English translations here according to the translation of Glarean by Clement Miller, *op. cit.*, pp. 131-132. The two following passages are from pp. 152-153 and p. 166.

7. *Mixolydius modus* (Latin), *Mode Mixolydien* or *Lydien melé* (French), *Modo Mixsolidio, Mixolydio* and *Missolidio* (Italian), *mixolydios* (Greek) or *mixtus Lydius* means: when a melody is contained between the notes *g* and *g'*, touches on the notes written down in example A4-15 within this ambitus, and makes its cadence on *G*, but in such a manner that no *f-sharp* enters in another voice. In order to avoid this the bass concludes not from *d* to *G*, but from *c* to *G*. Since it also does not admit the cadence on *B* for the same reason, but prefers the *C* cadence, it also cadences on *f*—from which it probably received its name, since the just-mentioned cadence is characteristic of the Lydian mode in the diatonic genus.

Example A4-15

1.   2.   3.   4.   5.   6.   7.

Since in this species of octave the semitone appears after the third and sixth degrees, the transpositions of this mode according to the signature [can be calculated]. Of the church songs set in this mode, other than *Ach wir armen Sünder unser Missethat &c.*, none can be procured which can show the legal and proper ambitus. [Andreas] Raselius [c.1562 or 1564-1602][14] and Snegassius[15] refer to this mode the song *Est is das Heyl uns kommen her &c.* [example A4-16], but the first of these writers recognized even then (1589) that it was commonly sung in a corrupt manner in the antistrophe or second part, and had been changed into the Ionian mode.

Example A4-16 [The melody as in *Cantata 86* by J. S. Bach.]

---

[14]*Hexachordum seu quaestiones musicae practicae* (Nürnberg, 1589).
[15]*Op. cit.*

Nowadays it is still subjected to the just-mentioned faulty alteration, so that in the first part *c* appears, but in the second *c-sharp* (because of the low register of the authentic and diatonic mode, in addition to the above factor, it is sung transposed to *D*); this causes bass progressions entirely different from those required by the proper mode. The variable ending notes of this melody also appear not to be accurate any longer, but probably [the ending of the melody] should remain on one [repeated] note on account of the authentic bass cadence of this mode, as happens at the end of, for example, *Diss sind die heilgen Zehen Gebot &c.* [example A4-17]

Example A4-17

In addition to this, on page 155 of the [*Erfurter*] *Gesangbuch* of [Nikolaus] Stenger [1609-1680][16] appears the song for the Ascension: *Auf diesen Tag bedencken wir &c.* [example A4-18], which goes, however, from *e'* to *f''*. Accordingly, it does not complete the proper octave species of this mode in the high register, but to the contrary has two more notes in the low register than it should.

Example A4-18 [Melody no. 5771 in Zahn.]

---

[16]Stenger was a musician and scholar in Erfurt, was author of the elementary manual *Manuductio ad musicam theoreticam* (Erfurt, 1635; in five editions though 1666), and was editor the *Gesangbuch* (Erfurt, 1663).

See Raselius's *Hexachordum*, chapter 6.[17] This song can also furnish an example of what was said above concerning the F cadence; for two such cadences appear twice in immediate succession before the end, and appear to be unavoidable in the bass.

8. *Hypomixolydius modus* (Latin), *Mode Hypomixolydien* (French), *Modo Hipomissolidio* (Italian), or Submixolydian (from *hypo* and *mixolydios*) means that mode which modulates in the same diatonic pitches as the preceding mode and also makes its final cadence on G in the same manner. But it departs from the former in that its ambitus is contained between the notes *d'* and *d"* (to calculate according to the discant) or between *d* and *d'* (according to the tenor), and thus proceeds a fourth below the former—example A4-19.

Example A4-19

The sustained or final note of the melody is notated in black.

Among church songs, the following are set in this mode:

1. Veni Sancte Spiritus &c., or Komm Heil. Geist, erfüll die Hertzen

2. Grates nunc omnes reddamus Domino &c., or Dancksagen wir alle, GOTT unserm HErrn Christo

3. O Lux beata Trinitas &c., or Der du bist drey in Einigkeit

4. Veni Creator Spiritus &c., or Komm GOTT Schöpffer Heiliger Geist

5. GOtt sey gelobet und gebenedeyet

6. Diss sind die heiligen zehen Gebot

7. Gelobet seyst du JEsu Christ, dass du Mensch gebohren bist

Among these the third is especially noteworthy [example A4-20], because writers on music have not been able to agree on which mode it truly is.

---

[17]Raselius, *op. cit.*

Example A4-20 [Melody from J. S. Bach's harmonization, *Gesamtausgabe*, vol. 39 no. 40.]

Thus some organists prelude to it on *D*, others on *F*, but only a few prelude to it on *G*. If, however, one knows that the end is proper and that the beginning and the middle are improper and corrupt, and that in both places the problem involves only a single note, namely *g*, which is commonly lacking or displaced in new as well as old song books, then all difficulty is at once removed. The true melody, as it is written in a Roman missal, is found in example A4-21.

Example A4-21

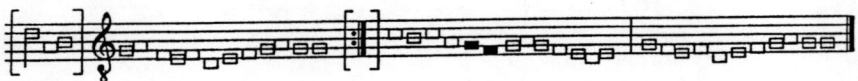

Concerning the melody of the fifth song, the following should be known: that in some places the same is no longer sung entirely purely according to this mode, but is changed to the Hypoionian mode by means of *f-sharp* which is insinuated especially at the end. The accurate melody is set down in example A4-22.

Example A4-22 [Dotted barlines added.]

In the middle of the seventh chorale: *Gelobet seyst du JEsu Christ &c.* [example A4-23], the most common bass progression which is made also does not look very well.

Example A4-23 [Melody from *Cantata 64* by J. S. Bach.]

And it is entirely plausible that if the *c* cadence in the beginning, and especially the iterated concluding notes, had not been retained, it would have decayed even further from purity. The *F* cadences in the first and sixth songs corroborate once again what was noted above concerning the name. Joachim Thuringus[18] asserts that the naming of the Mixolydian mode derives from the Mixolydians (who otherwise are called Mixo-macedonians or Mixo-tmolitans), an Asiatic nation of half-breeds descended from the muses and the Lydians, and accordingly could have been named Mixomacedonian and Mixotmolitan. In [Philippus] Ferrari's [?-1626] *Lexicon geographico*[19] one also finds concerning the Mixomacedonians that they were an Asiatic nation who lived near Ephesus in Lycia. But of the Mixolydians nothing is reported. Since, therefore, this mode has no region and nation (like other modes) from which it might derive its name, probably either the poetess Sappho, or Pythoclides was its inventor—see Alex. Sardum, *De rerum inventoribus*, I, 19.[20] Did not [Athanasias] Kircher [1601-1680] omit this mode intentionally in Book III, chapter 16 [of his *Musurgia universalis* (Rome, 1650)], because he could not bring forth proofs as with the others? And in [Zaccaria] Tevo [1651-1709 or 1712], Part 4, chapter 4, page 247 [of *In musico testore...* (Venice, 1706)], he says: "It was called Mixolydian by being related to and sharing in the Lydian," or, as [Vincenzo] Galilei [1520?-1591] on the 70th leaf of his *Dialogo della musica antica e moderna* [Venice, 1581] writes: "as if through the proximity which it had with the Lydian, it was mixed in with it." (Here once again no region or nation is thought of!) Even if the words of both authors, in the explanation found in them, aim at something else, it might still not be absurd to apply the F cadence to this mode, because experience teaches it.

9. *AEolius modus* (Latin), *Mode Eolien* (French), *Modo Eolio* (Italian) or the Aeolian manner of singing (which must have been used in particular by the Aeolians, a Greek nation), means: when a melody is contained between the notes *a* and *a'* or *a'* and *a''*, in which it makes the final, and touches upon the notes contained in example A4-24 within the ambitus. Since in this disposition the semitone appears after the second and fifth degrees, the complete transpositions of this mode [can be calculated according to the signatures].

[18]Joachim Thüring (?-?), *Nucleus musicus de modis seu tonis* (Berlin, 1622).
[19]Reprinted, edited by Michael Antonius Baudrand (Paris, 1670).
[20] Alessandro Sardi of Ferrara (1520-1588) annotated portions of the *Historia naturalis* by Pliny the Elder. This was published in Geneva in 1604.

Example A4-24

1.   2.   3.   4.   5.   6.   7.

Some church songs set in this mode are:

1. GOTT hat das Evangelium gegeben &c.

2. Magnificat; or Meine Seel erhebt den HErren &c., in the tonus peregrinus

3. Ich dancke dem HErrn von gantzem Hertzen

4. Ich ruff zu dir HErr JEsu Christ

5. Erhalt uns HErr bey deinem Wort

10. *Hypoaeolius modus* (Latin), *Mode Hypo-Eolien* (French), *Modo HipoEolio* (Italian), or Subaeolian (from *hypo* and *aeolios*) is the name of the mode which touches on the same diatonic pitches as the previous mode, and makes its final cadence on *A*. But whereas the ambitus of the former is contained between *a* and *a'*, or *a'* and *a''*, the ambitus of the latter is contained between *e* and *e'*, or *e'* and *e''*, and proceeds accordingly a fourth below the former—see example A4-25.

Example A4-25

Among church songs, the following are set in this mode:

1. Mag ich Unglück nicht wiederstahn

2. Allein zu dir, HErr JEsu Christ

3. Wär GOtt nicht mit uns diese Zeit

4. *Von allen Menschen abgewandt*

5. Wo GOtt der HErr nicht bey uns hält

11. *Jonicus modus* (Latin), *Mode Jonien* (French), *Modo Jonico* (Italian), or the Ionian manner of singing (which was especially used by the Ionians, a Greek nation dwelling in Asia Minor) means: when a melody is contained between the notes *c* and *c'* (to calculate according to the tenor) or between *c'* and *c''* (according to the discant), touches upon the notes written down in example A4-26 within this

ambitus, and concludes on *c*. Since in this disposition the semitone appears after the third and seventh degrees, the complete transpositions of this mode through all the keys on the keyboard [can be calculated].

Example A4-26

Some church songs which are arranged in this mode are:

1. Ein feste Burg ist unser GOtt
2. Vom Himmel hoch da komm ich her
3. Wo GOtt zum Haus nicht giebt sein Gunst
4. GOtt der Vater wohn uns bey
5. Jesaia dem Propheten das geschah
6. Sag was hilfft alle Welt

12. *Hypoionicus modus* (Latin), *Mode Hypo-Jonien* (French), *Modo HipoJonico* (Italian), or Subionian (from *hypo* and *ionicos*) is so named because it touches on the same diatonic notes as the previous mode, and also makes its final cadence on *c*. But whereas the ambitus of the former mode is contained between *c* and *c′* or *c′* and *c″*, the ambitus of this mode is contained between G and *g* or *g* and *g′*, and thus proceeds a fourth below the former—example A4-27.

Example A4-27

Some chorales set in this mode follow, which, however, are performed transposed:

1. Nun freut euch lieben Christen gemein
2. Es spricht der Unweisen Mund wohl
3. Wenn wir in höchsten Nöthen seyn
4. O HErre GOtt dein göttlich Wort
5. Aus tieffer Noth schrey ich zu dir

6. HErr GOtt dich loben alle wir

7. Nun lob mein Seel den HErren

8. Wenn mein Stündlein vorhanden ist

This was the first and older presentation of this teaching [of the modes], to which most musicians have adhered, as the writings already presented above indicate, and according to which the six principal tones or modes present 66 transpositions if they are transposed to all the notes found in an octave; of which some transpositions agree with others according to the signature, but not according to the fundamental note. And if one adds to these the said principal tones, 72 dispositions arise (expressing each note in only one manner; if some notes should be expressed in two manners, as they can, such as *d-sharp* and *e-flat*, or *g-sharp* and *a-flat*, then even more transpositions would arise).

The second and modern presentation of this teaching is more or less the following: one considers each note in an octave chiefly according to its minor and major third. Then, because there are twelve notes in an octave, there are that many dispositions of each species of third, and taken together these make twenty-four. Furthermore, in addition to the perfect fifth of each final note (which, together with the two species of third are called *Chordae essentiales*) two *Chordas naturales* are ordered, namely a major semitone below the final note found at the bottom or top of the octave, and a minor or major sixth (which is minor or major according to the quality of the third of the mode); and then two *Chordas necessarias*, namely a whole tone or perfect second over the final, and a whole tone between the third and fifth notes, which makes a perfect fourth with the final note.[21] Furthermore, four *Chordas elegantiores* are set, namely:

1. In a minor mode, the major semitone above the final; in a major mode, the minor semitone above the final.

2. In both types of modes the major semitone below the fifth.

3. In minor modes the minor semitone above the minor sixth, and the immediately following major semitone, which makes a minor semitone against the following *Chordam naturalem*.

---

[21]Of course Walther is in error here. The fourth degree is a whole step from both 3 and 5 in minor keys, but not in major.

4. In major modes the major semitone below the major sixth and the major semitone above the major sixth.

To these must be added a *Chorda peregrina*, which in minor modes is the major third, and in major modes the minor third. See example A4-28.

Example A4-28

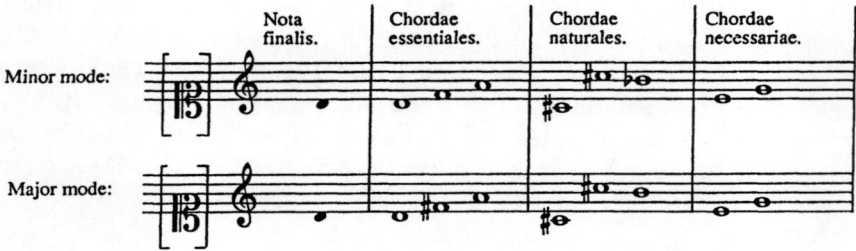

Since both types of teachings amount to the same thing in figural music[22] (as it seems to me), there is no need for dispute, all the more so because each appears to have some advantages over the other in certain pieces. In particular, this is the advantage of the first: that the signature is somewhat easier to find, and thus one can be more certain which notes belong and which do not belong. On the other hand, the latter is useful in that it shows what notes are used in the making of cadences as well as in other passages, and also what

---

[22]*Lexicon*, p. 433: "*Figural-Music* is that whose notes are of differing species and values [that is, of different durations]; likewise whose beat is sometimes rapid, sometimes slow."

pitches must be contributed to the content of the mode, even if the signature was set neither according to the first nor the second manner.

But the main reason why these twenty-four modes were discovered is that the whole tones found in a diatonic octave are not of the same size, but are different: namely *c-d*, *f-g*, and *a-b* are major tones, but the remaining ones, *d-e* and *g-a* are minor tones (the difference between these amounts to a comma); and accordingly none can truly be set and used in place of the other (which happens with the former and older type of modes in transposition). This is proper if it is agreed that the just-mentioned very small interval is perceptible to the ear in practice, which opinion many reject, and regard it as imperceptible.

I have, consequently, alluded to and explained briefly both types of teachings of the modes, in no way having taken sides in the heated disputes, both past and present—leaving it to each reader to decide which type he prefers, and I believe that either will lead to success in both figured music and chorale.

Index

Adlung, Jacob, 84, 140, 141-42, 146
Aeolian mode
  as model for minor, 12, 103
  in Glarean's nomenclature, 1-2
  in Zarlino's nomenclature, 11
affect, 206
  of modes, 27, 65, 116, 164-65
Agricola, Martin, 106
Albrecht, Hans, 69
Albrecht, Johann Lorenz, 142, 146
Allerup, Albert, 68
ambitus, 112, 173
  defined, xiii, 106
d'Anglebert, Jean Henri, 92
Apel, Willi, 56
arithmetic division, xix-xx
Arnold, Franck Thomas, 85, 116
Artusi, Giovanni Maria, 61
Atcherson, Walter, 20, 44, 78, 79, 94
authentic modes
  defined, xiii
  and harmonic division, xx
Avianius, Johannes, 15, 28-30, 31, 48

Bach, Carl Philipp Emanuel, 146
Bach, Johann Sebastian, 51, 89-90,
    109, 131, 141, 145, 211
  chorales, 156-58
  c-minor fugue, 152-55

Banchieri, Adriano, 50, 62
  and church keys, 78-79
Baryphonus, Heinrich, 27, 52, 57
Battiferri, Luigi, 145
Beethoven, Ludwig van, 148
Benary, Peter, 51, 129, 134, 137, 138
Benndorf, Kurt, 21
Berardi, Angelo, 193-94
Beringer, Maternus, 25-26, 63
Bernhard, Christoph, 58, 62, 66-68, 71,
    95, 109, 130, 206
Bertali, Antonio, 80, 105
Blankenburg, Walther, 119, 120
bocedisation, xviii, 43
Boethius, 121
Bononcini, Giovanni Maria, 62, 193
Brandenburg, Sieghard, 148
Brenet, Michel, 22
Brossard, Sébastien de, 99-100, 113
Bukofzer, Manfred, xi
Burmeister, Joachim
  on modes, 26-27
  on triads, 30-31, 33, 48
Buttstett, Johann, 59, 106, 142
  controversy with Mattheson, 117-
    25

cadences, 42, 61, 64-65, 67, 111-12, 173-74

Calvisius, Seth, 11, 21-24, 27, 33, 37, 68
  on major and minor, 23, 40, 44

Campion, Thomas, 33, 101, 103

cantus choralis
  defined, 23

cantus figuralis
  defined, 23

Carissimi, Giacomo, 67

chorales
  influencing modal theory, 48-51, 138, 139, 143-46

church keys, 62, 77-82, 94, 114, 148, 164
  as transposed modes, 79

Cima, Giovanni Paolo, 149

circle of keys, 90-92, 108-11, 116

Cohen, Vered, 7

Colhardt, Johann, 69

Crüger, Johann, 52-59, 66
  elementary manual, 68, 74, 75
  on ordering of modes, 13

Dahlhaus, Carl, viii, 11, 84

Dart, Thurston, 33

David, Hans, 89

Demant, Christoph, 23, 73

de Podio, Guillermus, 15

Diletskii, Nicolai, 92, 110

Diruta, Girolamo, 80

dominant
  defined, xiv

Dorian mode
  as model for minor, 12-13, 100

Duckles, Vincent, 131

dur, xviii-xix, 83-84, 89-90, 164, 165

Eberlin, Johann Ernst, 82

Eggebrecht, Hans, 138

Eichmann, Peter, 70

Eisel, Johann Philipp, 84

elementary manuals, 52, 68-76

Elsmann, Heinrich, 74

equal temperament, xx, xxiv

Erhard, Lorenz, 66, 76

Faber, Heinrich, 68-69, 70

Falck, Georg, xix, 98, 106, 115
  and church keys, 81, 83-84

Federhofer, Helmut, 66, 80, 105, 129

Feil, Arnold, 129

Ferrari, Philippus, 228

final, defined, xiv

Fischer, Johann Caspar Ferdinand, 82

Fischer-Krückeberg, Elisabeth, 53, 54, 55

Forkel, Johann Nikolaus, 148

Frère, Alexandre, 100

Frescobaldi, Girolamo, 145

Friderici, Daniel, 74

Froberger, Johann Jakob, 92, 145

Fux, Johann Joseph, x-xi, 3, 62, 145, 146, 148
  and solmization, xviii
  and Zarlino's modal names, 11
  correspondence with Mattheson, 123, 126-30, 133
  on modes, 127-28, 189-96
  translations of, 183-209

Gafori, Franchino, 14-15, 122

Galilei, Vincenzo, 228

Gasparini, Francesco, 145

Gaultier, Dénis, 11

Gehrmann, Hermann, 20, 137

Geiringer, Karl, 89

Gengenbach, Nicolaus, 75

Gesius, Bartholomäus, 73

Gibel, Otto, 57

Glarean, Heinrich, xi, xiii, xiv, xvi, 1-7, 44-45, 58, 60, 122, 209, 221-22
  ordering of modes, 26, 27, 72-76

Gossett, Philip, 12

Graun, Karl Heinrich, 142-43

Grimm, Heinrich, 22, 57, 59

Guido of Arezzo, xvii, 120, 121

Guillet, Charles, 11

Gumpelzhaimer, Adam, 65, 68, 69-71

Hahn, Georg Joachim Joseph, 81
Hahn, Kurt, 109, 137
Handel, Georg Friedrich, 126, 145
harmonic division, xix-xx
Harnish, Otto Siegfried, 31-33
Hase, Wolfgang, 75
Hawkins, John, 47-48
Heinichen, Johann David, 86, 104-5, 117
    on keys, 106-12, 134
Herbst, Johann Andreas, 63-66, 193
Hiller, Johann Adam, 131
Hilse, Walter, 66, 67
Hoffmann-Erbrecht, Lothar, 82
Houghton, Edward, 4
Hubmeier, Rektor, 22
Hüschen, Heinrich, 106
Humphries, Charles, 33
Hyperaeolian
    in Crüger, 55
    in Glarean, 5
    in Gumpelzhaimer, 69
Hyperphrygian
    in Crüger, 55
    in Glarean, 5
    in Gumpelzhaimer, 69

interval inversion, 38-39

Jackson, Susan, 61
Janowka, Thomas Balthasar, 12, 84, 117, 163-77
    and church keys, 81
    on major/minor keys, 105-6
Jensen, Claudia, 92, 110

Kellner, David, 134
key, as opposed to mode, xvii, 100, 104
key signatures, 92, 100, 147, 167-69
Kircher, Athanasius, 109-10, 228
Kirnberger, Johann Philipp, 48, 146
    and church keys, 81
    on modes, 142-46
Klein, Johann Joseph, 143, 146

Koch, Heinrich Christoph
    and church keys, 78, 81, 148
    on modes, 147-48
Kolb, Carlmann, 81
Kretzschmar, Johann, 72, 90, 149
Krieger, Johann, 126
Kuhnau, Johann, 90, 109-11, 137
    correspondence with Mattheson, 124

Langlütge, Ernst, 71
Lateinschul manuals
    see elementary manuals
Leo, Leonardo, 145
Lippius, Johannes, xix, 11, 21, 31, 51
    influence on Crüger, 52-54, 58
    on modes, 41
    on triad, 39-43, 48-49, 120-21
Lotti, Antonio, 145

Magirus, Johann, 63, 77
    on modes, 24-26, 27
    on triads, 33-34
Maillart, Pierre, 50
Majer, Joseph, 134, 139-40
major and minor
    absent from church keys, 82
    absent from Glarean's writing, 1-7
    absent from Italian tradition, 62-68
    in Calvisius, 22-23
    in Crüger, 53-54
    in Werckmeister, 88-89
    in Zarlino, ix-x, 13-20
Malcolm, Alexander, 104
Mann, Alfred, 114, 127, 128, 183
Marco, Guy, 7, 16
Marpurg, Friedrich Wilhelm, 141, 146
Matthaei, Conrad, 57, 58, 59-60, 63
Mattheson, Johann, x, 3, 85, 104-5, 109, 137, 140
    and Murschhauser, 131
    answering Buttstett, 121-25
    and church keys, 81
    correspondence re: Buttstett, 125-30, 133
    correspondence with Fux,

(Mattheson, cont.)
    on ordering of keys, 13
    on solmization, xviii
    on tuning, xxiv, 179-82, 213
    on twenty-four keys, 112-17, 134
Mendel, Arthur, 89
Mersenne, Marin, 11, 213
Miller, Clement, 1, 4
Mitchell, William, 114
Mizler, Lorenz, 129, 131, 141, 146, 196
modal theory, as comprehensive, xv-xvi
mode
    as fifth-species plus fourth-species, xiii-xiv
    as octave species, xiv-xv
    transposed, xix
modus
    meaning interval, 106
moll,   xviii-xix, 83-84, 89-90, 164, 165
Monteverdi, Claudio, 61
Morley, Thomas, 103
Mozart, Leopold
146, 147
Müller-Blattau, Josef Maria, 66
Muffat, Georg, 82
Murschhauser, Franz, 59, 120, 130-31, 148, 164
mutation, xviii
Mylius, Wolfgang, 57, 76, 83

Niedt, Friderich Erhard, 85, 98, 107, 115
Nivers, Guillaume, 98
Nolte, Eckhard, 24, 31
Nucius, Johannes, 49

octave species and mode
    criticized by Mattheson, 121-22
    in Calvisius, 1-4
    in Crüger, 22
    in Printz, 61

order of modes
    in Bernhard, 67
    in Calvisius, 22
    in Crüger, 55
    in Glarean, 2, 6
    in Magirus, 24-25
    in Praetorius, 27
    in Walther, 137
    in Zarlino, 8-13
Ozanam, 98-99

Palestrina, 145, 195
Palisca, Claude, 7, 16
Phrygian
    remaining along with major and minor, 98, 109, 124, 131, 145-46, 156-60
plagal mode
    and arithmetic division, xx
    defined, xiii
    in Fux, 191-96
Plato, 189
Playford, John, 101-4
Poglietti, Allessandro, 80
Praetorius, Michael, xvi, 27, 59, 60, 69
Preussner, Eberhard, 68
Printz, Wolfgang Caspar, 21, 60, 98, 120, 122, 148, 219
    elementary manual, 68
Purcell, Henry, 103-4
Puteanus, Erycius, xviii

Quantz, Johann Joachim, 147
Quirsfeld, Johann, xi, 76, 129

Rameau, Jean-Philippe, xvii, 160
    and Dorian mode, 12
Ramos de Pareja, xviii, 120
Raselius, Andreas, 223, 225
reciting tone, xiv
Reese, Gustave, xi, xviii
repercussio
    defined, xiv
    redefined by Printz, 61

Rid, Christoph, 69
Riedel, Friedrich Wilhelm, 130
Riemann, Hugo, vii, 129
Rivera, Benito, 14-15, 28, 29, 38, 39, 48,
    50
Roggius, Nicolaus, 71
Rousseau, Jean, 97
Ruhnke, Martin, 26, 31

Saint Lambert, 100, 104
Salinas, Francisco, 38
Sardi, Alessandro, 228
Sartorius, Erasmus, 26, 75
Scheibe, Johann Adolph, 134
Schneider, Herbert, 11, 81, 98
Schütz, Heinrich, 61, 66
semitone placement
    as criterion in modal differentia-
        tion, 2-3, 8, 44-45
            in Buttstett, 120, 125
            in Fux, 189-91
            in Magirus, 24-25
            in Marpurg, 141
            in Walther, 135, 212-13
Shirlaw, Matthew, xiii, 14
Siefert, Paul, 66
Simpson, Christopher, 101-2
Smith, William, 33
Snegassius, Cyriacus, 220, 223
solmization, xvii-xix, 9-10, 26, 126
    in Buttstett, 120
    in Fux, xi, 150, 197-98
Sorge, Georg Andreas, 89, 141, 159
species
    defined, xiii-xiv
    see also octave species
Speer, Daniel, xix, 84, 98, 106, 115, 134

Speth, Johann, 164
Spiess, Meinrad, 59, 120, 131-32
Stenger, Nikolaus, 224

Stevenson, Robert, 103
Stössel, J. C. and J. D., 140
Sweelinck, Jan, 66

temperament, 123
tenor
    primacy of
            in Herbst, 64
            in Nucius, 49
            in Zarlino, 15
Tevo, Zaccario, 228
Thüring, Joachim, 228
Tinctoris, Johannes, xii
tonic, as term, 100-1
transpositions
    in lists of twenty-four keys, 99,
        101, 136
    in Mattheson-Buttstett controver-
        sy, 122-23
    in Werckmeister, 90
Treiber, Johann Phillip, 85
triad
    and harmonic/arithmetic division,
        xx-xxi
    in Brossard, 100
    in Crüger, 53-56
    in Lippius, 39-43
    in theory before Lippius, 28-36
    in Zarlino, ix-x, 14-20
Trost, Johann Caspar, 22
tuning
    Mattheson's, 179-82
    Pythagorean, xxi-xxii
    syntonic, xxii-xxiii, 9
Türk, Daniel Gottlob, 56, 143, 146
twenty-four keys
    earliest listings, 98-117

Vogel, Martin, 52
Vogler, Abbé, 148, 155
Vulpius, Melchior, 69

Waelrant, Hugo, xviii
Walther, Johann Gottfried, xi, 30, 51, 80, 82, 106, 109, 145, 155, 158, 164
   influence of, 139-40
   on modes and keys, 135-39
   translation of, 211-33
Weber, Carl Maria von, 155
Weinandt, Elwyn, 134
Werckmeister, Andreas, xix, 86-93, 98, 110, 111, 123
   and equal temperament, xxiv
Wienpahl Robert, 20

Zahn, Johannes, 211

Zarlino, Gioseffo, xiii, xvi, 7-20, 38, 57, 58, 192-93, 212
   and syntonic tuning, xxii-xxiii
   aspects borrowed from Glarean, 7-9
   influence on Calvisius, 21-24
   new names for modes, 10-11, 195, 196
   on major and minor, viii-x, 13-20, 28, 40, 44
   on triads, ix-x, 14-20
   ordering of modes, 8-13, 26, 27, 72-76, 196
Zelenka, Johann, 145
Ziller, Ernst, 120